Know Your Soul

"We have fallen out of touch with our soul, both individually and collectively—thus the mess we are in. Joseph Howell prophetically witnesses to a recovery of soul. This is where our true strength lies. A remarkable book, full of redemptive insight and practical guidance for the harnessing of ego and the rebirth of soul."

—**JOHN PHILIP NEWELL**, author of *Sacred Earth Sacred Soul*

"Joseph Howell's profound journey into the Enneagram invites us to transcend mere personality traits and explore the soul's lush landscapes. This transformative book, rich with wisdom and personal stories, guides readers through deep introspection and self-discovery. Howell reveals the soul child—the Enneagram's less-talked-about gem—encouraging us to unveil our true authenticity and collective consciousness. This odyssey into our genuine selves bridges personal and collective egos to a shared soul."

—**ANNA SORKO**, board member, International Enneagram Association, Finland

"Read this book carefully for you will uncover a magnificent story of transcendence. This book illuminates the journey of transcending the bonds of ego and unleashing the soul. It's the road map to move from personality to souality, from the mind to the heart, from I, me, and mine to Thee, Thou, and Thine. An enriching read to transcend knowledge and move into the realms of experience to become one with your soul child and enter the sacred oasis within."

—**DAAJI (KAMLESH D. PATEL)**, global guide, The Heartfulness Institute, and author of *The Heartfulness Way*

"In this book, psychologist and master teacher Joseph Howell draws on extensive longtime study and use of the Enneagram, as well as his own life experiences. It is a unique addition to the Enneagram world and an invaluable guide to the deepest wisdom of the Enneagram. Howell effectively explains the mystery of the soul while preserving the wonders and the power of the soul. He is a trustworthy guide. This book is soul-work at its best."

—**Jeanie Miley**, author of *Fierce Love*

"Joseph Howell takes the reader on a journey of spiritual adventure. Using the Enneagram Theory of Personality as both map and compass, he invites the reader to discover one's soul child in the turbulence of life's flowing river."

—**Patrick H. O'Leary**, founder, International Enneagram Association

"*Know Your Soul* is filled with poignant stories about the soul's journey from ego to essence. Joseph Howell calls this a journey from Enneagram personality type to souality. It is a journey that helps us to 'unblock the obstacles to that sacred part of ourselves,' our true nature that is crying out to be seen. I have read many Enneagram books over the years, and this one has become a favorite. I highly recommend Howell's spiritually uplifting book."

—**Deborah A. Ooten**, CEO, Conscious Dynamics

Know Your Soul

Journeying with the Enneagram

Joseph Benton Howell
Foreword by Phil Cousineau

CASCADE Books • Eugene, Oregon

KNOW YOUR SOUL
Journeying with the Enneagram

Copyright © 2024 Joseph Benton Howell. All rights reserved. Except for brief quotations in critical publications or reviews, no part of this book may be reproduced in any manner without prior written permission from the publisher. Write: Permissions, Wipf and Stock Publishers, 199 W. 8th Ave., Suite 3, Eugene, OR 97401.

Cascade Books
An Imprint of Wipf and Stock Publishers
199 W. 8th Ave., Suite 3
Eugene, OR 97401

www.wipfandstock.com

PAPERBACK ISBN: 979-8-3852-1572-0
HARDCOVER ISBN: 979-8-3852-1573-7
EBOOK ISBN: 979-8-3852-1574-4

Cataloguing-in-Publication data:

Names: Howell, Joseph Benton [author]. | Cousineau, Phil [foreword writer].

Title: Know your soul : journeying with the enneagram / by Joseph Benton Howell.

Description: Eugene, OR: Cascade Books, 2024. | Includes bibliographical references and index.

Identifiers: ISBN 979-8-3852-1572-0 (paperback) | ISBN 979-8-3852-1573-7 (hardcover) | ISBN 979-8-3852-1574-4 (ebook)

Subjects: LCSH: Enneagram. | Spiritual life. | Personality assessment. | Self-evaluation. | Typology (Psychology). | Spirituality—Christianity.

Classification: BF698.3 H69 2024 (paperback) | BF698.3 (ebook)

VERSION NUMBER 09/04/25

Written in thankfulness for our children,
Ben and Lauren,
whose dear souls speak to me every day.

Contents

Foreword by Phil Cousineau | ix
Preface | xv
Acknowledgments | xxiii

1. The Enneagram: An Overview of Basics | 1

PART ONE: What Is Soulality?

2. Soulality: The Qualities of Our Unique Soul | 37

3. Who Is the Soul Child? | 63

4. Who Is Your Soul Child? | 95

PART TWO: Exploring Your Soul

5. The Enneagram of Soul | 109

6. The Soul Types of the Enneagram of Soul | 137

7. Spiritual Transformation and Amalgamation of Our Ego and Soul | 164

8. Three Major Levels of Soul Development | 182

9. The Enneagram's Passageways to Inner and Outer Peace | 195

Ego/Soul Traits | 223

Bibliography | 229
Index | 233

Foreword

TWENTY-FIVE HUNDRED YEARS AGO, the Greek philosopher Heraclitus of Ephesus said, "You could not discover the frontiers of the soul, even if you traveled every road to do so." The humility and wisdom of this ancient aphorism came to mind while reading Dr. Joseph Howell's new book, *Know Your Soul*.

Growing up in Detroit, the city that gave us Motown and soul music, the greatest thing you could say about a person was "She's got soul," or "He is a soulful dude," meaning *genuine, real, authentic*. When I attended the University of Detroit, I learned for the first time, from my Jesuit teacher on world religion, the aphorism of Meister Eckhardt, that the soul is the "God-spark," as if our very essence flew off the flint of God.

Since then, working as an author and filmmaker in cultures the world over, I discovered a common thread—from the Americas to Australia, Iceland to Ireland, Sumerian myths to medieval European theology—between breath and soul, so much so that in American Sign Language the gesture for soul and spirit is of the hand drawing a thread out of the belly. Everywhere I've looked is a belief that we are declared alive when we draw our first breath and regarded as having passed on every we draw our last.

My own search appears to be part of a wider phenomenon, identified by the American novelist Rebecca West, who wrote that the twentieth century would be marked by a "desperate search for a pattern." A pattern that makes sense of the chaos in every facet of modern life, from religious teaching to political beliefs. In a world that appears more bewildering by the day, one suffering from a surfeit of information and a dearth of wisdom, the recognition of a pattern in the outside world—and on the inside, in our very being—is a welcome and comforting thought.

This was anticipated by the German Romantic poet Novalis, who famously said, "The soul is there where the inner and the outer world overlap." So mysterious is the life-and-death power of the soul that it is used to name the overpowering experience of emotions, dreams, fears, and desires. The wonderful word "quickening" expresses not only the mythic moment when the soul enters the fetus in the mother's womb, but also those numinous moments in life when we feel more alive than ever before.

Still, we look for the all-seeing pattern. Over the millennia we have musings on the soul from Gilgamesh to Odysseus, Parmenides to Plato, Plotinus to Augustine, Origen to Hildegaard, Aretha Franklin to Sam Cooke, plus plenty of poetic commentators writing about soul food, soulful architecture, and soul friends. So much so it sometimes feels as if everything that could be said has been, written, sung, painted, or sculpted.

Until the musings of Dr. Joseph Howell, that is.

His timely new work, *Know Your Soul*, I like to think is a modest but wise paraphrase of the immortal advice from the Delphic Oracle: *Gnothic sauton*, "Know Thyself." Considering the vast amount of ancient Greek writing on the topic, it is fair to suggest the early Greeks meant the well-lived life began with knowing your *deep* self.

Dr. Howell is a profoundly compassionate psychologist who describes himself as being "intensely interested in a spiritual approach," and has been on a lifelong search to create a system that reflects the best teachings from what the historian of religions Huston Smith called the world's wisdom traditions. For Howell, this process has led to an uncanny blend of insights from the ancient psychological and spiritual discipline of the mysterious spiritual map called the Enneagram, with Christian theology, and Jungian studies, to "reflect who we are," especially in the depths of the soul.

But Howell isn't content to merely rehash these ancient beliefs, fascinating as they are; he proposes the unique idea of the getting in touch with our "soul child," a poetic image that names the archetype he believes lies at the root of our personality.

While reading about this thrilling idea and perusing his complex model of the many facets of the soul, I thought of the great scholar William Irwin Thompson's tantalizing line, in *The Time Falling Bodies Take to Light*, "The nursery-rhyme is a memory of the soul." Or Frank L. Baum's bold practice of making a break with European fairy tales and conjuring up new and decidedly American stories for his children every night before bed, which we know now as tales from *The Wizard of Oz*.

For this reader, Howell's breakthrough idea conjures up a concatenation of soul images. I see in my mind's eye the haunting sculpture of a grieving mother and her dying daughter on a funeral stele at the National Archaeological Museum in Athens. I recall the shadow-strewn medieval engravings of the alchemical homunculus, and remember Giotto's gold-hued, radiant image of "The Ognissanti Madonna and Child Enthroned." And I hear the contagious rhythm and blues song "O-o-h Child," by the Five Stairsteps.

For me, the most moving image that corresponds to Howell's notion of the soul child can be found in the film *Immortal Beloved*, which contains the haunting image of the young Beethoven running away from home in the middle of the night to escape his cruel father, dashing through a moonlit forest to a pond that he leaps into and floats on his back while gazing at the night sky as the first notes of "Ode to Joy" play on the soundtrack.

Soulful, numinous, incandescent images of the child within and without us.

The healing glow of the soul child mythologem also happens to be the point of this book. What Dr. Howell has accomplished here is no less than handing the reader a spiritual map that shows us the long and winding road, at once Sisyphean and Ozian (as in Wizardly), that is intended to guide us from childhood to adulthood, grief to joy, paralysis to *exstasis* (ecstatic), or, in a word, transformative. This is that rare kind of book that fulfills the task that both ancient and modern writers have faced, which is to write something to help readers feel less alone in their struggles to be free of the past and exhilarated to move into the future.

As I read the manuscript, I thought of the insight from George Gurdjieff, the mystic philosopher and first person to make the Enneagram publicly known, that "Man lives in sleep, and in sleep he dies." By sleep he meant unconscious to the point of being automatons, out of touch with the miracle of being truly alive and as such we often lose touch with the glory and miracle, the divine gift of being alive. For Gurdjieff, as for many other spiritual masters, the task of tasks is to Wake Up! to the full vitality of what it means to be human.

This *cri de coeur* for spiritual awakening is at the heart of Howell's book as well, a cry of the heart to awaken from the deep sleep of ignorance of who we are, and to gain access to the wisdom of our souls, which is to say of that part of us that knows it knows. The notion of self-remembering is the leitmotif in all memorable art and the wisdom traditions, a recognition, to be sure, of the sorrow and disappointment and pain that silences many of us. But the transformation also allows us to wake up to the beauty of the human adventure and the divine spark inside each and every one of us.

One of the great artists of our time, the dancer and choreographer Jean Erdman Campbell, told me in an interview, in 1985, that she thought of the different aspects of her creative life as "rooms in her mind," aspects of the mansion of her soul, as the Swiss psychiatrist Carl Jung had told her and her husband Joseph Campbell, when they visited him at his home in Switzerland. These capacious rooms in her innermost being, Erdman came to believe, were where she was free to roam and do as her spirit allowed. I remember being overjoyed to hear about such a generous and kinetic image, a natural one coming from a dancer, which I have been grateful for ever since in my own creative life.

Years later, I find a similar exuberance in Howell's description of psychological types as rooms, which are not only useful but buoyant as he describes the often painful movement from victimhood to accountability as the essence of soul work, or what he calls "the conscious re-habiting of our true selves."

Dr. Howell's philosophy is rooted in the profound early mysticism of the desert fathers, and Plato's idea of Eternal Forms, Pythagorean mathematics, and Jungian archetypes, and gleaning of these ancient wisdom paths reminds me of the Irish poet and mystic John O'Donohue's revival of the Celtic belief in *anam cara*, the soul friend, as being the most profound aspect of a healer's work. Howell's writing here reveals how much he cares about the souls—the inward life—of his patients, students, and readers. So much so, his description of the deepest purpose of the Enneagram reveals it to be more of a beautiful *form* than a reductionistic *formula*. As such his work is redolent of the immortal poet Emily Dickinson, who wrote,

> The soul should
> always stand ajar
> ready to welcome the
> ecstatic experience.

The sublime connection between the soul and the ecstatic here was also at the heart of the work of one of my own mentors, Dr. Robert A. Johnson. Robert wrote movingly about the elegant beauty of the gold in the soul, the ultimate and radiant treasure within us that needs to be rescued from the claws of the possessive dragon in our nature. For Howell, the gold in the soul is a glowing reminder of our inner nature, our deepest gifts.

Finally, these fine pages bring back a memory of my time living in Paris, in the late 1980s, when I befriended an elderly woman who had studied with Gurdjieff himself in the early 1920s, in a chateau, in Fontainebleau, France. The self-described seeker told me, over a strong café crème, at the venerable La Coupole, that after an all-night lecture at the chateau dawn was approaching and the group of students she was part of grew weary and expressed a desire to leave for home.

"We can't go home yet," Gurdjieff objected. "We haven't proved that God exists!"

While some may object to the philosopher's uncertainty about the Divine or the rigorous demands he had on his students, I admire the spiritual tenacity, the utter devotion to the living reality of what Joseph Howell calls "sacred wisdom." And one other element that is often overlooked in spiritual and psychological work, the irrepressible urge for companionship in our pursuit of spiritual truth.

In *Know Your Soul*, I find a similar passion, a spark off the divine flint, evidence of the cry of the soul to be recognized, honored, and if necessary, healed on its holy path. Not unlike the advice of Howell's marvelous mentor, Henri Nouwen, who "was a proponent of examining the soul. Within our academic conversations, I felt his passionate drive to know more about our divine selves."

"Seek the depths—or else!" wrote Saul Bellow, in *Henderson the Rain King*.

So too does Joseph Howell exhort us to probe the depths of our childhood, our midlife, and in our elder years, as an echo of the ancient wisdom that "the unexamined life is not worth living."

In turn, in this book, Dr. Howell shows us how, through the mystery and beauty of the Enneagram, the fiery writings of the desert fathers, the piercing insights of modern depth psychology, that the pursuit of our personal truths in our "soul child" will help wake us up, even rekindle the spark our wayward souls.

Phil Cousineau
San Francisco
Summer 2024

Preface

We were a young, married couple who wanted to have a child but couldn't. After five years of infertility, Lark and I decided to try in vitro fertilization (IVF). In the early 1980s, it was a relatively new procedure; it offered us hope. Yet after multiple tries and finally a miscarriage, we gave up; it seemed we'd never have a child.

However, our need to be parents never left us. It came from the depths of our souls. To desire something so natural and so worthwhile was hard to give up, especially while all of our friends were raising families. Our lives seemed to be on hold.

In the past, my soul had made itself known many times, especially in crises. When it looked as if we would never have a child, Lark's soul and my own surfaced in unmistakable ways. The cries of our souls were constant and their desires didn't diminish but grew. So, we lived in a liminal space with constant reminders that reality wasn't making room for our desires, however heartfelt our cries may be.

Then one day, out of the blue, a dear friend asked if we would be interested in adopting a soon-to-be-born baby. We then realized that reality had been working behind the scenes to fulfill our souls' desires. One month later, the miracle we'd hoped for was placed into our arms. We named him Ben. Finally, we were a family! Three years later, our daughter Lauren was also placed into our arms.

The soul satisfaction of parenthood so completed us that deep joy had replaced our worries and anxieties. We had learned much about our souls, the most significant of all being that all our immediate desires pale in the face of our souls' desires. I didn't know about the Enneagram at this time of my life, but I had certainly experienced the truth it reflects: that our true nature, our essence, cries out for expression.

In the tremendous state of soul consciousness described above, we had entered what I have come to call the Enneagram of Soul. Many of us enter the Enneagram of Soul when we are open to something beyond ourselves and we are in touch with our very depths. The Enneagram of Soul, which I describe in detail in this book, is about becoming conscious of the soul's qualities and evolvement.

Many of us have memories of early childhood when we felt safe, peaceful, and loved. In soul we experience transparency to the Divine that connects us with these memories on a visceral level. Our soul emerges for a while; we feel reconnected to our long-lost selves. Then, as quickly as it surfaces, like an apron of surf upon the sand, the soul seems to disappear. Many of us work on enlarging these periods of soul so that we can become conscious of the foundational growth going on inside us. The Enneagram of Soul is a beautiful map of this spiritual growth in consciousness. In soul, we are growing in much deeper ways than in our egoic personality.

This book was born of a need to know our own souls and how to live within them. Grief, loss, and suffering push us to reach into our depths to meet such gigantic challenges. However, we cannot reach our depths if our ego—and its personality—bar the passageway to our soul. The soul cannot be fully expressed unless we unblock the obstacles to that sacred part of ourselves. Deep peace is a valued feeling but the ego, regardless of how valiantly it tries, cannot provide the peace that our souls provide. Gratefully, I experience deep peace much more frequently than I ever used to. I also know many others who experience the peace of having a deeper reconnection to their souls. The major question is, "How are we prevented from living in soul?"

While our egos want us to remain in control of our lives, their having complete control eclipses our soul. As long as the soul is ignored, our suffering increases.

This book came about because of my personal suffering and the alternatives that I found to that anguish. True, some of the suffering I endured was necessary, but I could have avoided much of it if I had been more aware. Of course, along the way, all of us experience peaks in our misery. The most sudden and excruciating ones are aptly called shock points because they shake our very foundations. Such shock points include the loss of a job, the end of a marriage, the devastating effects of an illness or addiction, and the loss of a loved one. Because these occurrences unexpectedly catapult us into a strange and frequently torturous land, our consciousness must expand to survive the new reality. If consciousness does not expand, we are prevented from living in soul, and our suffering continues.

My family experienced a seismic shock with the disease and death of our son Ben in 2008. Until Ben's death at twenty-six years old, my wife Lark and I managed to endure most of our shocks with fortitude and spiritual growth, relying on our faith and our mental and emotional faculties. We were so devastated by the loss of Ben, however, that our former methods of coping brought little relief. So, we searched for something that could.

Lark and I began studying the Enneagram in the late 1980s. It provided profound wisdom that helped us through many difficulties. We'd spent years delving into the Enneagram and teaching it to various groups across the southeastern United States. However, our application of it had been confined to personality typing and incorporating the healthy aspects of the personality found at the Point of Integration into everyday life.

Presented in a spiritual context, this approach was healing and positive. Our attempts to apply what we knew of the Enneagram to our suffering after losing Ben met with limited success, though. We were still lost in a desert of grief. Yet the life-altering experience that I discuss in the last chapter of this book prompted me to delve deeper into the Enneagram. I knew it to be an infinite well of wisdom, so we searched for more profound realizations, beyond what we already knew. We eventually found that the Enneagram has profoundly multidimensional aspects and contains much more nuanced information than we had previously realized or experienced.

In my searches and inquiries, it dawned on me that my suffering was caused by a very stubborn ego mind. Despite the reality of Ben's death, my ego refused to accept the loss. My egoic reaction was rage, which flared up every time I re-lived my failures to save Ben. Overwhelmed with guilt and self-condemnation, I irrationally punished myself and even blamed Ben for leaving us. My ego was trying to save me but, instead, it was destroying me.

When I looked at the Enneagram more closely, I saw that my ego and personality are actually mental structures. There are basically nine types of egos which are depicted on the Enneagram of Personality. So, the Enneagram of Personality is an Enneagram of Egos. As part of my personality, my ego acts in what it thinks is my interest, just as it was developed to do. In self-inquiry, my particular fear-based ego was making "restitution" for my failures in an attempt to balance out my psyche. It didn't work. Regardless of how much I punished myself or shifted the blame to others, the suffering continued.

As I studied the Enneagram of Personality and integrated the healthy characteristics of my Point of Integration, I improved somewhat. It was spiritual transformation, however, not an intellectual process, that began my healing. One day, I discovered a core of life-giving energy within my Point of Integration: this powerful energy was beyond the characteristics of my personality . . . it was my soul child: my soul. I had experienced this divine aspect of myself at times in my life.

The soul child reveals a unique and sacred dimension to our being. Instead of a collection of personality traits, the soul child embodies sacred qualities that express our divine identity, one that is much deeper than our personality alone. By following my Enneagram's passageway to integration, I discovered my soul child, and with it, my truest nature, which was far more capable, sure, and strong than my personality. Our soul child is a huge gateway to our soul. This book concentrates on the soul child and how we can come to know his or her qualities.

I found that our ego keeps us away from our soul child by tricking us into believing its own particular narrative. It does this by distorting our perceptions so that we see the world as the ego wants it to be. Many of us view life through our ego's lenses, which are difficult to remove. Indeed, we have been aligned for so long with our ego's perceptions that we trust them as real. But when the resilient soul emerges and the ego vies for dominance, we have the opportunity to let the soul lead our ego. The soul sees the world only through the lenses of love and does away with the ego's narrative. The spectrum of love has created soul types just as there are Enneagram personality types. This work explores the soul types as well as the soul points on what I call the Enneagram of Soul.

The soul has an entirely different manner of perceiving our self, others, and the way we move in the world. Besides love, our soul expresses other awesome qualities, including presence, surrender, peace, compassion, humility, and courage. Tethered to the Divine, our soul manifests itself through our mind, heart, and body. The discovery of my soul child happened only when I was ready for it. I found that re-embodying him was never a completed job; it is, instead, a daily accomplishment that I have made part of my spiritual practice. In this book, I present the steps to actually re-embody your soul child and how to discern its various and particular qualities. Reconnecting with our soul child may be a lifelong process; however, with every soul quality of which we become conscious, we manifest that quality and have more peace.

This book is not an Enneagram primer, although chapter 1 lays out the basics for beginners among the reading audience. Nor is this a religious book, though it relates to Christianity and all pathways to whomever we conceive the Divine to be. This book is not a work on personality or personality typing, though I address that as an important aspect of ourselves. It is not a scientific study in psychology, but it pulls from psychological principles.

This book is about how to know our own soul by consulting the Enneagram. It is a combination of the different schools of Enneagram teaching that influence me. These include my first Enneagram teachers in 1988, Patrick O'Leary and Maria Beesing at the Jesuit Retreat House in Cleveland, Ohio. I collaborated with my friend Don Richard Riso and co-taught the Enneagram to medical residents with him in the early 1990s. I am greatly influenced by my relationship with Father Richard Rohr, whose early teaching on the Enneagram were profound for me. Likewise, my ongoing study of the Diamond Approach with Sandra Maitri is life-changing for me. My studies have also benefited from the wisdom of amazing Enneagram teachers such as Russ Hudson, Helen Palmer, A. H. Almaas, and Beatrice Chestnut. I am honored to be among these teachers at The International Enneagram Association's many conferences around the United States and the world.

By using the Enneagram and the stories of this amazing journey, I hope you will shift the command center from your personality to your *soulality*: your amazing compendium of sacred qualities. I hope you will derive great peace from reuniting with your depths and that you will share this peace with everyone whose life touches yours. In this way, not only will individual lives be transformed but the ripple effect will shift the consciousness of the collective. A conscious collective mind will preserve the earth and our species.

The book begins with chapter 1 on Enneagram basics, which reflects the classical Enneagram as initially taught by Oscar Ichazo and Claudio Naranjo. I also refer to the influence of George Gurdjieff, the first teacher of the Enneagram. This chapter is for novices who need familiarity with the rudiments of the Enneagram.

Then we progress to Part One of the book, "What Is Soulality?"

Chapter 2 is on Soulality, which, using the lens of the Enneagram, explains what our soul actually is. Here, we look at the concept of the soul and its qualities and embark on self-remembering to learn our Soulality.

Chapter 3, "Who Is the Soul Child?," deals with the soul child as the gateway to our truest nature and explores it as the only structure in our psyche free of ego dominance.

Chapter 4, "Who Is Your Soul Child?," explores the many aspects of the soul child's life cycle and components of the inner child, including its traumas and foibles. Chapter 4 also presents methods of finding and reconnecting with your soul child. I lay out actual exercises for reconnecting and communicating directly with this energy.

Part Two is entitled "Exploring Your Soul."

Chapter 5, "The Enneagram of Soul," reveals the hidden Enneagram of Soul that works together with the Enneagram of Personality to evolve our beings.

Chapter 6, "The Soul Types of the Enneagram and Soul," presents the nine types of souls and their components that correspond to each ego type.

Chapter 7, "Spiritual Transformation and Amalgamation of Our Ego and Soul," explores the process of spiritual growth reflected in the Enneagram: by way of spiritual alchemy, the ego and the soul blend to create a new creature.

Chapter 8, "Three Major Levels of Soul Development," delineates the three major levels of soul consciousness.

Finally, chapter 9, "The Enneagram's Passageways to Inner and Outer Peace," explains the implications of how working in the Enneagram of Personality and the Enneagram of Soul of one person can eventually affect the collective.

You may sometimes be overwhelmed by the amount of information presented in this book; therefore, it is important to enter it in the same way you would enter a cool river. First, you survey the river. Then, you step into the shallow part, starting with only one foot, followed by the other. You enter the river slowly, so your body has the chance to adjust to the temperature and currents. Like salmon who swim upstream to their spawning place, this book invites you to swim against the river's flow, all the way to your soul. For this reason, you may want to take each section slowly and not read this book as you would a novel or an academic work. It is a blend of over thirty years of experience with the Enneagram and how it is reflected in me, my family, and other dear souls whom I have had the honor of working with professionally.

As you read this book, I pray your own soul will resonate with these ancient principles and that this will lead you to remember, acknowledge, embrace, and heal many forgotten aspects of yourself.

This book, five years in the making, shares my personal struggles and my spiritual searches before and after I learned about the Enneagram. My pathway is not yours and I offer it only as an illustration of how the Enneagram helped me to do that much-needed inner work. I sincerely hope that you may apply those truths that you learn from this book to your own spiritual journey and to the world around you.

I add this note: since completing the writing of this book, Lark and I lost our only other child, Lauren. At age thirty-six, Lauren was a psychotherapist and had accomplished many things, even while battling the disease of alcoholism that plagued her for the last ten years of her life. After a two-year period of sobriety, and having run in various marathons during that time, Lauren experienced a relapse and died in her sleep in August of 2022. Lauren and her brother Ben are in our hearts and souls forever. We continue to share and teach the Enneagram with hundreds. Its truths grow our souls and guide us to the Divine within and beyond ourselves. Its truths help to heal us.

Namaste,

Joseph Benton Howell
Hyderabad, India
February 20, 2023

Anniston, Alabama
January 2021

Acknowledgments

Several dear people have helped me in the process of bringing this book to life. First of all, Denise White tirelessly and generously edited my first drafts. Her extraordinary analytical skills gave the work its foundational structure. My appreciation always, Denise.

And a huge thank you goes to my friends and leading members of The Institute for Conscious Being, Erika Jobes, Scott Smith, Nanette Mudiam, Terri Bailey, and Nan Hornsby. They generously gave time to discuss the book's ideas and proofread chapters.

I would like to thank my long-time administrative assistant, Bekah Wilson Sudsberry, for her unrelenting support for this and many other projects over the years.

Our dear friends Charlotte and Buddy Mullis have been a constant source of inspiration and support for this book. They have been loyal friends in good times and not-so-good times. Their continued inspiration and spiritual support helped to make this book a reality.

My editor for the entire book before it went to the publisher was Sonya Landau, who not only put my words into a reader-friendly form but also creatively found ways to present the most difficult concepts. Sonya has the gift of saying, "Please tell me what you are trying to say here because it doesn't make sense the way it reads." My heartfelt gratitude, Sonya.

Lark, my spouse of fifty years, my anchor, and the loving mother of our two children, Ben and Lauren, has been the most steadfast support for this project. She very patiently gave of her time and talent at all times of the day. During my years of writing this book, Lark's joyful spirit always pointed me in the right direction whenever I got off track or felt discouraged about the book's progress.

I am grateful to Emily Callihan, assistant managing editor, Wipf and Stock Publishers, who graciously makes herself available for expert direction and advice. I am also thankful to my editor at Wipf and Stock Publishers, Robin Parry, who, from the beginning, has been enthusiastic about this book and its purpose.

Finally, I thank my friend and colleague Phil Cousineau, whose guidance and support have been invaluable in writing and journeying in the pilgrimage of life itself.

I

The Enneagram

An Overview of Basics

THIS CHAPTER IS FOR novices to the Enneagram who have an interest in soul exploration. It explains the basics of the Enneagram in preparation for using it in the transformational work of the soul. If you are already familiar with the Enneagram's essential history, structure, and processes, you may want to begin with chapter 2.

My First Encounter with the Enneagram

In the late 1980s I flew to Cleveland, Ohio, to attend a week-long workshop on the Enneagram. The event, conducted by Patrick O'Leary, Maria Beesing, and Robert Nogosek, was held at the Jesuit Retreat House. My first exposure to the Enneagram was expansive, revelatory, and, in short, mind-blowing. As a psychologist intensely interested in spiritual growth, I was astounded at how the Enneagram brilliantly blended both of these disciplines to accurately reflect the truth of who we are.

At one point in the workshop, we students were asked to go down a corridor and visit nine consecutively numbered rooms. Supposedly, the room where the people were talking about subjects that resonated with us reflected our personality type (also called our ego type). Our teachers said that in the room of our personality, we would feel like we were talking around the kitchen table at home.

There was one room I thought would be mine for sure, but it wasn't. There was another close second, but I didn't find much in common with those people either. I was about to give up when I thought about a certain personality type that I distinctly disliked. I entered that room just to observe, but the people there expressed my thoughts, preoccupations, desires, and fears. This began my long journey of over thirty-five years with the Enneagram. Each day, I learn more from it.

Having learned from my main teacher, Patrick O'Leary, who attested to the profound spiritual nature of the Enneagram, I eagerly delved further into this amazing wisdom. My search revealed that the Enneagram is an instrument for understanding the nature of all things. It has a vast and overarching scope, stemming from a slew of early spiritual sources, including early mysticism, the desert fathers and mothers, the Platonic forms, and Pythagorean mathematics.

The Enneagram is a system by which we discern the properties, interrelationships, and dynamics of foundational subjects, such as history, mathematics, economics, physical science, biology, astronomy, medicine, the arts, music, psychology, spirituality, and theology, as well as death, birth, and being. Personality is only one variety of the Enneagram; the number of possible Enneagrams is infinite. I learned it is not a static classification system but a fluid method of comprehending the ever-changing dynamics of things. It is not a tool for divination, entertainment, labeling, or controlling others; it is most essentially a spiritual map of reality.

On its most elementary level, the Enneagram is visually represented by a circle with nine points spaced around its circumference. Each of the nine points represents one of the nine fundamental and irreducible energies of the universe. Like a clock, barometer, or compass, it indicates certain information. But the Enneagram yields much more than a measurement.

The Enneagram of Personality

The Enneagram of Personality is enormously popular because through its wisdom we gain essential understandings about our personality's healthy and unhealthy coping strategies, and how our personality can be improved. Besides our personality traits, we learn the antidotes to their dilemmas. Though the Enneagram of Personality was initially born of and embraced by those interested in the mysteries of spiritual growth, in the last few decades, the secular worlds of business, industry, technology, government, education, psychology, rehabilitation, medicine, etc., have also applied its truths. These sectors have developed their own sets of information about the Enneagram that fit their specific needs.

Understandably, many organizations have moved away from its original usage as a spiritual tool.

More than a personality type indicator, the Enneagram of Personality presents a method for determining each personality type's optimum way to move through the world. It also explains forces such as the avoidances, traps, virtues, passions, fixations, and other essential components that shape our thoughts and behavior.

Figure One
Enneagram of Personality

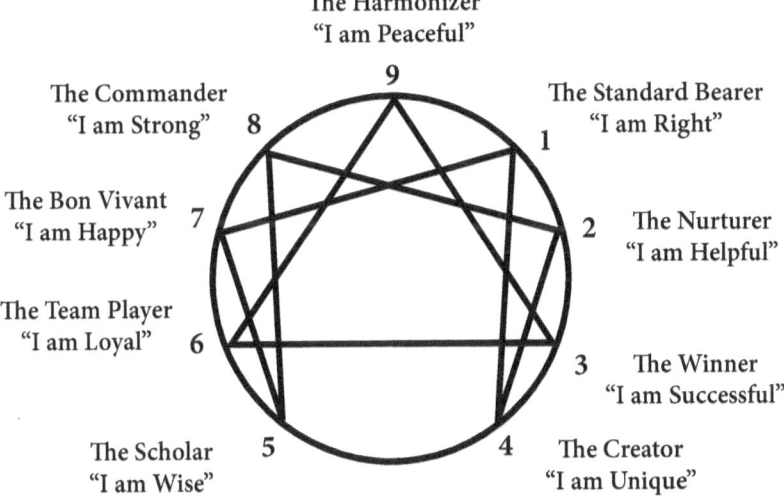

The Enneagram's Nine Ego and Personality Types

When understood in its greatest depths, the Enneagram not only helps us identify who we are at our worst and best, it reveals why and how we arrived at our type, with all its attributes, flaws, capacities, and associated pain. It also reveals the passageway to integration and self-realization, and how to minimize the suffering our ego causes us. In its spiritual depths, the Enneagram goes beyond personality into the realm of soul.

Our personality type actually describes our ego and is located at one of the nine points on the Enneagram. The antidotes for our deficiencies are the qualities of another point on the Enneagram called the Point of Integration, Heart Point, or Soul Point. It contains counter-intuitive information that, if embodied, improves our psychological balance and our effectiveness. But the gold within the Soul Point is much more valuable than achieving our optimal personality functioning; it contains the higher-ordered qualities of our truest nature, our soul. We must identify our personality type in order to find our corresponding Soul Point. Then how much of its gold we want to mine is for us to decide.

A Brief History of the Enneagram and Its Development

George Gurdjieff

The Greek-Armenian spiritual teacher and mystic George Ivanovich Gurdjieff (1866–1949) is credited with having first discovered the Enneagram and having brought it to the West. It is believed that the Enneagram was part of the sacred spiritual teachings of a Sufi monastic group located in the mountains in the heart of Asia about twelve days' journey from Bukara, Uzbekistan. This monastery was said to be the home of the Sarmoung Brotherhood, a religious order descended from Zoroastrian schools in Mesopotamia that had migrated to Asia. Gurdjieff visited this monastery and other sacred sites in Asia from 1890 to 1912. His work, called "The Fourth Way," is the application of specific daily spiritual practices to the Heart, Head, and Body Centers of Intelligence. The result is a greater awareness of our truest selves and our purpose. After his time at the monastery, Gurdjieff taught in various places in Russia and Europe but finally established a more permanent school in Fontainebleau, France. He also made several teaching visits to the United States.

Gurdjieff taught that the Enneagram was a system of energies that fundamentally underpin the universe. According to him, three universal laws order all being.[1] There is the Law of One, which says that there is no duality: everything is connected to everything. The Law of Three holds that every phenomenon is a manifestation of three definitive lines of action: holy affirming, holy denying, and holy reconciling. And the Law of Seven is explained by Jeanne de Salzmann,[2] a student of Gurdjieff's, as follows:

1. Webb, *Harmonious Circle*.
2. de Salzmann, *Reality of Being*, 296.

All matter in the universe consists of vibrations descending toward manifestation of form ("involution") or ascending in a return to the formless source ("evolution"). Their development is not continuous but characterized by periodic accelerations and retardations at definite intervals. The laws governing this process are embodied in an ancient formula that divides the period in which a vibration doubles into eight unequal steps corresponding to the rate of increase in the vibrations. This period is called an "octave," that is to say, "composed of eight." This formula lies at the basis of the Biblical myth of the creation of the world, and our division of time into workdays and Sundays. Applied to music, the formula is expressed in the musical scale do-re-mi-fa-sol-la-si-do, with semitones missing at the intervals mi-fa and si-do. The inner movement toward consciousness requires a "conscious shock" at these two intervals in order to proceed to a higher level, that is, a new octave.

Gurdjieff proposed that we are party to these laws but have lost touch with them. As a result, we have devised our own ways of perceiving reality. Gurdjieff's teachings are based on these laws and his methods of re-aligning with them, including meditation, dance, music, and living in the present moment. He taught his students to use passing through any doorway as an occasion to be more conscious of the present moment. He also used mealtimes to practice presence.

Only one facet of Gurdjieff's teaching addressed personality. He believed that most people are sleepwalking through life, unconscious of who they really are and why they are here. He said that most of us are machines who simply go through the same motions over and over without knowing why. For Gurdjieff, personality was an expression of the false self we adopted when we lost our connection to the natural order and our true nature. He described the false self in unflattering terms. He said that it emerges in specific ways: arguing with people about everything all the time, not being present, lacking a conscience, not letting anyone see who we are, having no shame, talking when we should be silent, and being silent when we should speak.

Gurdjieff asserted that we belong to groups that share the same chief features (failings) but his list was not confined to nine. Our chief feature is simply the most pronounced way we manifest our false self and, because of its pejorative nature, something we work hard to disguise. We are so adept at hiding or ignoring this aspect of ourselves that we are completely unconscious of it. Gurdjieff maintained that only a teacher can make us aware of our chief feature by helping us to *self-remember*. Self-remembering is the process of combining so completely with our true nature that, like a flash of light, we exit our false self and experience again our essence or *true self*. At that moment, we remember who we really are and re-inhabit our true selves. While this experience can last mere seconds or minutes, it can also be so transformative that it lasts a lifetime.[3]

Gurdjieff never wrote a book about the Enneagram as such, but his writings are said to implicitly refer to its truths. His student, Peter Ouspensky (1878–1947), who wrote *In Search of the Miraculous* (1949), claimed the spiritual teachers who taught Gurdjieff instructed him never to translate the sacred knowledge into written form, lest it be misused. Thus, Gurdjieff taught the sacred wisdom by other means: live interactions, lectures, dance, and music that he composed. Human movement in individual and group dance were the mainstays of his teaching method. His original music used harmonics based on integrals within the Law of Seven.

Oscar Ichazo

The Enneagram of Personality was conceived by the Bolivian Oscar Ichazo (1931–2020). In his youth, Ichazo was regularly exposed to Gurdjieff's teachings and was so inspired that he reportedly journeyed to the same monastery Gurdjieff had visited many years before (though he never actually confirmed this). After his spiritual journey to the East, Ichazo returned to South America, where he taught his in-depth expansion of the Enneagram—one that he alone put together. Ichazo's teachings eventually led to the establishment of the Arica Institute in the northern desert of Chile. At the Arica Institute, Ichazo taught his methods of self-realization, including the Enneagram of Personality. He discerned and created over one hundred Enneagrams, which he referred to as "enneagons." Each presented the properties and dynamics of universal, spiritual fundamentals. Gurdjieff's teachings laid the groundwork for Ichazo's later development of his enneagons and the Enneagram of Personality, but it was Ichazo who named and delineated the nine personality types—their passions, virtues, and Holy Ideas, etc.—that are taught today. He also created and taught the Enneagrams of the traps, avoidances, and fixations, among others.[4]

3. Bennett, *Gurdjieff*.
4. *Interviews with Oscar Ichazo*, 54.

Claudio Naranjo and Other Formational Teachers

Claudio Naranjo (1932–2019), a Chilean-born psychiatrist of Arabic/Moorish, Spanish, and Jewish descent, was one of Oscar Ichazo's students. He brought the Enneagram of Personality and other teachings from the Arica Institute to the United States. A widely traveled student and teacher of Gestalt therapy,[5] Naranjo developed his own teachings that added substantially to the body of knowledge of the Enneagram. Naranjo also developed the concept of the Instinctual Subtypes and the wings (which I will not go into in this book), and the inner flow of the Enneagram, some aspects of which were not necessarily taken directly from Ichazo.

Naranjo first taught the Enneagram in the early 1970s at The Esalen Institute in California at Big Sur. With a handful of students, he taught a SAT group (Seekers After Truth) for four years. Among these students was Robert Ochs, a Jesuit priest whose Enneagram teachings later influenced Catholic theological studies in seminaries.

The first Enneagram book in the US, *The Enneagram: A Journey of Self Discovery* (1984),[6] was authored by Maria Beesing, Patrick O'Leary, and Robert Nogosek. Their book was inspired by the teachings of Catholic priest and professor Father Bob Ochs, a student of Naranjo, whose teachings brilliantly depicted the Enneagram in Christian terms. Patrick and Maria taught me the Enneagram in a group at the Jesuit Retreat House in Cleveland, Ohio (now the Jesuit Retreat Center) in the late 1980s. Patrick is a friend of mine and one of the founders of the International Enneagram Association. Today, he actively teaches and consults on the Enneagram.

Don Riso, who learned the Enneagram from one of Robert Ochs' students, wrote ground-breaking works on the Enneagram. He eventually collaborated with Russ Hudson; together, they wrote *The Wisdom of the Enneagram* (1999), a classic in Enneagram studies. They also co-founded the Enneagram Institute. I contacted Don after his first book appeared and we collaborated and taught the Enneagram to medical residents in the early 1990s.

Another of Naranjo's students, A. Hameed Ali, who writes under the pen name A. H. Almaas, went on to establish the Ridhwan School in Berkeley, California, and Boulder, Colorado, which now has national and international branches. Its Diamond Approach teaches the spiritual

---

5. Perls, *Gestalt Approach and Eye Witness to Therapy*.
6. Beesing et al., *Enneagram*.

nature of life, the spirituality of the Enneagram, and the progression of the soul, among many topics. A. H. Almaas is the author of *Facets of Unity* (2012) and many other ground-breaking, seminal contributions to the field.[7]

Sandra Maitri, another of Naranjo's other students, joined The Ridhwan School and also teaches the Diamond Approach to consciousness and spirituality. She authored *The Spiritual Dimension of the Enneagram* (2000), which has become a seminal text in these studies. I have been a student of Sandra's and the other teachers associated with her since 2017, in the Diamond Heart Retreat Group of the Ridhwan School.

Helen Palmer, a pioneering author in the Enneagram, and another founder of the International Enneagram Association, studied under Naranjo. She teamed up with David Daniels, MD, to create the narrative tradition in Enneagram studies.

Jerry Wagner, PhD, is a clinical psychologist and author of *Nine Lenses on the World: The Enneagram Perspective* (2010). He is an early builder of statistically validated materials, including the Wagner Enneagram Personality Style Scales (WEPSS). His work is so esteemed that he was named an honorary founder of the International Enneagram Association.

The monumental contributions of these teachers and many others led to the creation of the International Enneagram Association, which promotes the study and application of the Enneagram in many settings around the world.

The First Step: Discovering Our Type

We develop our coping strategies from childhood, under the influences of our parents, family, and genetic make-up. The Enneagram describes the nine broad strategies for coping, around which our specific personality types evolve. We discover our Enneagram type through reading, self-observation, assessments, consultation, and/or an interactive group process (like the rooms I spoke of earlier). Then we settle on one of the nine personality types as our own. As an aspect of our ego, our personality expresses higher or lower aspects, depending on our level of consciousness and stress.

For example, I am the personality type number Six on the Enneagram of Personality. Sixes live in fear when we are not healthy, when we

---

7. Such as Almaas, *Diamond Approach to Inner Realization*.

are under extreme stress, or when we are not conscious. Although Sixes have a storehouse of courage, we spend much of our time defending against harm, danger, and all that terrorizes or unsettles us. Though I don't want to admit it, fear distorts my perception of things and prevents me from experiencing reality accurately. In general, Sixes view people and circumstances with suspicion, guessing at their potential to harm us. We assume the hidden motives of others but these are often projections of our own imaginings. Anticipating worst-case scenarios, unhealthy Sixes live in readiness for disaster, betrayal, rejection, and loss. Our root fear is that of being annihilated because of our deviance and inner flaws. We believe that membership in a group protects us. Such a group includes family. We also long for the protection of an Alpha figure and/or the umbrella of a group, agency, or organization. Our very survival is threatened if we feel unprotected from being fired, punished, shunned, disqualified, and/or ultimately rejected. Though reality is rarely as cruel as we imagine it to be, our fearful perceptions make us live as if it were.

I recall a harrowing experience as a young father, shopping in a large toy store with my three-year-old daughter. Before we left home, my wife, Lark, cautioned me to keep my eyes on Lauren because she was such a wanderer. Therefore, I kept her at my side in the store, but when I took my eyes off her to reach for something on the top shelf, she vanished in a flash. A flood of hysteria seized me and I took off running down each aisle, frantically screaming out her name. Imagining an abductor with my daughter in his arms, I darted past the check-out and, with my back to the front doors, yelled in a loud voice, "I have lost my three-year-old daughter. Have you seen her?" I must have looked like a mad man because the manager was more interested in calming me down than in finding my daughter. Then, out of nowhere, Lauren came up to me and asked, "Daddy, where were you?" This is an example of how, when fear overtakes us, our perceptions are distorted. As a Type Six under that stress, I quickly disintegrated into seeing the world only through the lens of fear.

Often, the key to finding our type is in exploring our primary dilemmas, our overriding emotions, and our avoidances. I discuss these later, along with passions and virtues, other key markers of type.

A Brief Description of the Nine Personality Types

Throughout this work, I describe all nine Enneagram energies in great detail. For the purpose of initial introduction, however, below is a brief and basic description of each of the nine types.

Type One: The Standard Bearer. This person upholds standards and seeks to do the right thing. In their healthiest state, this person is a brilliant light who leads others in the right direction, with empathy and optimism. In their unhealthy state, they are critical, demanding, and full of resentment. They are apt to think the world is going to hell in a handbasket despite all their efforts to put things in order.

Type Two: The Nurturer. This person fosters personal connections and relationships through giving and sharing. In their healthiest state, they give humbly and altruistically while acknowledging and meeting their own needs. In an unhealthy state, they create dependencies and co-dependencies to ensure that they are always in demand. In that state of unhealthy functioning, they are unaware of their own needs and are trapped in service.

Type Three: The Winner. This person takes solid action for the success and progress of the entire family, group, or collective. In a healthy state, they are tireless achievers, driven to perform for the good of all. In an unhealthy state, they forget their commitments and fall into self-centered activities. They have abandoned their standards as they selfishly pursue their personal agenda and image that now supersede the greater good.

Type Four: The Creator. This person is a unique and creative being. In their healthiest state, they bring a special contribution to all endeavors and have empathy for those who are neglected, abused, or left out. In an unhealthy state, they are envious, self-absorbed, and enveloped by melancholia that proceeds from focusing solely on their own tragic life.

Type Five: The Scholar. This person holds a plethora of information. In their healthy state, they use their knowledge as a source of power to move effectively in the world and to guide others. In an unhealthy state, they hoard their knowledge and withdraw from the world, which they perceive as a drain on their time and information.

Type Six: The Team Player. This person is a loyal family and group member. In a healthy state, they deepen community by keeping people together, courageously leading teams, and inspiring common bonds. In an unhealthy state, they seek the security of authority figures and the pack but don't easily trust because they believe something is fundamentally abnormal about them. Paranoid that their secure pack will kick them out for being deviant, they are anxious and fearful.

Type Seven: The Bon Vivant. This person loves life. In a healthy state, they are enthusiastic and bring an optimistic, joyful note to all circumstances. They can face the pain of life with strength and acceptance. In an unhealthy state, they avoid pain by satiating themselves with all that is pleasurable and distracting. They say, "If some is good, more is better."

Type Eight: The Commander. This person has a mixture of power and compassion. In a healthy state, they tend to rise to positions of leadership. They envision and carry out the big picture while seeking the truth. In an unhealthy state, they can be tyrannical, oppressive, and obsessed with enacting their version of justice.

Type Nine: The Harmonizer. This person is an agent for peacemaking. In a healthy state, they see all sides of a situation and mediate by finding common ground between people on opposite sides. In an unhealthy state, they sink into laziness and apathy to avoid conflict.

Figure Two
The Three Centers

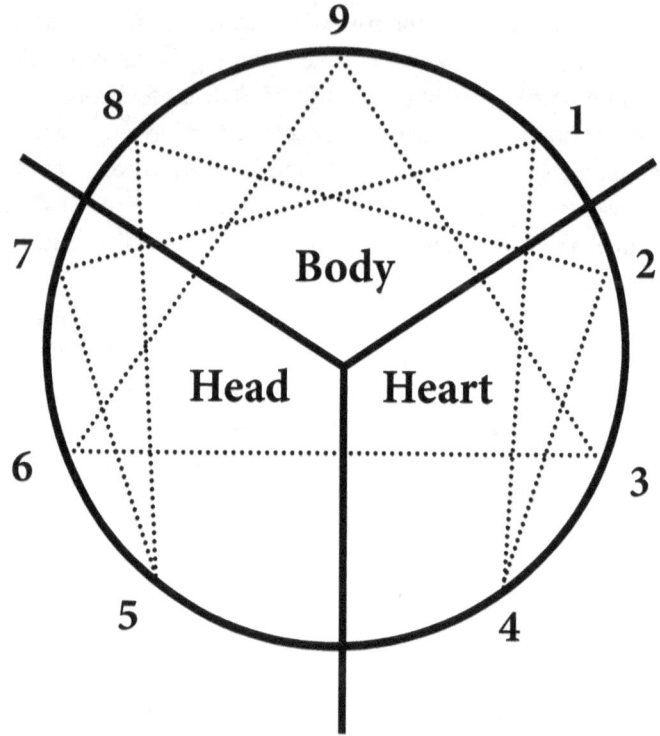

**Diagram of the Types Here on the Enneagram Diagram,
Including the Three Centers of Intelligence**

The Types within Each of the Three Centers of Intelligence

The personality types fall into three overarching groups called the three Centers of Intelligence. The Body Center of Intelligence is composed of Points One, Eight, and Nine. This center receives, processes, and transmits intelligence through our physical senses—by understanding the deeply rooted knowledge inherent to our physical body. The Heart Center of Intelligence comprises Points Two, Three, and Four. Those in this center receive, process, and transmit information through emotions. The Mind Center of Intelligence is made up of Points Five, Six, and Seven. It receives, processes, and transmits information through thinking and cognitive processes. Each center has a dominant motivating factor.

For the Body Center, that factor is its overwhelming anger over the limitations of being restricted to a body. Each of its three ego types expresses that anger differently. Ones do so by controlling their personal universe, monitoring others' behavior, and suppressing their anger, which leaks out in resentment. Eights do so with outright rage, intimidation, and maintenance of power. Nines detach and try to sleep on their anger.

The Heart Center's motivating factor is coping with the belief that it must do something specific to be loved. This center remedies this by striving endlessly to earn that love. Twos do so by being helpful and giving, Threes seek to be loved for their success, and Fours hope to be loved for their uniqueness.

The Head or Mind Center's motivating factor is coping with their fear. Fives are fearful that they are vulnerable because they are empty of substance. Frequently, they hoard information as a source of inner power. Their dilemma is how to stay full of knowledge, which protects them from their inner emptiness and void. Sixes are fearful of annihilation, exclusion, and their own deviance. They seek the inclusion and safety of the group. Their dilemma is how to remain a part of the group for security in a world that cannot be trusted. They solve this by being loyal team players who always side with the power base. Sevens are fearful of deprivation and pain. They arrange a continuous supply of activities, distractions, and indulgences, hoping to avoid pain in whatever forms it takes.

The Dominant Emotion of Each Type in the Three Centers

Each center has one dominant emotion. Those in the Body Center have the overriding emotion of anger. Ones funnel that anger into reordering the universe according to their standards, Eights use it to fight, and Nines shut down (go to sleep) to avoid it. Ones are angry at imperfection—both their own and that of the world around them. Their anger cannot be healed until they reconnect with the optimism, humor, and wholeness found at their core. Eights, who are enraged at the limitations and constraints they must live with, can only move through the world in peace when they discover their core of empathy and benevolence. When Nines no longer merge with others to escape conflict or go to sleep on their life, they have accepted their right and responsibility to show up for their own life. This happens as they integrate into healthy action, which has been at their core but obscured. Their anger, masked as sloth and passive aggression, dissipates.

The types in the Heart Center feel shame because they question whether or not they are loved—or even lovable. Twos find love by incessantly giving to others and denying their own needs. If they can learn to accept and meet their own needs first, they can heal from their compulsion to give all of themselves to others. Threes use accomplishment as a way to "win" love. Self-absorbed, they compete for the prize and the admiration it gives them. Only when Threes embrace the connection to family and community and let their accomplishments be for the collective benefit do they find the authentic love for which they search. Fours seek to be loved by being different, significant, and lamenting the sadnesses of their pasts. They learn to love themselves by finding the right path and outlet for their life and emotions. This brings them the authenticity they have always sought, and love comes their way, naturally.

The Head Center's dominant emotion is fear. Fives retreat into their world of stored information, hoping to assuage their fear of emptiness by accumulating knowledge. Sixes crumble into cowardice for fear of being repudiated and even exiled for their deviance. They react by clinging to external security. Sevens, who fear deprivation and pain, consume everything around them, staying in constant movement to distract them from deprivation and suffering.

When Fives detach from their reliance on hoarding information, they are able to find inner fullness and power. Sixes realize their inner strength when they embrace their virtue of courage. When Sevens embody their virtue of sobriety, their frenetic activity to avoid pain gives way to accepting and experiencing the present moment. Once in balance, the folks of the Mind Center are no longer consumed with and motivated by fear. They then approach life in touch with transparency to the Divine (Fives), inner strength and faith (Sixes), and reliance on presence and the divine plan (Sevens).

When these centers are healthy, they perceive, process, and store vital information. In their healthy state, each Center of Intelligence provides a clearer understanding of others and the world as a whole. When these three centers are balanced and interact healthily, we have access to the body's immortal spirit, the heart's overwhelming love, and the mind's divine intelligence.

The Antidote to Our Distortions and Suffering: The Soul Point

The qualities of our Point of Integration offer the antidote to our personality's suffering.

At their highest function, the qualities of our Point of Integration counterbalance the deficiencies of our personality type, also called our ego type. We find this all-important Point of Integration by going against the arrow that points to our type's number to find the number at its source. Each point has an arrow to and from it. For example, if we trace the arrow that points toward Point Six to its beginning, we find Point Nine. Some of the positive and healthy characteristics of the Nine are peacefulness, relaxation, good self-esteem, trust in the outcome, going with the flow, and the ability to look at all aspects of any given problem. These traits are opposites of my Six personality's unhealthy aspects of hyper-vigilance, self-doubt, suspicion, anxiety, and emotional projection onto others. By fully embracing the healthy traits of Nine and including them in my personality, I become a healthier individual.

When I lost my young daughter in that huge toy store, I was shaken. However, if at that time I had known about the Enneagram and the qualities of the healthy Nine, I would likely have handled the situation with much more composure. Thankfully, I have worked on incorporating a fair number of the Nine's healthy qualities. My Six ego's once-familiar frenzy for security has greatly diminished and been replaced by a settled feeling that "all is well." Also reduced is much of the anxiety over gaining others' approval in order to prevent my being "exiled." Now, I am grateful for a healthy sense of being my own authority instead of relying on a protector. I am not as hyper-vigilant now as I was then because, thanks to my experience with the Enneagram's map, I have realized that much of life happens in the present moment and that I am OK. Now, I take time to look the checkout clerk in the eyes, stop and have a chat with a neighbor, or stand in the sun feeling the warmth on my face. These are benefits of the exhilarating present. It requires courage, strength, and faith to speak my truth independently when before I would have spoken from the ego's primary need to maintain security within a group.

The Enneagram's Inner Flow: The Arrows

For us to follow the inner flow of integration, we must understand the directionality of the arrows that connect the numbers. To journey from your ego type to your Point of Integration/Soul Point:

1. Locate the arrowhead that points *to* your ego type's number.
2. Follow the arrow shaft backward until you reach its origin.
3. The number at the other end of the arrow is your Point of Integration.

The flow toward integration requires effort. Like a salmon swimming upstream to spawn, we go in the opposite direction of the arrow from our ego type to our Point of Integration. Going against the flow to our Point of Integration represents the great effort it takes to go against entropy, the tendency for energy to dissipate or devolve.

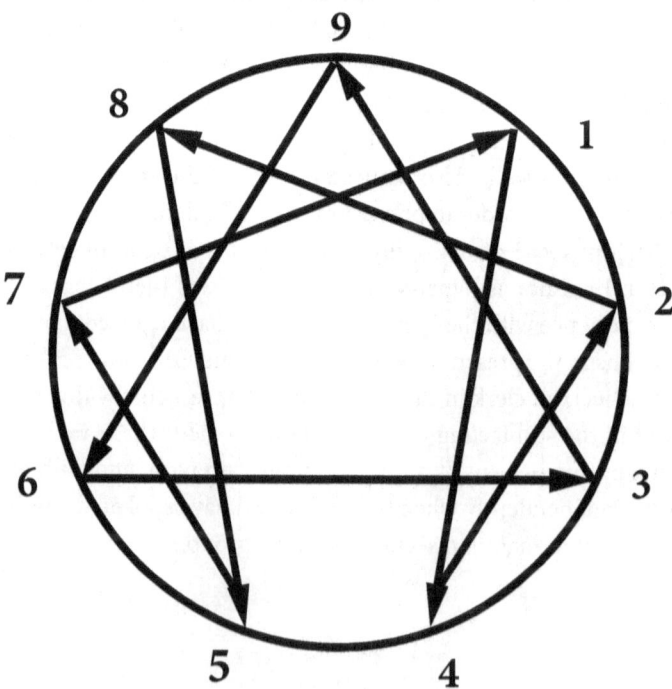

**Figure Three
The Inner Flow**

The inner flow of the Enneagram also takes us in the opposite direction, from our ego type to our Stress Point/Point of Disintegration. This is the path of least resistance: what happens when we go with what seems the easiest and takes the least effort. To journey from your ego type to your Stress Point:

1. Locate the arrow that extends *from* your ego type's number.
2. Follow its shaft until you reach its arrowhead.
3. This arrowhead points to your Point of Disintegration/Stress Point.

The inner flow of the Enneagram does not end at the Points of Integration or Disintegration. Instead, we advance, flowing against each consecutive arrow to the next number on the Enneagram until we return to our ego type at a higher level of functioning. Then we continue our trip around, over and over, in an upward spiral of growth and consciousness. Likewise, when we flow with the path of least resistance, we follow the arrows and enter a downward spiral of entropic disintegration and lower levels of functioning.

In the flow of integration, only the healthy aspects of each point become part of us; in the flow of disintegration, only the unhealthy characteristics of each of the nine energies become part of us.

Figure Four

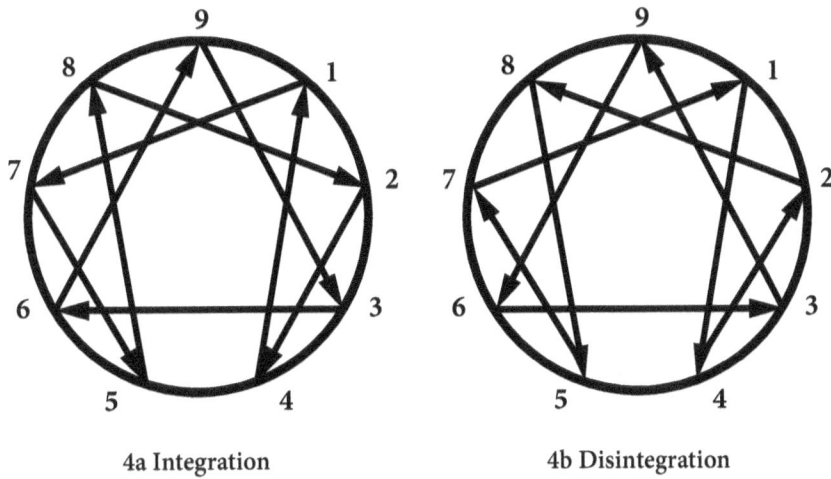

4a Integration   4b Disintegration

Each Ego Type's Integration into Its Soul Point

The Point of Integration for each of the nine types is also called their Soul Point or Heart Point. In this work, we will refer to it as the Soul Point. The Soul Point contains not only the characteristics of personality that are the antidotes for that personality's suffering but also the deeper qualities of that type's soul.

Ones integrate into the optimism of the healthy Seven and abandon the critical controller role.

Twos integrate into the healthy Four, where they are aware of what they need and able to meet those needs.

Threes integrate into the healthy Six, where they reconnect with the sense of integrity spawned in the family, group, and community, and therefore shed their focus on themselves and their achievements.

Fours integrate into the healthy One, which points the way out of self-absorption and to just the right action that puts them in contact with their true nature.

Fives integrate into the healthy Eight, where they exit their withdrawal and boldly move in the world to share their knowledge.

Sixes integrate into the healthy Nine, where they receive a peace that displaces anxiety.

Sevens integrate into the healthy Five, where reflection, contemplation, and stillness of the present replace constant movement, indulgence, and distractions.

Eights integrate into the healthy Two, where they recontact their true nature as an empathic servant.

Nines integrate into the healthy Three, where they receive the action and motivation to move effectively in the world.

In chapter 5, we will discuss how the process of integration becomes a process of transformation when we shift from our ego to the Enneagram of Soul as the base of operation.

The Number That Disintegrates Us: The Stress Point

Our ego type's number on the Enneagram also has a line that joins it to another point: our Point of Disintegration, also called our Stress Point. In stress, under pressure, or in taking a shortcut, we gravitate to this number. In doing so, we express its unhealthy traits, which may at first seem to be the solutions to our dilemmas but actually become our downfall. These unhealthy traits work hand in glove with our ego to create our hoped-for life. The problem is that the unhealthy aspects of this point are not compatible with our true nature and instead disrupt us on a deep level.

For example, my Point of Disintegration as a Type Six is found at Point Three. When fears are high and I need security and protection, my first "go-to" coping strategy is to accomplish as much as possible. This method reassures me that I am secure in my position and my place in the relationship, the group, the family, or the community. Overcompensating, maintaining a reputation for unsustainably high productivity, craving affirmation, and making yourself irreplaceable are all rabbit holes for the Six, who can still never achieve the security desired, even with these obsessive routines. Three is my Stress Point. The healthy application of Three's characteristics is not inherently negative; the unhealthy aspect is my fear-based expectations of what they should afford me.

I was in midlife before I was thoroughly convinced that my staying late at the office, working on weekends, and excelling beyond expectations did not secure my position. Despite my continuous accomplishments, I still had to deal with disagreeable people, office politics, threats to my position, and the fear of rejection. Though these are all part and parcel of the workplace for most folks, I felt unduly targeted. I perpetuated the delusion that by overachieving, I would never be questioned, targeted, or rejected. This delusion brought suffering.

Each Ego Type's Disintegration into Their Stress Point

The Stress Point is the number on the Enneagram whose unhealthy characteristics we exhibit when we are disintegrating. Our ego is attracted to this number because it appears that it will solve our dilemmas; instead, it tears us down.

Ones pick up Four's depressive energy, creating more hopelessness and negativity.

Twos take on Eight's tyranny of ruling those whom they "serve."

Threes languish in Nine's laziness and relax their standards and ethics, leading them to accomplish without integrity.

Fours take on Two's dependent relationships in hopes the other person will recognize their unique worth and save them from their sadness.

Fives adopt Seven's fantasy life, which puts them in another world far from reality.

Sixes use Three's unhealthy frenzy to accomplish as a way to build security in their position.

Sevens emulate One's perfectionist approach by planning every last detail to ensure perfect happiness.

Eights disintegrate into Five's detachment from others and enact revenge by withdrawing their strength and support from those who do not comply with them.

Nines' laziness goes too far and their lives disintegrate so seriously that they become alarmed. They adopt the anxiety and panic of the unhealthy Six.

The Levels of Consciousness within Each Type

There are three broad levels of consciousness for each ego type. The highest is Level One: Healthy/Conscious. Below that is Level Two: Average. Level Three is called Unhealthy/Unconscious. Each type has a different way of expressing itself within all three of its levels. For example, Type Eight at Level One is a servant leader with great strength and compassion. At Level Two, they are a strong bully who intimidates others and picks fights. At Level Three, the Eight is a tyrant who suppresses those they lead and makes up the truth to fit their objectives. Most of us are at the average level. But at times, all of us penetrate the highest and lowest levels.

When we are at Level One and remain there, that means there has been a tremendous amount of transformation. For a detailed discussion of the levels of consciousness, see my first book on the Enneagram, *Becoming Conscious: The Enneagram's Forgotten Passageway*.[8]

The Enneagram of Personality: Categories of Its Applications

There are several broad areas in which the Enneagram is applied. These include the Enneagram of Personality, which is used for general personality typing and integration, the Enneagram of Business, the Enneagram of Transformation, and the Enneagram of the Soul.

---

8. Howell, *Becoming Conscious*, ch. 5, pp. 93–97.

The Enneagram and Personality Typing

The aspect of the Enneagram currently captivating thousands is personality typing. In my experience, some of us are absolutely entranced with typing our personalities and even the personalities of others. Personality typing is used in general life situations by people at various levels of understanding and competency. Many of us use it to better know ourselves and others in a range of situations, including our personal lives and how we interact with people in our family, clubs, organizations, relationships, and various other circumstances.

Learning about our personality type gives us new insights into our needs, our innate strengths, and those phenomena that trap us. Typing helps immeasurably because it augments healthy introspection and self-observation. Further, it leads us to identify the personality traits that counteract our unhealthy ones. We can gain substantial insights into the complexities of human personality through typing, which can have many positive results, including self-awareness, greater tolerance of ourselves and others, and self-improvement.

Typing inspires lively conversations in which we compare personalities with one another. In such conversations, we exchange experiences and stories about personality similarities and differences. Sharing helps us grow in awareness that, while we see the world through different lenses, we are not restricted to those lenses. These are often affirming and positive exchanges because, in them, we acknowledge our humanity and even learn to laugh at ourselves.

Conversely, typing can be misused, as when we assume we know someone else's type, and therefore their motivations and intentions. Speculation about another's motives and behaviors by labeling and analyzing them may cause negative consequences for all. Typing another person runs the risk of typing them incorrectly. We may be a Five who has so disintegrated into Seven that we appear to *be* a Seven. We may be an Ego Type Three who has done much inner work and exhibits many positive qualities found at Point Six. We will see that there are many more factors that shade our expression of who we are. In short, we may be incorrect about the underlying motivations affecting other people's behaviors and therefore interact with them under a set of false assumptions.

Another concern about erroneous typing is that it increases the focus on ego characteristics. Fascination with the ego feeds the ego and gets in the way of our work on consciousness. Identifying more qualities, characteristics, and stories about our ego can entrap us within the surface layer of ourselves. As Eckhart Tolle said about our fascination with our ego and its characteristics, "It only makes more me."[9]

Fortunately, many of us eventually lose interest in fixating on types, comparing traits, and talking about their various facets. Many finally drop this when they have a fairly good feel for all nine types. This marks the end of the journey for some. Others use knowing their type as a gateway into the transformational aspects of the Enneagram.

Plenty of individuals use professional Enneagram personality typing. This service is not an amateur attempt to define someone's type. An Enneagram professional is trained to help their client accurately find their type, based on solid assessment, self-report, and other methods such as typing panels. They also work with their client to improve their lives by applying the knowledge of the types to real-life circumstances.

The Enneagram in Business, Education, and Government

As I mentioned earlier, businesses and the corporate world also find applications for the Enneagram. Most specifically, they use typing to identify personality traits in their disintegrative and integrative aspects. This application of the Enneagram improves business environments, job satisfaction, job placement, team compatibility, and overall productivity. This use of the Enneagram of Personality is also geared toward understanding the behavior of board members, executives, managers, and the general workforce.

Typing is also used to improve individual and staff competence, communication, group dynamics, and staff cohesion in the education, government, business, and corporate worlds. When the personality types are understood, essentials such as written communication, employee incentives, and role definitions can be improved. In the realm of consumer advertisement, businesses employ the Enneagram to target specific audiences. The Enneagram also solves problems in any workplace by understanding certain audiences' motivations, such as how and why the types spend money in certain ways. This application of typing emphasizes the inherent potential of each ego type. Functioning at our most healthy level of personality improves the quality of our business, educational, and governmental worlds.

9. Tolle, "Small Group Lectures."

Secular institutions are understandably hard-pressed to avoid the use of spiritual language in training and development. Many Enneagram teachers in the secular areas have reformulated the original language of Oscar Ichazo's Enneagram of Personality. Much of the newer language emphasizes functional improvement of personality without Ichazo's foundational spiritual aspects of transformation and references to the Divine. This is expected, considering that secular businesses and institutions contain a broad range of people, and a spiritually formulated learning format might present formidable problems. Trainees can be spiritual, non-spiritual, religious, or non-religious. Understandably, many employers prefer secular educational training that fits with a secular workplace. Businesses are not aiming for spiritual transformation. Rather, they use the Enneagram to improve job satisfaction, working relationships, and communication.

The Enneagram and Transformation

A third use for the Enneagram is for life transformation. Professionals such as nurses, ministers, psychologists, life coaches, rehabilitation professionals, reconciliation workers, mediators, counselors, spiritual directors, pastoral counselors, chaplains, social workers, psychiatrists, and others use the Enneagram. Though to date, few studies have been conducted on the efficacy of the Enneagram in correlation to psychological science, for many practitioners, it has become a tried-and-true tool for understanding and changing human behavior on the deepest levels. The Enneagram used in transformation uses personality type for us to understand ourselves and others more completely. Knowing our ego type is the first step in transformation; without knowing our ego type, we cannot know our soul. This sort of spiritual transformation is beyond a cognitive shift; it changes our identity, from our surface all the way down to our depths.

Transformation raises our level of consciousness as we increasingly see our ego's distortions of reality. When these distortions are removed, reality appears. When we get past our ego's fear, shame, or anger, we see the truth more clearly and our beliefs and behaviors change. Likewise, we learn to understand the deeply rooted nature of our distortions and the sheer effort it takes to shed the old concepts and transform ourselves at our depths.

Using the Enneagram in assessment and therapy/counseling—whether in clinically oriented therapy, life coaching, rehabilitation, or spiritual direction—provides a model for pinpointing our strengths and weaknesses. From there, we can work toward transformation in both clinical and non-clinical contexts.

A huge part of the transformation is that we see, for the first time, a pathway out of our unhealthy cycles. There can be a substantial overlap between the psychological and spiritual transformation. Indeed, many health professionals, including psychologists like myself, use the Enneagram to guide the healing and wholeness of our clients and patients.

Reading the Enneagram's Map

The diagram of the Enneagram of Personality is a map of nine points around a circle. Each point, or ego type, represents an energy that is described in terms of personality attributes, strengths, weaknesses, and defenses. Each of the nine energies also has a much deeper aspect. In its purest form, each is a reflection of our divine qualities: the essence of our being. Our Soul Point contains the divine qualities of our personal essence, our soul.

Figure Five
The Primary Triangle and the Hexad

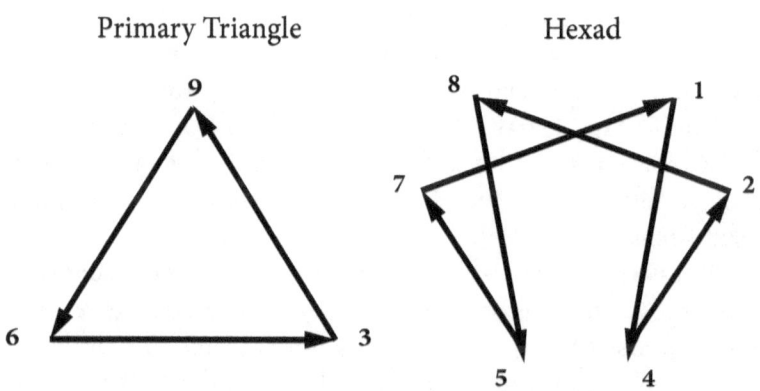

Triangle and Hexad Side by Side

Points Three, Six, and Nine make up the inner triangle on the Enneagram's "map." An irregular hexagram called a hexad is superimposed on the inner triangle. The hexad's six points are One, Two, Four, Five, Seven, and Eight. A circle surrounds the triangle, the hexad, and the nine points they contain.

The map of the Enneagram contains pathways of flow from point to point, as indicated by the arrows. Yet, our movement from point to point is only a portion of this dynamic map. There is more going on than our moving to or away from our Soul Point. We are assimilating and transforming on many dimensions as we move. To read the map, we must be familiar with the various dimensions of transformation. Here, I refer to dimensions presented in Sandra Maitri's *The Spiritual Dimension of the Enneagram*.

These dimensions include:

1. **EGO TYPE:** this is the point on the Enneagram that contains the characteristics of our personality in both its healthy and unhealthy aspects. Our ego type helps us move through the world. It can also be a source of pain when maladapted to our circumstances and thereby prevents healthy adaptation. Some refer to our ego type as our Ennea-type. We often use tests, interviews, self-assessments, and self-inquiry to determine our ego type.

2. **WINGS:** on either side of our ego type is another ego type. The two ego types flanking us are our wings. These are like alter egos from which we operate at various times. They also integrate and disintegrate in parallel with our ego.

3. **POINT OF INTEGRATION:** this point, also called the Heart Point or Soul Point, is one of the nine points on the Enneagram. The healthy aspects contained here are the antidote to the suffering caused by our ego type. Our Point of Integration contains more than healthy qualities; it holds the vital energy called our essence. Our essence is deeper than our personality alone. It is the core of our being, our very first identity: our soul child. This energy is a treasure trove of essential qualities that compose our soul. The Soul Point is found at the origin of the arrow that points to our ego type's number.

4. **POINT OF DISINTEGRATION:** this point, also called the Stress Point, is the point on the Enneagram where we gravitate when at our unhealthiest. The energy contained here in its more unconscious and unhealthy forms seems to hold the answer to our dilemmas.

However, this point ultimately disintegrates us and causes great suffering. When we follow the arrow that begins at the number of our ego type, we reach our number of disintegration. We disintegrate by moving toward the unhealthy characteristics of this point.

5. **AVOIDANCES:** each ego type has something they avoid. We avoid that which brings us face to face with our major fears, anger, or shame. For example, the powerful Eight avoids their weakness and the unique Four avoids anything common, typical, or run-of-the-mill.

    Avoidances by Ego Type:

TYPE ONE: Anger/Being wrong	TYPE FOUR: Despair/Loss of true self	TYPE SEVEN: Pain
TYPE TWO: Neediness	TYPE FIVE: Emptiness	TYPE EIGHT: Weakness
TYPE THREE: Failure	TYPE SIX: Deviance	TYPE NINE: Conflict

6. **PASSIONS:** the passion is the blind spot of the ego. It is our ego type's expression of fear, anger, or shame, our ego's way of evening the score—of establishing equilibrium and restoring our sense of worth. The problem is that the passion doesn't actually accomplish its intended purpose. For example, the passion of Ego Type Two is pride. Pride nurtures our self-worth in a distorted way, by demanding admiration, respect, love, etc. When Twos don't feel they are needed or wanted, they react by saying to themselves, "See how wonderful I am that I give you so much? You need me. . . . You owe me respect and love." For Twos, their passion of pride demands love from those they "help," but love given on demand is not real love. In the end, their pride causes them suffering.

    Passions by Ego Type:

TYPE ONE: Anger	TYPE FOUR: Envy	TYPE SEVEN: Gluttony
TYPE TWO: Pride	TYPE FIVE: Avarice/Greed	TYPE EIGHT: Lust
TYPE THREE: Deceit	TYPE SIX: Fear	TYPE NINE: Indolence/Sloth

7. **FIXATIONS:** we are commonly controlled by preoccupations and behaviors caused by our ego type's unconscious compulsions. The fixations are rigid ideas at the core of each ego type that distort reality. We are at the whim of our ego's fixation. For example, Ego Type

One's fixation is resentment. Because Ones are preoccupied with right and wrong, they fixate on resenting those whom they judge to be wrong.

Fixations by Ego Type:

Type One: Resentment	Type Four: Melancholy	Type Seven: Planning
Type Two: Flattery	Type Five: Avarice/Stinginess	Type Eight: Vengeance
Type Three: Vanity	Type Six: Cowardice	Type Nine: Indolence

8. **Traps:** our egos fall into traps that cage us in our fixation. For example, the trap of Ego Type Three is efficiency. Doing things faster, and producing greater quantities while being driven to win the race or sales contest, etc., forces the Three onto a never-ending gerbil wheel of activity. Efficiency may produce something faster but its quality may suffer. The trap of efficiency perpetuates a fixation on achieving success and admiration. Each ego type eventually runs aground because of the trap in which it finds itself.

Traps by Ego Type:

Type One: Perfection	Type Four: Authenticity	Type Seven: Idealism
Type Two: Freedom	Type Five: Knowledge	Type Eight: Justice
Type Three: Efficiency	Type Six: Security	Type Nine: Seeker

Type One is trapped by their relentless drive for perfection in all things.

Type Two's trap is their desire for freedom from their compulsive slavery to the dependencies they created.

Type Three is trapped in efficiency, always struggling to accomplish more.

Type Four's trap is their relentless search for their own authenticity, which they are convinced will enable them to live their real life.

Type Five's trap is becoming an observer; their quest to amass knowledge isolates them in their heads. They take in information by observing the world instead of participating.

Type Six's trap is their insatiable preoccupation with security, which they believe will completely protect them from danger.

Type Seven's trap is their idealism: the desire for a painless and totally positive existence.

Type Eight's trap is to impose their form of justice on the world around them.

Type Nine's trap is to be a seeker of others: to merge with them, and in doing so bypass their own inner life and identity.

9. **VIRTUES:** these are obscured soul attributes within our ego type. They are the inner goodness and strengths that animate us from our core. They help pull us out of the cycle of disintegration and into the spiral of integration. A virtue is an attribute that originates in our essence; it is the counterpoint of our passion. For the Ego Type Four, the virtue is equanimity. This is a counterpoint to their passion of envy. In equanimity, there is a balance of emotion, a quiet calm that replaces despair. In equanimity, the frenzy to have what others have subsides as the Four contacts the beauty of their own true nature.

Virtues by Ego Type:

Type One: Serenity	Type Four: Equanimity	Type Seven: Sobriety
Type Two: Humility	Type Five: Non-attachment	Type Eight: Innocence
Type Three: Veracity/Truthfulness	Type Six: Courage	Type Nine: Action

Type One's virtue is serenity, which is the inner composure and tranquility they manifest when connected to their depths. This virtue displaces their passion of anger evoked when things go wrong.

Type Two's virtue is humility, which comes with a genuine understanding of their true nature. In humility, they accept their own neediness and are grateful for help and assistance from others. Humility displaces their passion of pride, which motivated their compulsion to give.

Type Three's virtue is veracity/truthfulness, which is expressed when connected to their higher self. Truthfulness displaces their passion of deceit, which otherwise creates a false image of themselves.

Type Four's virtue is equanimity, which balances their emotions, especially when driven by the passion of envy of others. Equanimity emerges when Fours stop envying others and embody their own indisputable significance and purpose.

Type Five's virtue is non-attachment to their amassed knowledge and the various totems they hoard. When connected to their true nature, they become conscious that all knowledge is at their fingertips. No longer driven by their passion of avarice (stinginess), they loosen their hold on their reservoir of knowledge and share with the world.

Type Six's virtue, courage, has always been at the core of their essence. Courage displaces Six's passion of fear of rejection, repudiation, and loss. Sixes are not aware of their courage until they embrace their essence and reconnect to it. Then, their passion of fear gives way to their essential courage.

Type Seven's virtue of sobriety displaces their passion of gluttony. Sobriety in this sense is the tempered approach to all types of over-consumption. In their essence, they become conscious of their own inner wisdom that, when accessed, provides a fulfillment that consumables can never yield.

Type Eight's virtue of innocence vaporizes their passion of lust for domination, control, and ownership. Angry at injustice, they have forced their own brand of justice on the world around them. Their virtue of innocence returns them to the simplicity of their essence and the innocence of childhood. Now, they experience the world through the eyes of compassion and divine justice.

Type Nine's virtue is diligence, which moves them out of their passion of indolence (sloth). By taking action instead of avoiding conflict through self-narcotizing, or going to sleep on life, Nines move in peaceful diligence.

10. **HOLY IDEAS:** these are the fundamental divine energies inherent to all things. In their totality, the nine sets of Holy Ideas express nine Essential Aspects of the Divine. Each ego type's soul child was once very connected to its Holy Idea and, in fact, lived from its energy more than any other expression of the Divine. When the ego came into being, however, we lost connection to that Idea. For example,

the Holy Idea of Ego Type Eight is Holy Truth. Eights lost contact with this Idea when their ego began to take over in childhood. By losing the connection to that Idea of Holy Truth, the Eight became so strong that it thought it could create its own truth. Eights' re-embodiment of Holy Truth reconnects them with their Soul Point at Point Two, where they see the truth of who they are and of reality. Then, Eights return to their true nature of compassion.

Holy Ideas by Ego Type:

Type One:
Holy Perfection

Type Two:
Holy Will and Holy Freedom

Type Three:
Holy Law, Holy Hope, and Holy Harmony

Type Four:
Holy Origin

Type Five:
Holy Transparency and Holy Omniscience

Type Six:
Holy Strength and Holy Faith

Type Seven:
Holy Wisdom, Holy Work, and Holy Plan

Type Eight:
Holy Truth

Type Nine:
Holy Love

11. **Soul's Essential Aspects:** There are many divine aspects of our soul. These are called the Soul's Essential Aspects. There is one Essential Aspect, however, that is the core of our soul's individual essence. It is imperative that we re-contact it in order to live in our true nature.

12. **Ego's Idealized Aspects:** The bliss of being in our essence as a soul child was sublime. From the moment that we separate from our soul child, we seek to rejoin that bliss. There is a particular state of being associated with each soul child that is a living aspect of the Divine. Our ego's attempt to embody that aspect, however, is doomed to fail. Only when we have journeyed in integration past the ego's control to our essence can we truly understand and express this as the Authenticated Idealized Aspect that it is meant to be.

(See chapter 3 of this work or Sandra Maitri's book *The Spiritual Dimensions of the Enneagram* for more on Essential and Idealized Aspects.)

The Enneagram and the Soul

The Enneagram of Personality is the gateway to identifying our Soul Type. The Soul Type is our essence and our true nature, found at the depths of our being. The alchemical processes involved in combining the ego with the soul transform us so radically that we no longer express an ego type in the way we once did. Instead, we express a one-of-a-kind amalgamation of our ego and soul. The new amalgamation is created by the transformation of our ego from egocentric leadership of our being to acting in service to the soul.

The soul continuously transforms on this journey to integration as we reconnect to all the aspects of our true nature at each point of the Enneagram. The continuous journey around the Enneagram burns away veil after veil that cover our soul's full expression. We become one with our soul. This phenomenon is articulated by Enneagram teacher Sandra Maitri, in her book *The Enneagram of Passions and Virtues*: "the rigid structure of our personality melts and our infinite potential becomes accessible."[10]

The Enneagram of Soul considers the personality as the outer layer of ourselves, which early teachers like Gurdjieff referred to as our false self. On the other hand, our soul represents our true self—that is, the real, fundamental, and enduring self at our depths. Our soul animates our being and it desires to grow. As long as our false self (our ego) is our major identification, however, our soul is limited in its expression and growth. Fortunately, when our personality and its ego journey back to our soul, we transcend our false self and undergo the alchemical process of blending the ego's wisdom into our soul: that which we learned from the pain and joys we have experienced. At this point, we realize spiritual transformation as the ego becomes the servant of the soul, and we move from the Enneagram of Personality to the Enneagram of Soul. This is not a one-way journey. Throughout life, we inevitably have periods of ego domination and therefore discontinue our travels around the Enneagram of Soul and revert to the Enneagram of Personality.

---

10. Maitri, *Enneagram of Passions and Virtues*, 129.

The Enneagram's Religious Roots and the Soul

The early Christian desert mothers and fathers have been associated with the truths of the Enneagram. By the time Christianity became the Roman Empire's official religion, many churches arose all over its territories. Gradually, the church was under the political influence of Rome and therefore had little resemblance to the earliest church. To preserve the ideas of holy discipleship, and closeness to the Divine, as many as five thousand people took to the desert of Egypt to conduct private lives of asceticism and devout prayer. These devout individuals, later called the desert mothers and fathers, did not live in communities but as individual monks in their own caves. Their suffering, insight, and wisdom were written down and passed to others.[11] Some of these materials contained the rudiments of our nine virtues and passions.

Greek monk, ascetic, and desert father Evagrius of Ponticus (AD 345–399) contributed the eight deadly sins to early Christian theology. Evagrius also added the preliminary (and therefore separate) sin of love of self, composing a total of nine deadly sins, which directly correlate to the nine passions of the Enneagram. Pope Gregory later pared these down to the seven deadly sins.[12]

Ramon Llull (1242–1315) of the Third Order of St. Francis, who was beatified in 1847, was a mathematician, philosopher, writer, and mystic who fashioned a wheel with nine points that illustrated the virtues, vices, and divine qualities.[13]

Athanasius Kircher (1601–80), a German-born Jesuit scholar and mathematician, wrote about a wide array of studies, including medicine, Egyptology, and music. He compared these disciplines and cataloged the underlying mathematical and pedagogical correlations between them. He featured an Enneagram-like configuration as the frontispiece of his 1665 book, *Arithmologia*.[14]

Jesus himself, as told in the Gospel of Matthew, gave nine blessings, which reflect the nine Enneagram types in their most spiritually conscious state.[15] The Hebrew Kabbalah parallels the nine energies of the

---

11. *Wisdom of the Desert Fathers and Mothers*.
12. Casiday, *Evagrius Ponticus*.
13. Llull, *Ars Brevis 1313*.
14. Kircher, *Arithmologia*.
15. Howell, *Becoming Conscious*, 285–98.

Enneagram in the Sephirot.[16] In Islam, the eight doors or gates of Jannah also bear a striking correlation with the Enneagram: "The Eight Gates of Jannah are the sub-gates that will be accessible by the believer who gets through the main door."[17] Counting the main gate, this makes nine gateways through which to enter the Muslim paradise (Jannah), each specific to a certain type of believer.

In other words, we do not know who actually originated the Enneagram. We only know that it reflects certain preexisting truths. The remainder of this book is about the Enneagram and the soul. Just as we cannot get to our Point of Integration without first knowing our ego type, we cannot perceive the Enneagram of Soul without first knowing of the Enneagram of Personality.

In short, the deepest Enneagram, the Enneagram of Soul, reveals the many qualities and dimensions of the infinitely powerful soul we were born with. This soul of ours is our truest self to which the Enneagram leads us. Therefore, in its depths, the Enneagram guides us back to our true nature, our essence: our soul. With this reconnection comes infinitely increasing levels of consciousness, purpose, and abilities, as well as freedom from needless suffering. The implications are exponential. In this work, I name each of the points on the Enneagram of Soul based on their essential energy and qualities.

---

16. Addison, *Enneagram and Kabbalah*.
17. Kahn, "8 Gates of Jannah."

Part One

What Is Soulality?

2

Soulality

The Qualities of Our Unique Soul

The Quest for Soul and Its Nature

WHEN FRIGHTENED OR SURPRISED, my grandmother would exclaim, "Lord, have mercy on my *soul*!" One day I asked my mother, "What is Grandmother's soul?" She answered that it is an invisible self in everyone. She added that it is a part of God in us and that it goes to heaven when we die. I remember asking her where our souls are. Placing her hands over her chest, she said, "I believe our souls are here."

I couldn't quite imagine another, separate self inside me. Now I know why. At that time of our lives, we *are* our souls and are unaware of any other self. Nevertheless, I kept asking questions about the soul and God. This book tells many stories of what I've been privileged to learn over my lifetime.

Amazingly, at this point in life, after years of serious inquiry into spirituality—academically as well as experientially—I have returned to my mother's simple explanation of the soul. For me, it is indeed invisible; it is also in everyone, is tethered to the Divine, and continues to exist after the physical body dies. As for the soul's location within our body, according to Greek philosophers, such as Socrates and Plato, it resides in the area of the heart and lungs. The Greek word *psyche* can mean both "soul" and "breath" and the Greek word *pneuma* can mean "spirit" or "breath" (and is unsurprisingly related to the word *pneumon*, meaning "lungs"). This area, the center of our life force, is where my mother had placed her hands.

Whenever I ask an audience to point to their *selves*, they inevitably point to the heart region of their chests. Next, I ask them to point to their *souls*; without hesitation, they again point their fingers toward their hearts. This signifies to me that many of us consider our souls to be in our bodies' upper region, even if there's no scientific proof of the soul's existence, much less its location.

I have always been intrigued by the soul. In my early years, at Christmastime, my mother would read a book to me and my little brother, Trevor. I loved that book and went on to read it to my own kids. *The Littlest Angel*[1] is the story of an angel child who was to bring a gift to the infant Jesus but was ashamed of his offering. It was a small box of items that he'd had in life and brought with him to heaven:

> . . . a butterfly with golden wings, captured one bright summer day on the hills above Jerusalem, and a sky blue egg from a bird's nest in the olive tree that stood beside his mother's kitchen door. Yes and two white stones found in a muddy creek where he and his friends had played like small brown beavers, and, at the bottom of the box a limp, tooth-marked leather strap once worn as a collar by his mongrel dog who had died as he had lived, in absolute love and infinite devotion.

This story holds many concepts that children can relate to. I saw myself in the littlest angel. Like me, he'd had friends, found happiness in the creek, collected pretty rocks, and loved and missed his dog. Now in heaven, he loved the memories of these things: these tokens which he had brought with him from earth. For me, the story made the point that the littlest angel was the same being in heaven as he had been on earth. This resonated deeply with me as a child. Now as an adult, I have different words for this same point: our constant self, our essence, is always our truest self, regardless of how we appear to ourselves or others and regardless of what realm of consciousness in which we find ourselves. Our essence is our enduring soul, our most real identity.

My fourth-grade teacher, Mrs. Anna Jones, read *Angel Unaware*[2] to our class. It was written by the television star Dale Evans and talked about the author's baby, who was born with Down Syndrome. While that child, Robin, lived only two-and-a-half years, her life of complete love so profoundly changed the entire family that its ripple effect was

---

1. Tazewell, *Littlest Angel*.
2. Rogers, *Angel Unaware*.

tremendous. Evans wrote in the voice of her daughter in heaven as she reviews her life and purpose on earth. Robin beautifully describes the continuity between earth and heaven.

In the early 1970s, while I was a student at Yale Divinity School, I worked as an aide at a state facility for the intellectually disabled. The residents sometimes made allusions to "others" whom they saw in the room. Whenever I asked about these invisible "others," I was ignored. I kept asking until one of the young residents—I will call him Tommy—told me that the invisible people were angels. He warned me I was not to tell the staff. The residents kept it a secret; in the past, those who had told the staff they saw these beings were given a medicine that made them sleepy. As I learned more, I discovered that these "others" were an everyday element of life for the residents. One day, Tommy himself pointed out one of the "others," whom he said was standing in the room with us. While I could not see this "other," the rest of the residents said they did.

At the time, I was fortunate to be studying under Henri Nouwen, who was my faculty adviser and mentor at Yale. In one of my individual reading courses with Henri, I wrote a paper about "The Others," based on my work at the facility. In our discussions about this paper, Henri was unusually interested in the subject matter and asked if he could keep a copy. He said that he related to the themes of the paper because his sister in Holland was "mentally retarded" (the term used for the disability then). He was especially intrigued by the residents' transparency to another world, which she reportedly had also experienced.

Henri was fascinated by the soul and remarked that he always felt nearer to his own when he was with those like his sister, who saw things without the layer of ego. Henri's interest in the subject came into its fullness later in life, when he gave up his academic posts to become chaplain at the L'Arche community in France. He lived there, among the intellectually disabled, for the remainder of his life. His 1997 book, *Adam*, is a testimony to his devotion to and his learning from those with mental disabilities.

Henri was a proponent of examining the soul. Within our academic conversations, I felt his passionate drive to know more about our divine selves. His interest in the soul was academic, scriptural, and pastoral, so he frequently drew parallels between the soul and the woundedness of all human beings. Henri influenced me profoundly, both as a person and through his interest in transcendence.

As a graduate student, my constant immersion in religion saturated me with dogmas, scriptural debates, and the fiscal and business aspects of the church but most of all with continuous preaching. It was a breath of fresh air when I came upon the Society of Friends (also known as Quakers). Their major theological point, as espoused by their founder George Fox in the seventeenth century, was "There is that of God in every [hu]man."[3] Fox later added that all people have an inward light.

In the early 1970s, the Friends in New Haven met on Yale's old campus. Meetings were mostly silent, with no preaching, no rituals, and no distractions: just what my soul needed at the time. It was a community that was more transparent to the Divine than I had ever encountered. Their reverent silence, heartfelt kinship, and acceptance of everyone fed me spiritually when nothing else did. I distinctly remember feeling that I was not sitting with *people* in a circle but with *souls*. Whenever a person in the meeting spoke from the silence, I felt their truth emanating from an inward light: their soul.

In the mid-1970s, as a graduate student in clinical psychology at the University of Virginia, I met psychiatric resident Raymond Moody, who had just released his book, *Life After Life* (1975). In his work, Raymond coined the term "near-death experiences" (NDEs). He chronicled real-life examples and commonalities among NDE reports. I met some of the people whose NDE descriptions he mentioned in his book. I found them all to be convinced that our soul survives our physical death. I am still friends with Raymond and his seminal work continually reminds me of the idea that our consciousness—or soul—is not dependent upon being in a physical body.

While I have included other stories in this book regarding encounters with my own soul, I have paired them with subjects pertinent to the part of the book in which they appear.

After my wife Lark and I married and began our careers and our family, my soul work took the form of a practicum. My young children (later teens), my patients, and my father's illness forced me to either put into practice much of what I had learned about the soul or to disregard it all and play it by ear. Soul work was important to me though, so instead of just sleepwalking through this phase of life, I made a conscious decision to become my own guinea pig. I was faced with big challenges and my question was, how would I spiritually handle them?

Only six years after I married Lark, my father suffered a sudden and incapacitating stroke and I had to draw on previously untapped spiritual

---

3. Fox, *Works of George Fox*, 111, 55.

capacities within myself. Having just begun my first professional position as a psychologist at a medical residency program, I also had to help my mother with my father's physical and mental conditions while living three hundred miles away. Besides the constant travel and time off work that took, negotiating the complicated sale of my dad's business also fell on my shoulders. Unaware I was capable of handling all these things, I was shocked at the capacities that manifested from what I now know were my depths. I did not know at the time that these were part of what I would come to know as my "soulality."

Real truths repeat themselves. One day, in my late forties, I was visiting a friend's mentally disabled son—I will call him Daniel—in a nursing facility. Thoughts of our invisible selves—our souls—flooded my mind. Daniel, who was about my age, was terminally ill. His mother, my friend, was exhausted from continuous caretaking so I sat with him for a while. At some point, Daniel looked up into the corner of his room, pointed, and identified "The watchers and the lookers." His eyes followed something that I could not see. When I told his mother what had happened, she reported that Daniel had seen "lookers and watchers" that no one else could see since he was a child. This brought back the memories of a lifetime ago: the mentally disabled residents who also saw invisible "others."

As I will discuss later in this book, I came to know my soul in profound ways as Lark, Lauren, and I endured Ben's long illness. Though my son's illness ended in his death, the amazing things we learned about the ego, the soul, the Divine, and of course the Enneagram, changed our lives forever.

As life has unfolded, I have gathered aspects of my soul and witnessed them ripen within me. I have known people in my life whom I recognized were living from their souls. There are those in our daily lives who, like the residents in the state facility, see through the eyes of their soul much of the time. They operate differently from most of us, able to not only see past the dread, confusion, frustration, and conflict of life but to participate fully in the present moment. A sense of joy permeates everything they do, even if it is mundane or unpleasant. Certainly, they have individual personalities, but another subtly powerful and luminous energy also shines through them. I believe these dear people live so differently because they are rooted in their souls. Their identity is not found in their personality but from their depths, where the qualities of soul compose their "soul-ality."

Beneath and Beyond Our Personality: Our Soul

We all know our personalities. We know our sense of humor, our likes and dislikes, our fears, and our vanities. We know our strong points and weak ones. We know if we are extroverted or introverted, intuitive or more empirically oriented. We know our tempers and our tender spots, our pet peeves and our indulgences. We know our capacities for sadness and merriment, as well as how we express those emotions. While hugely important, these elements still make up only our outer edges. Though we may see these traits as being the key to our identity, we are much more. Our truest selves are our souls and the qualities within them are their "bones." These fundamental spiritual qualities support our personality and provide the inner structure of our entire being. When we become conscious of these soul qualities, we operate from the depths of our wholeness. When these qualities are not recognized, however, we operate from personality alone, disconnected from what supports us from the inside out.

The bones of our soul are the infrastructure of our being and include such qualities as compassion, sacrifice, deep joy, unconditional trust, vision, hope, perseverance, truth, tranquility, peace, faith, self-realization, consciousness, and love. Without these qualities, we would be only a personality living on our outer surface, disconnected from our amazing soul. Our link to our soulality has vast implications, not only for ourselves as individuals but also for the collective destiny of humanity.

To determine the particular qualities of our soulality, we first have to know the basic components of any soul. In this work, I have derived major components of the soul from theology as well as foundational teachings of the spirituality of the Enneagram. The Enneagram contains the major dimensions of our soul. As we study these components, we are in a better position to discern our particular soulality—both how it is spontaneously expressed and how we can use our consciousness to manifest its many aspects.

Following the Enneagram's inner flow helps us slowly unfold our particular soulality. Once our soul qualities are illuminated, we can embody them. This is not to say that our soulality makes us angels on earth, but that spiritual consciousness increases with soul discovery and embodiment. Our soulality is not a product of intellect, money, status, power, or notoriety. It is inherent in all of us; our soulality is our particular set of soul qualities, expressed as our true nature.

Though they are very important, our acquired ego personalities are not the skeletons that support us. If we come to know our soulality and relate to the souls of others, our lives will continue to "flesh out" our spiritual bones and we become "the fulfillment of the seed planted in us at our making."[4]

Concepts of the Soul and Its Progression

The Greek philosopher Plato believed the soul is our truest self, is unseen on the physical plane, and is immortal. Plato espoused the pre-existence of the soul, a foundational precept of Platonic innatism.[5] The second- and third-century Christian church father Origen was also a proponent of the pre-existent soul.[6] According to some theologians, Jesus himself acknowledged this concept of soul.[7] The concept of the pre-existing soul is likewise described in the Jewish texts, like Wisdom of Solomon 8:19–20, and Islamic theology.[8, 9] However, it is more common for Christians, at least, to believe that, rather than pre-existing, the soul is created by God at or after conception.

Whether our soul is created with the body upon conception (or at some other point before birth) or pre-exists the body, most of the world's major spiritual pathways acknowledge our souls as our fundamental identities. The concept of soul qualities that I have called our soulality is consistent with the archetypal soul referred to by the major traditions. The level of transparency between our ego and soul and the number of soul qualities that we can become conscious of help determine the spiritual progress we can make. The Enneagram holds the code for us to understand our soul and how to live in it.

Most of us spend much of our lives on the level of the ego. However, when the suffering mounts and the ego cannot relieve that suffering, we reach into our depths for respite. Why do we reach into our depths? That

---

4. Appleton, "Gathering Prayer."
5. Plato, *Plato's Meno*.
6. Tripolitis, *Doctrine of the Soul*.
7. One of Jesus' disciples asked Jesus if the man born blind was being punished for his past sins (John 9:1–12). How could he be punished for past sins if he had no past, i.e., no pre-existence? Jesus did not negate the disciple's possible explanation, which is why many think that Christ himself may have thought the soul was indeed pre-existent.
8. Porter, "Pre-Existence of the Soul," 53–115.
9. Gulpaygani, *Discursive Theology*, vol. 1.

is where we find the impressions, sensations, and memories of a time long ago when we were supported by the world around us and experienced no suffering. Once we are overrun with suffering, we seek that sort of painless bliss again. Though we lost touch with our bliss, we know somewhere in the recesses of our minds that we once lived in such a way and we desire to live in it once more. To return to our true nature's bliss and peace, our ego must abdicate to the soul. There is a set trajectory to our souls' forward progress.

The Spiral Continuum of Being

The Enneagram reflects the truth that there are gradations of soul progression. We express these gradations as we pass through different stages of our lives. The Spiral Continuum of Being illustrates the broad stages of spiritual progression. At its bottom is our origin, called Essence/Soul Child. At the upper regions is our Essence/Transformed Soul. In between these two extremes in ascending order are the three stages of Egocentricity, Coexistence, and Soulcentricity/Soulality.

When we leave our childhood state of Essence/Soul Child, we spiral upward to the next stage of Egocentricity. In this stage, we are increasingly centered on ego-based proclivities, traits, expressions, strengths, weaknesses, avoidances, preferences, and fixations. Our personalities develop in concert with these egoic needs and drives.

Then we spiral upward from Egocentricity to the middle of the continuum, where there is a flux between our ego and soul. This is sometimes a contentious zone of internal conflict. At other times, it is the place of spiritual alchemy wherein the ego and soul can peacefully integrate. On the Spiral Continuum of Being, neither the ego nor the soul dominates. This state is called Coexistence.

As we spiral upward from Coexistence toward Soulcentricity/Soulality, we see that our soul qualities are the very bones of our souls. When we become conscious of these qualities, we realize that—like our body's bones—they compose the unseen structure that supports us. By the stage of Soulcentricity/Soulality, our ego and our personality have transformed from being dominant to being in service to our soul.

At the top of the Spiral Continuum of Being is Essence/Transformed Soul. This stage includes and transcends Soulcentricity/Soulality. In pure soul, we live in God, conscious of our divine nature.

Figure Six
The Spiral Continuum of Being

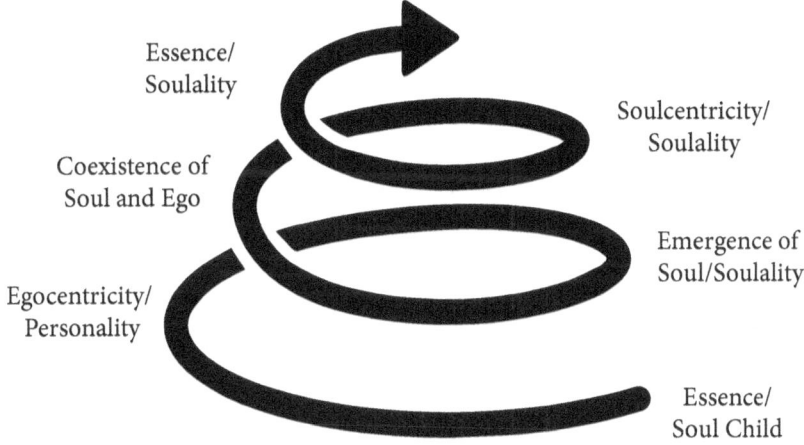

The Spiral Continuum of Being

Our stage on the Spiral Continuum of Being depends on many converging factors, such as our stress level, life experiences, resolution of loss and trauma, level of consciousness, and our accumulated spiritual development. As we progress up the spiral, our consciousness transforms and creates vastly new thoughts, feelings, and ways of moving in the world. The soul is returning to itself in a much higher state of consciousness than it had at the beginning of life.

The progressive levels of the Spiral Continuum of Being mark how the soul deals with its corresponding ego. Many of us do not progress past the egocentric stage. If, however, we can progress to the coexistent stage, the ego is transformed and we can progress further toward embodying our soul qualities. The next section discusses several methods by which we can discern the qualities of our soulality.

Self-Remembering, Soulality, and the Shadow

Paradoxically, many qualities that compose our soulality are opposite to those of our expressed personality. This phenomenon can be understood by exploring an unconscious aspect of our psyche known as the shadow. The shadow is composed of our repressed, unexpressed aspects and includes many energies that are opposite from the personality we portray to the world or ourselves. For example, we could be unaware that we have the repressed urge to have a lot of money that we show off with a flashy car and house. Because of our sense of humility and discretion, however, we may not even be in touch with this drive. Indeed, we might repress it, but it leaks out as we dwell on it, and as we repeatedly claim that we would never want those specific things.

In the therapeutic process of shadow work, we journey into repressed, unconscious emotions, drives, proclivities, fantasies, capacities, talents, and motivations, allowing ourselves to consciously experience these for the first time. Knowing and dealing with these facets of ourselves is a key part of learning to maintain equilibrium and wholeness. Delving into our unknown shadow is best done with the guidance of a reputable spiritual director, therapist, or pastoral counselor who is trained in this method.

Importantly, the shadow holds both negative and positive repressed aspects of ourselves. Many hidden strengths reside in our shadow. A person may have a great aptitude for cooking but could go a lifetime without unearthing this talent, while it stays unknown and unexpressed in their shadow.

Though obscured from conscious awareness, our shadow greatly influences our avoidances, virtues, motivations, and most importantly, our passions. Shadow energy is denied or turned inward, which causes us great internal conflict. As the shadow's energies push for expression, we lock these "monsters" in the cellar of our being and deny their existence.

How does the shadow relate to knowing our soulality? Psychologist Carl Jung said the following of the shadow, "To confront a person with his shadow is to show him his own light."[10] Paradoxically, the shadow can lead to the soul. Sandra Maitri, in her work *The Enneagram of Passions and Virtues*, says:

> . . . if our practices and our orientation toward our personal processes are those congruent with the ways our deepest nature operates and the ways that it affects the human soul, our inner

---

10. Jung, *Good and Evil in Analytical Psychology*, 872.

work is likely to bring us closer to our depths. If our practices and orientation are those of the personality, they will only lead us deeper into enmeshment with that structure of the virtues.[11]

Our ego distorts our virtues into passions. The following list illustrates each type's passion and its corresponding virtue. Our passions may be part of our unknown shadow or we may know them well.

Ego Type	Ego Virtue	Passion
ONE	Serenity	Anger
TWO	Humility	Pride
THREE	Veracity/Truth	Deceit
FOUR	Equanimity	Envy
FIVE	Non-attachment	Avarice/Greed
SIX	Courage	Fear
SEVEN	Sobriety	Gluttony/Overindulgence
EIGHT	Innocence/Simplicity	Lust/Arrogance
NINE	Action	Indolence/Laziness

From this list of passions, which are also the foundation of our shadow material, it is easy to see the corresponding virtue. Our virtue, whether repressed or unrecognized, is a primary soul quality within each of us, whereas, our passion, which often drives us, is frequently something we are unconscious of or deny. Through shadow work, once we recognize our unconscious passion, we can trace it back to our corresponding virtue and have access to one of the most fundamental and powerful qualities of our soulality.

Self-Remembering, Soulality, and the Enneagram of Holy Ideas

Soulality is the composite of our soul qualities that pre-date our personality and fundamentally compose our truest selves. Self-remembering, named by George Ivanovich Gurdjieff,[12] is the process of recalling and re-knowing our essence. Personal essence is our particular combination of soul qualities. It is the quintessential, distilled, fundamental identity that reflects the divine in us.

11. Maitri, *Enneagram of Passions and Virtues*.
12. Gurdjieff, *Views from the Real World*, 79–80.

In self-remembering, we become aware of our essence and of all the particular qualities of our soul-self: our soulality. When we were children, we had never been separated from the Divine or lived outside of our soulality. In our innocence, we simply reflected and expressed divine qualities; we naturally trusted, loved, worked, and co-created. Later in childhood, however, we became disconnected from that sacred self. Self-remembering is a type of self-inquiry that helps us recall our true nature. In self-remembering, attention shifts from ego to utter openness to the divine mystery. This process can include the revelation of our soul child, who has been preserved in our psyche.

Through the process of self-remembering, we can more fully comprehend the soul's immense power and beauty. Our consciousness of our soulality enables us to contrast it with our personality. For many of us, this contrast brings awe-inspiring realizations. For instance, it is possible to realize that the soul has completely different intentions than those of the ego and its personality. We begin to comprehend that our soul is completing its purpose and fulfilling its contract with the Divine, yet our personality alone may be completely unaware of this. Caroline Myss discusses the concept of our individual soul's purpose in her book *Sacred Contracts*. Myss proposes that every soul is working its way back to wholeness and that there are specific divine purposes it must complete to progress. The self-rememberer finds that the soul is forever tethered to the Divine and their sacred contract with the Divine. Our ego, however, is about fulfilling its own narrative, avoiding its fears, and imitating the bliss of early childhood that we lost contact with.

Though we may go through the process of self-remembering and successfully reconnect with our essence, we can remain in the state of essence only if our ego submits to our soul. To do this, we acknowledge that trying to make the ego's narrative come true is futile. We must also accept that the ego's avoidances, traps, passions, etc., will not ultimately satisfy us. When we self-remember our essential nature, our soul becomes our chief executive officer. Our soul's purpose and divine expression are to manifest its Holy Idea and other qualities.

The nine Holy Ideas are the nine essential expressions of Divine Love.[13] The soul's Holy Idea is what the ego has been trying for years to imitate under its own steam, albeit based on its distorted perception of reality. To fully express our Holy Idea, our ego submits to that Idea.

---

13. Erikson, *Childhood and Society*.

The Holy Ideas were developed by Enneagram teacher Oscar Ichazo,[14] founder of the Arica School. Ichazo is the originator of the Enneagram of Personality and conceptualized 108 enneagons in all. The Holy Ideas, elucidated by A. H. Almaas,[15] are:

Type One: Holy Perfection: I am perfect because my wholeness is complete, not flawless.

Type Two: Holy Will and Holy Freedom: I can rely on divine will to know that all is taken care of, leaving me able to be free, full, and happy.

Type Three: Holy Harmony, Holy Law, and Holy Hope: All is run by a harmonious upward movement undergirded by fixed laws. All is being accomplished; therefore, I am hopeful.

Type Four: Holy Origin: I am one with my true source and therefore I know who I am and what I am to do.

Type Five: Holy Omniscience and Holy Transparency: The Divine and divine knowledge are accessible to me everywhere at all times. In being transparent to these, I may move in the world, sharing them.

Type Six: Holy Strength and Holy Faith: I have inner capacities of strength and faith and I manifest these always.

Type Seven: Holy Wisdom, Holy Work, and Holy Plan: In seeking wisdom, I know my work and, in it, I discover the Holy Plan.

Type Eight: Holy Truth: Reality is true and if I see the truth and embody it, I will understand that the world beyond me is made of love.

Type Nine: Holy Love: I love myself and, from there, I take action to love others.

The Holy Ideas all proceed from and are aspects of Holy Love. They are the purest and most fundamental perceptions of reality: states of pure being. These nine expressions of love are each associated with a corresponding personality type on the Enneagram of Personality. We are most connected to our Holy Idea before the ego forms and, until then, we express it naturally. When the ego emerges, we forget it; the ego distorts that Holy Idea into passions and fixations.

14. Ichazo, "Arica Psycho-Catalyzers."
15. Almaas, *Facets of Unity*.

As a child, I lived in strength and faith, but as my wounds accumulated, fear, shame, and inferiority set in. Having been disconnected from my Holy Idea, my ego took over and tried to reconstruct the absolute love, trust, and peace of my earlier days. It was incapable of giving me these holy qualities, so it tried to imitate them by making my life secure. My ego gained supreme importance in my life when it promised it could reunite me with Holy Strength and Holy Faith, but it delivered only a facsimile of these.

As with most of us, when life took off, my ego became my main identity. As a teen, it seemed like I knew most everything or could at least figure it out. In young adulthood, my ego ran on certain presuppositions about how life worked and how to negotiate the world. When the ego was successful in solving problems and defending me, I had good feelings that I mistook for peace, trust, strength, and faith. I took for granted that my ego was who I was. Eventually, I reached the point in life when I had to accept that my ego was not foolproof. Sometimes, its narrative *didn't* come true. I realized there must be a deeper layer within me. To relieve the suffering, my ego had to forgo its prior narrative and begin to merge with my soul. Only then could it healthily begin to submit to my soul. In this alchemical process of blending, my ego is not "killed" or silenced; it is transformed into an arm of my soul. This is a daily process, not a sudden change.

Self-Remembering and the Three Centers of Intelligence

Our three Centers of Intelligence—Mind, Heart, and Body—have their own "brains." Respectively, these are our intellectual/cognitive processes, our emotional life, and our physical body. Each can be used on both the ego and soul levels. On the soul level, the soul shines through these three centers to express itself. Therefore, the mind becomes the receptor, processor, and storage for divine intelligence. The heart does the same for divine love, as does the body for the Immortal Spirit that underlies all physical manifestations of life. Each center is used in sync with the other two, in transmitting our soul's qualities. All three centers—rich with impressions, memories, sensations, and much more—are treasure troves for self-remembering.

Self-Remembering, Soulality, and the Body Center of Intelligence

The fundamental nature of the physical senses makes the Body Center of Intelligence the first through which we perceive the world. At the beginning of life, the other two centers depend on the Body Center to receive outside information.

Our physical sensations inform us about the world, but they also tell us an amazing amount about our souls. We experience physical sensations long before we develop our ego, language, intricate cognition, or emotions. For example, we feel our first experiences of love through our physical sensations, even in the womb. We can re-experience that love now through the deep memories that our five senses have encoded into our body memory. Because they were our first receptors of love, when triggered today, these senses elicit those same deep feelings.

In our process of self-remembering, we first imagine the soul qualities we most value, list them, then search our memories for instances or people associated with those qualities. Even the act of selecting or identifying which qualities we will focus on reveals a lot about our soulality. We have many facets within us but this choice reflects that which we deem important. While it might seem arbitrary to "pick" them, we are naturally drawn toward those soul qualities that reflect our truth.

Alternatively, we may search for sensory experiences associated with positive memories. These memories usually trace back to a soul quality anchored into the body long ago. The search takes the form of sensory memory review. Once we detect a sensory anchor, we then try to discover its experiential origin. It could be a circumstance, a setting, a situation, an action, and/or a person. This leads to early memories of our first experiences and takes us deeper into the particular layers of the soul.

Sensory review is an easy practice. We simply identify and inquire of ourselves the origins of the sensory experiences that bring us the most profound peace, calm, and atmosphere of support. We can trace some of the most soulful sensory experiences back to early childhood.

One of my soul qualities is deep relaxation. In my sensory review, I learned that the sound of running water anchors that relaxation within me. I discovered the origins of this when I remembered the long drives we often made to see my father's family, three hundred miles from our home. Inevitably, we stopped along the way so that Dad could take me to the gas station or restaurant lavatory. Often, to help me start the process of emptying my bladder, he would turn on the water in the sink. Immediately, things began to flow. To this day, the sound of running water positively affects me in mind and body. It helps me experience the soul quality of deep relaxation through tranquility and serenity.

A woman who went through this process told me:

> In searching for trust as a quality of my soul, I found myself wondering how trust first smelled, tasted, sounded, felt, and appeared to me. In my "sensory review," I immediately associated the feeling of deep trust with—of all things—the taste of vanilla milkshakes. I would always, even as a child, order the thickest shake possible; now I realize that in order to taste the shake, I would have to suck hard on the straw; this simulated my early breastfeeding, I suppose. The rich taste may be paired with my early breastfeeding and the trust I had in my mother or it may be that the richness of a shake anchors in me the safety and nurturance from my mom and dad when they took me to the Dairy Queen. The sweetness and even the shake's aroma immediately return me to a state of trust that conveys to me, "all I need is here." I relax; this sweetness is beyond words. There is no bitterness or anxiety. This is the sweet trust of love. I know trust is a major quality of my soul.

Another person in the process of self-remembering most associated his soul quality of trust with his kinesthetic senses. He said:

> I link trust to touch. I remember the hug from my mother as she dropped me off at school and when she picked me up. I feel trust within the tightness of an embrace. My mother's hug was tight; I could count on her. For me now, close and tight embraces are an embodiment of trust. My mother is no longer alive, but I never lost my connection with the trust she placed in me. But I wouldn't say that I generally trust well; I am in the military and suffer from Post-Traumatic Stress Disorder. I am overly cautious. But in re-experiencing my mother's hugs, I re-enter the state of trust I lived in as a little boy.

A college student anchored one soul quality to her olfactory sense. "At college, I keep a pillow from home. It has the smell of the house in it and when I put my face in the pillow, I breathe in 'home.' In the first whiff, I immediately feel secure and loved."

For another man in his fifties, trusting is directly related to a body sensation. He said, "When I trust, I have warm feelings in my stomach; I feel secure like a child in the care of my parents. I specifically remember sitting on my father's shoulders, his hands grasping my ankles and balancing me perfectly. But when I feel off-kilter, unbalanced and unanchored, my abdomen area churns."

Still another example is the sense of hearing, especially certain sounds. Music is paired with many sensations. A brother and sister who are now in adulthood both remember the classical music their mother played during their nap time when they were toddlers. Both still associate classical music with security, love, and relaxation. Auditory perceptions embedded in them the soul qualities of peace and contentment, which they continue to feel today.

The breath too is a very important sensory experience that pairs with soul qualities. Tied mostly to the kinesthetic sense, the physical feelings associated with our lungs' rhythmic inhalations and exhalations begin with our emergence from our mother's womb. Once we are outside of her body, breathing marks the beginning of our own body's independent life. The rhythm of our breath links to our heartbeat and provides life's tempo.

Of his breath, a gentleman in his late eighties said:

> I have done breath meditation for decades. Taking me right to my center, I become one with all. I am renewed in that oneness and feel most secure and alive there. It is difficult for me to leave the distractions of my waking life and travel to that oneness unless I follow my breath. I pair my breath with the deep feeling of peace I had as a child while going to sleep in my bed alone. I would listen to my own breathing as I peacefully fell asleep. Every time I follow my breath to my center, I trust that journey and the place to which it takes me.

The breath elicits the soul qualities associated with aliveness and oneness with the Divine.

Self-Remembering, Soulality, and the Heart Center of Intelligence

Our heart is the first organ we develop and it is the center of our aliveness. It is also the region in which we receive, process, and store our emotions. Heavy-heartedness is synonymous with sadness, lightheartedness is associated with happiness, and wholeheartedness signals full commitment and enthusiasm.

As babies and young children, we express our inborn emotions in an unfiltered manner. Fundamentally, the Heart Center is the emotional domain of our lives. We channel all of our emotional states—such as equanimity, tranquility, serenity, empathy, humility, accomplishment, hope, creativity, fulfillment, and authenticity—through it. Likewise, this is where we process and express hatred, envy, anger, rage, resentment, and exasperation.

The infant's natural state of well-being is most interrupted by physical distress. Anger is a natural reflex in response to distress. The first feelings of shame arise in early childhood when we sustain an embarrassment; these first occurrences of shame and anger are the very beginnings of our ego. Babies have few fears: loud noises, falling, and people who are unknown to them. As the ego develops, however, shame becomes a more prevalent emotion.

In the process of self-remembering, we access our Heart Center as we search for our first recollection of our feelings. These memories may be preverbal and therefore deeply rooted in the five physical senses. In postverbal development, we associate the feeling of love, for example, with certain words and actions of our caretakers and loved ones. Therefore, the very presence of one of these people can prompt those feelings of love.

Also anchored in our hearts are pain and other unpleasantries, great and small. However, these can lead us to our soul qualities. When I was four or five, the paperboy was killed on his motorcycle in front of our apartment. His brakes failed and he had run into the back of a garbage truck. Even now, the sound of a garbage truck triggers uncomfortable feelings in me. My soul dealt with this tragedy in many ways, some of which ended up being positive. Even though I experienced horror, the event prompted my soul quality of deep compassion. I recall my sadness for the paperboy, whom I had admired from behind my screen door as he gallantly threw newspapers onto each doorstep from atop his blue motorcycle. The sorrow I felt at losing him developed into compassion, which became an important part of my emerging soulality.

As a young boy, I'd often spend the night with my grandmother, who lived nearby. She made me feel cherished. My grandmother took pains to keep me from falling down the stairs at night by moving a piece of furniture in front of the stairway. Though I was not fearful of falling, her vigilance made me feel treasured and loved. Those memories continue to resonate with these same soul qualities today, as does any instance in which someone else demonstrates that they value my welfare.

Self-remembering reveals our highly charged emotions. When I was six years old, and before I had learned to swim, I fell into a neighbor's swimming pool. As I was sinking, a teen standing nearby jumped in and pulled me out of the deep end. I had an emotional imprint of gratefulness. I still remember the young man's face and name and am most thankful to him.

In another example of emotional imprinting, I met a woman who pairs the feeling of being cared for with the sights and sounds of the circus. As a little girl, her father invited her to go with him as his special guest to the circus that was coming to town. She said, "He told me that he didn't want anyone other than me to go to the circus with him. During the entire time, he held me on his lap while I watched the show and ate cotton candy." Her soul pairs the qualities of being desired, valued, and cared for with being held. These are part of her soulality.

Self-Remembering, Soulality, and the Mind/Head Center of Intelligence

In babyhood and early childhood, the youngster learns by building mental structures that developmental psychologist Jean Piaget defined as "schemas."[16] These are the categories of every subject the child knows. Each subject has a heading or title. For example, there is a schema for animals, which includes a list of all the kinds of animals the child can name. Schemas are the building blocks of information, from which we organize such methods of thinking as memory, processing, differentiating, and intuiting. Of course, these schemas expand as life progresses.

The soul needs the Mental Center of Intelligence to grow and to express itself. For example, the soul uses the mental function of memory for reflection. In reflecting on its memories, the soul builds energy, enthusiasm, and power. Memories of helping and being helped, of creating, of succeeding, and of taking in new knowledge, etc., are memories that not only build ego but, in their deepest sense, reflect the soul. The most vivid memories can be either wonderful or terrible. The Mind Center's memory function is essential to the soul. We recall not only mental memories but those of the body and heart. The Mental Center processes and catalogs these. Finally, it is the Mind Center that puts words to and expresses them.

16. Piaget, *Origins of Intelligence in Children*.

Therefore, the Heart and Body Centers also make use of cognitive memories. A gentleman told me:

> I have a memory of playing in my little sister's baby bed when I was just five or six. My mother saw me, and instead of scolding me, she wrapped me in a blanket and patted my back until I fell asleep right there. That memory is huge for me because I was very sad in thinking that my sister had taken my place. I connected the dots that when my mother did that for me, she affirmed that I was still her baby boy and was not displaced. I would say that because of my Mind Center, I was able to reason out that I was still valued by my mother. The Mind Center must have immediately sent the message to my heart. I felt so loved.

This soul quality of security through reasoning is a part of this gentleman's soulality.

We learn the particularities of objects, situations, memories, and people, and we create mental associations with each, a process called differentiation. At the start of our babyhood, we see everything as concrete and take it all at face value. When we later realize that all things are not as they appear, the processes of assimilation and accommodation come into play. We categorize information before we include it into our repertoire of skills and knowledge. If the experience does not fit into our current mental structures, we build new ones to accommodate it. We test this information to see if it meets an acceptable level of truth or if we should file it in the mental compartment of "untrue."

The cognitive process of differentiation is essential to the soul. A young woman said that she had an experience in which her soul took on new energy and greater depth. Though her father had severely abused her as a child, there had been times when he had seemed quite caring. She loved him but was never really sure if he had ever truly loved her. He died suddenly when she was eleven years old. Now, in her thirties, she was doing forgiveness and differentiation work in spiritually oriented psychotherapy, finally confronting the mixed signals she received from her father and her lack of closure due to his early death.

In therapy, she was able to separate the man from his alcoholism, a process that she was unable to do as a child. This categorization in spiritual form led her to be able to forgive. She said:

> I had heard many times the phrase, "I don't know where to put this," referring to something that we don't know what to do with mentally. It's like, how am I supposed to deal with it? Now my

soul has a place for a very disturbing set of circumstances. My soul now trusts that those events of childhood were exactly what I needed to develop into the teacher that I am now.

This is an example of soulality in development. The years of ambiguity regarding her father were years that stirred the soul. Yet, when the time was right, her soul was able to find a much-needed resolution to one of the most vital issues of her life. Her persistent reaching for peace was an underlying soul quality that finally brought her a long-sought conclusion to her grief, anger, love, and confusion.

The very night she finally forgave her father, she stopped at a large shopping center for groceries on the way home. In the parking lot, when she opened the door of her car, she found a golden necklace on the pavement that spelled out the words "Your Daddy Loves You." This event caused her to create another schema of "soul messages from beyond." This expectation of divine happenings became one of the strongest components of her soulality.

Intuition is another mental process that the soul uses to discern things. It is the ability to sense a truth that may not be obvious—a way of knowing without actually knowing the facts. Intuition comes naturally for some and can be developed in others. What does it have to do with soulality? Our soul spiritually intuits and discerns the truth about a person, decision, or circumstance, regardless of appearances.

Intuition in its advanced functions includes pre-cognition, the foreknowledge of what may be going to happen, what someone thinks or feels, and religious experiences such as epiphanies that may not be logically explainable. The Mind Center is the key to the soul's ability to receive information conveyed in a vision or message from another realm. Pioneer psychologist William James explains this phenomenon in his classic work, *The Varieties of Religious Experience*. He writes, "They are states of insights into depths of truth unplumbed by the discursive intellect. They are illuminations, revelations, full of significance and importance, all inarticulate though they remain; and as a rule, they carry with them a curious sense of authority for after-time."[17]

Intuition may be a mental faculty but it is also related to the Heart and Body Centers. The mind relays the message to the other centers. Our soul's intuition leads us to those people who become our friends, our partners. It leads us to our life's work and sometimes to the very city,

---

17. James, *Varieties of Religious Experience*, 371. See Lectures 16 and 17.

state, and house we live in. It also can steer us away from those people and situations that would not be best for us. The soul knows who is medicine for us and who is poison. Its intuitive senses know whom we need to play with, wrestle with, and learn from. The more conscious we are, the more we can understand our intuitive capacities and rely on what they tell us.

When I was five, my soul's intuition led me to my best friend, Freddie. At first, I just loved the fact he could climb a tree faster than anyone I knew. Now that I look back on that friendship, I see my soul quality of "seeking the mystery." If my five-year-old mind hadn't somehow known that Freddie was the very friend I needed, I would never have picked him out of all the kids of the neighborhood to be my best buddy. I couldn't see it then, but now I see that Freddie was the one who taught me courage. It was a latent quality, deep within me, that was getting covered over by fear. Freddie helped it emerge.

A teenager recounted how intuition led him to recognize one of his soul qualities:

> I knew I was adopted but my parents never told me. I'll never know how I knew it because I actually looked just like both my adopted parents and there were never any references to any adoption. This feeling kept growing in me, as I began to put two and two together. My parents never mentioned my mother's pregnancy, my birth, or the hospital stories that all my friends and their families spoke of. I found a soul quality of mine due to this situation. That quality was compassion. I felt sorry for my folks because they obviously thought that adoption was a second-best way to have a child. I felt the opposite, though. That adoption was a great way to have a child! It made me feel like taking their shame away from them because they really didn't need to keep the truth away from me; I was fine with it! My heart ached for them until I was fourteen and finally told both of them that I knew. They thanked me. We all wept.

Soulality in the Beatitudes

Of course, our souls have numerous qualities corresponding to the many aspects of love. Soul qualities are found in the Holy Ideas, the virtues, and the many other fundamental positives on the spiritual upward spiral. Nine major groups of soul qualities correspond to nine major types of people, blessed by Jesus in the Sermon on the Mount.[18] These nine blessings are the Beatitudes. Everyone contains all nine groups of soul qualities, yet each of us has one in particular that appears most prominently. Each ego type is blessed for going against its arrow to its soul type.

Type One: Beatitude: Those who are reviled and persecuted for Christ's sake

Blessed for: Returning to their essence of gladness and optimism

Holy Idea: Perfection

Examples of soul qualities: patience, endurance, discernment, acceptance, sacred joy, serenity, and brilliancy

Type Two: Beatitude: The meek

Blessed for: Returning to their essence of self-awareness and creative receptivity

Holy Ideas: Will and Freedom

Examples of soul qualities: surrender, non-attachment to the temporal, humility, grace, and sacred creativity

Type Three: Beatitude: The poor in spirit

Blessed for: Returning to their essence of integrity and emptiness of ego

Holy Ideas: Harmony, Law, and Hope

Examples of soul qualities: truth, hope, divestment of self, alignment with the Divine, transparency, perseverance, interdependence, sacred kinship, and embodiment of the image of God

Type Four: Beatitude: Those persecuted for righteousness' sake

Blessed for: Adopting causes for those who are excluded, abused, or victims of injustice; returning to their essence that is one with right action: The ability to discern and apply—through attitudes and behavior—the principles that guide and support consciousness in ourselves, the collective, and the environment.

Holy Idea: Origin

---

18. From the Sermon on the Mount in Matthew 5:3–10, King James Version.

Examples of soul qualities: equanimity, transparency to creation, inspiration by moral action, advocacy of the neglected, oneness with the Divine, ability to create beauty, groundedness in being, and sacred righteousness

TYPE FIVE: BEATITUDE: THOSE WHO HUNGER AND THIRST FOR RIGHTEOUSNESS

Blessed for: Returning to their essence of power, compassion, and alignment with the Divine, which fills them with righteousness

Holy Ideas: Omniscience and Transparency

Examples of soul qualities: wholeness, divinely empowered wisdom, strong presence, guidance, and sacred power

TYPE SIX: BEATITUDE: THE PURE IN HEART

Blessed for: Returning to their essence of wholehearted reliance on the Divine

Holy Ideas: Strength and Faith

Examples of soul qualities: faithfulness, trust, peace, courageous strength, loyalty, loving-kindness, group-mindedness, inclusivity, kinship, sacred loving

TYPE SEVEN: BEATITUDE: THOSE WHO MOURN

Blessed for: Returning to their essence of reflective, grounded acceptance of pain

Holy Ideas: Wisdom, Work, and Plan

Examples of soul qualities: vision, contemplativeness, industriousness, restraint, balance, sacred wisdom

TYPE EIGHT: BEATITUDE: THE MERCIFUL

Blessed for: Returning to their essence of compassion

Holy Idea: Truth

Examples of soul qualities: alignment with divine truth, empathy, charisma, powerful protection of others, ability to lead from a position of service, intense strength, vulnerable power, and sacred benevolence

Type Nine: Beatitude: The peacemakers

Blessed for: Returning to their essence of peaceful action

Holy Idea: Love

Examples of soul qualities: love, peace, ability to see unity, ability to understand all sides, affirmation, diligence, healing, and sacred action

The nine Enneagram types depicted in the Beatitudes correspond to similar representations in the Hebrew Kabbalah. Rabbi Howard Addison, in his book *The Enneagram and Kabbalah: Reading Your Soul*, provides the Kabbalah's correlations with the ego types:

Enneagram Ego Type	The Kabbalah
One	*Chochmah*: The all-knowing, correct, internalized Father, Abba
Two	*Binah*: The understanding, controlling, supernal Mother, Ima
Three	*Gedulah*: The impetus to be great
Four	*Tiferet*: Beauty and romantic longing
Five	*Din*: Bound, enclosed, and limited
Six	*Netsach*: Enduring and seeking authority
Seven	*Hod*: Splendor
Eight	*Yesod*: Seminal force
Nine	*Shechinah*: The accepting presence

From the Hebrew tradition, we see the correlation with the same truths that the Enneagram reflects.

The Soul and Its Pain

The Body Center also holds energy of negative weight. For example, the body stores memories from early trauma or wounds, which are also part of the soul's journey. Babies and young children store many early preverbal memories in their tissue. These wounds are expressed through the distortions of love, peace, and the life force's courage; they manifest as rage, shame, and fear. The soul carries these wounds and is called to do the work of healing painful body memories. Eckhart Tolle describes such pain stored in the body as the "pain-body."[19] If appropriate inner work is not done, this type of pain-body can overtake and obscure the vibrant, positive qualities of one's soul.

A baby can be born with these genetically encoded wounded and or undeveloped qualities, which express the pain of their ancestors. Other pain-bodies can be passed down in families through social learning and generational psychological inheritance. Weariness, despair, rejection, inconsolability, inferiority, defectiveness, deviance, turbulence, resentfulness, abandonment, and ugliness are all examples of painful soul wounds which are evoked by the pain-body's rage, shame, and fear. Collective pain-bodies can also result from shared persecutions, slavery, genocide, mass murders, or other joint tragedies.

Many soul qualities, including deep compassion, are elicited to deal with the pain-body. Once elicited, the soul qualities enlarge and, like a muscle that is exercised, grow in strength. For every pain-body characteristic, there is a soul quality that is its antidote.

In conclusion, the soul, our most primary identity, is made up of many qualities that govern our ego and our personality. The various combinations of our soul qualities make up our soulality.

We can know our soul to a greater extent by using the Mind, Body, and Heart Centers of Intelligence to delve into our own depths. This chapter has reviewed several methods for self-remembering our souls. By understanding our truest inner nature, we know the issues that form the fundamentals of our journey in this life. As we progress in the real work of becoming, the distractions of the false self naturally diminish in focus.

---

19. Tolle, *New Earth*.

3
Who Is the Soul Child?

WHEN I SPEAK TO audiences about the soul child, I naturally share stories of my own childhood. In doing so, I re-experience my soul child in real-time. Because of the vivid and lively descriptions, the audience is right with me and each of them is reminded of how they saw the world as a very young child. Whether by myself or teaching in front of groups, I re-embody that energy daily and reconnect with the qualities of my soul.

One of my earliest memories from my soul child era is when I awoke from an afternoon nap to find my mother fast asleep with my new baby brother. I took this opportunity to explore the house on my own. After finding my mother's chocolate bars and disposing of at least one, I ventured into the bathroom, where I climbed up to the medicine cabinet. There, I removed the scissors and promptly cut off a handful of my hair down to the scalp. Returning to bed with my bald spot, I was lulled back to sleep by the droning window fan on that hot summer's day.

Suddenly, I was shaken out of my nap by my panicking mother, who demanded to know who had come into the house and cut my hair. As you can imagine, the rest of the story didn't go well for me. But this memory—one of many of my first self—is of my soul child. Besides mischief, this child was full of inner confidence and strength. He held a deep connection to family and had faith that all was well. Today, when living from my essence, I have reconnected to these traits. I am self-assured, steady, and close to my loved ones. I feel held and supported. Once again, I have the sense that all is well, even when appearances may be to the contrary.

To question my security would be like my soul child questioning whether the parent holding me was going to drop me: unfathomable.

Memories of my soul child are prompted not only by stories but by smells, sights, sounds, and even tastes. All these—including the sensation of the wind on my skin, the caress of someone who cares for me, the warmth of the sun, or the feel of certain smooth fabrics—place me right inside that small body once more. I spend a lot of time these days in that body, re-experiencing the world through the freshness and freedom I enjoyed.

In that body, I see the world as I saw it when I first arrived and during my earliest childhood. Through those eyes, colors seem brighter, the shapes more distinct. By re-experiencing the senses in that body, I am once again closely connected to the natural world and all that's greater than myself. Through those ears, music takes on a different quality, as if it's intimately related to my childhood body's vibrations and inner rhythms. Movement is more than just "second nature"; it's spontaneous.

Each awareness I experience as my soul child is familiar but somewhat vague because those times are mostly forgotten. Just the other day, I was walking on the beach in the Gulf of Mexico where I grew up. As the sea air filled my lungs, I recalled the very first time I had inhaled that fragrance: a mysterious mixture of salt water and sea life. Immediately I was with my parents, who showed me the blue-green expanse for the first time. I recalled a memory I had long forgotten: My father put sand over one of my feet and packed it down. Then he slowly took my foot out of the wet pile and what was left was a small sand igloo. Amazing! The newness and freshness of the sea that day will forever be paired with my mother and father's all-encompassing love. Today, when I breathe in that same sea air, I immediately return to my parents' arms.

Besides the reunion with loved ones, another inherent value in reconnecting to the child within is to directly experience my soul's emotions. The unconditional love of my parents was only one of many emotions. I also experienced fear of the unknown, compassion for those who were hurt, jealousy when my little brother received more attention, sadness over disappointments, and awe for the endless discoveries of every day. Our body and emotions are the primary sources of our first thoughts.

Our soul child's memories and their stories, body's sensations, and emotions are rooted in soul, not in ego. These pieces sit far deeper than personality; they are our expressions of the Divine. Yes, even our earliest mischief and the unveiled need for love join with everything else to express our divine identity.

As parents, Lark and I witnessed the soul children of both our son and daughter. Each was distinctive but shared similarities with all soul children in that their souls, not their emerging egos, were their essential energy. To say that life is simple for most soul children is an understatement. For most of us at that age, life is full of being held, supported, and nurtured. Our main problems so early in life are hunger and soiled diapers. The soul child may be mischievous but not flagrantly devious or maliciously violent. However, when we face life's hardest demands and woundings, our soul child needs the protection of our ego, which we enlist to protect us. Then, for the most part, our soul child is forgotten under a protective crust. Up until the ego and its fixations take command, however, we live as unfettered expressions of our essential nature, our original divine being.

Lark and I often walk on the beach as the sun is setting. At this time of day, our children used to chase down the sand crabs with nets as the clawed creatures scampered in and out of their holes in the sand. The children scooped the crabs into their nets but always let them go. Once nighttime arrived, flashlights appeared and the fun continued. Now, as an older couple, when we stop and become fully present in the moment, we can hear our children's squeals of joy on those beach time capers. It takes stillness for the soul to make itself known.

Life, however, has a way of distancing us from our soul. As psychologist Erik Erickson points out, each stage of life presents its own dilemmas and we can't competently move forward until we address them.[1] Sadly, we employ our egos to solve these life problems; it isn't until the second half of life that we are apt to conclude that our ego doesn't have all the abilities we once thought.

By midlife or by the time we reach a critical mass of suffering, many of us begin to search for a better way to live. Deep in the recesses of our being, we vaguely recall when life was simple, joyous, and even blissful. Amid the pain, we ask ourselves, "How can I find that state of peacefulness now?" This essential question prompts our journey back to soul. Our soul child is an exclusive gateway to our soul; it's the only part of us that existed before our ego ran the show. As this child, we had only one

---

1. Erik, *Childhood and Society* (1993).

identity: our essence. This is why our soul child is the most qualified to re-acquaint us with living in soul!

As I stated, after we reach a critical mass of suffering, we naturally reach back to our origins—our core, our soul—to remember our identity and our purpose. Self-discovery and healing are our greatest motivators for transformation.

Unfortunately, merely going back to this inner child and noticing their world and feelings isn't sufficient to drive transformation. Real transformation re-incorporates our soul's individual qualities and expresses them through our minds, hearts, and bodies. It is then, and only then, that these qualities thrive in us once again. Living in soul is light years away from living fully in ego.

This chapter covers how we can know our own soul. It first presents the Holy Ideas foundational to our essence and then describes each soul child in light of their specific Holy Idea. I explain the soul's Essential Aspects and the ego's Idealized Aspects. I look at the soul child's predilection for naughtiness and human mischief, as well as their inevitable wounds and subsequent concealment. I will familiarize you with the nine steps in the soul child's journey and how their connection to the inner flow of the Enneagram can lead toward wholeness. Much of the latter depends upon the process of spiritual alchemy, which I will address in later chapters.

The Holy Ideas: The Foundations of Our Soul

When all is said and done, what ultimately defines a person? Taking myself as an example, if I went beneath the level of my personality and distilled everything, there would be two foundational aspects of my being: my strength and the grounded peacefulness provided by faith. Emerging from these are the qualities of my soul. Granted, my studies of the Enneagram have led me to identify these two characteristics, yet, I maintain that they are the base of my core identity and would be whether or not I knew their names.

If it is normal that we lose contact with our soul child and the foundational aspects of the soul, then how can these aspects find expression in us? The answer is that our soul itself speaks throughout our life, even in rumblings beneath the crust—that unseen barrier separating our ego and soul. The soul's most sincere desire is to express its divine identity. Therefore, our soul emanates its true nature at life's shock points, its turning points, and even in everyday life. It is the still, small voice,[2] the clarity in confusion, and the soul's wisdom to which we finally gravitate.

I found myself unsettled during the Vietnam War; it was expected that good patriots would be willing to sacrifice themselves for this great country, as my parents and thousands of others had done in WWII. As a college student, I found it difficult to give up my future to fight a war that had never been adequately justified. It was not clear at that time that the US was losing the war, but the mounting rates of American deaths meant the public was slowly turning against it. I couldn't understand why—with so many losses—we were making no gains against the North Vietnamese. I could see no reason why I should lose my life to such a hopeless cause without any apparent rationale, but I did not want to be unpatriotic. I was paralyzed with indecision and fear. However, the still, small voice within me insisted I remain in school, even it meant that others would see me as a coward—and that I would sometimes see myself as such.

I continued with an educational deferment until the war ended. But what pulled me through this labyrinth of fear, self-doubt, and confusion was my core—my soul. My faith and strength made me aware of my courage and my soul's other qualities; they helped me pursue life with honor rather than shame. It wasn't until my thirties that I learned, according to Enneagram teachings, that Strength and Faith are the two halves of my Holy Idea.

Finding our Holy Idea is one of the most important pieces of self-discovery for healing and wholeness. These holy words serve as a reminder, a link to how we perceived reality as a soul child. Our ego, though, disconnects us from these Holy Ideas so completely that we forget them, until—from time to time—our soul briefly emerges from under the crust of our ego and we see life once again through its eyes. Soon, however, the ego retakes control and we quickly forget our Holy Idea once again.

Our soul's bedrock is Holy Love, out of which our essence emanates. Oscar Ichazo refers to a spectrum of ideas that comprise nine specific ways of perceiving and living in divine love. These holy truths about how life really is are called the Holy Ideas in Ichazo's original Enneagram teachings.[3] Let us look at the origin of these Holy Ideas and how they each represent one of nine fundamental expressions of the Divine.

---

2. As Elijah heard in 1 Kings 19:11.
3. Ichazo, "Arica Psycho-Catalyzers."

Oscar Ichazo developed the Enneagram of Personality and proposed that each of the nine personalities arose from what he conceived and described as the Enneagram of Holy Ideas. Simply put, the Holy Ideas are nine fundamental and irreducible expressions of divine truth that were set into motion by divine intelligence. They are the mechanisms that run the cosmos, including the natural order of all. They are nine particular perceptions that together comprise the divine mind.

Each personality type emerges as a reaction to having lost contact with our Holy Idea. It follows that—before our personality and our ego become our primary mechanisms for moving in the world—our soul child is our only identity. Therefore, our soul child once lived exclusively in their Holy Idea.

Ichazo's Enneagram of Holy Ideas is consistent with concepts presented by the Greek philosophers, most specifically, in the Platonic Forms.[4] The basic premise of Plato's forms (and solids) is that everything in the material world is grounded in some non-reducible spiritual truth. Therefore, all things must first exist in the form of a spiritual idea before they can ever manifest in their material form. Ichazo described each of the Holy Ideas as one and the same as the natural laws undergirding the universe. Like Plato, Ichazo perceived that our souls are manifestations of the spiritual idea that preceded us.

On Ichazo's Enneagram of Personality, each personality type is an ego, which is why I refer to each of the nine personalities as an ego type. According to Ichazo, when first created, we were each simply a Holy Idea; then, other soul qualities were built around that initial idea to constitute our true nature. For us to express an aspect of God such as our Holy Idea, we require neither language nor ego. The baby and small child exude spirit and soul without the developed personality that will one day become what defines them most. Their communication, reciprocity, and love are among their many expressions of the Divine. Many of us refer to this state of being as bliss.

Sadly, the demands of the world around us and the wounds to our innocent selves make us disconnect from both our soul child and our Holy Idea. Our ego then takes over and convinces us of another, less vulnerable way of moving through the world. Our ego acts, looks, and feels vastly different from our original state but it goes about trying to reconstitute our bliss in its own way.

---

4. Dancy, *Plato's Introduction of Forms*.

When life brings us to the search for our real self, our soul child is an amazing gateway to our soul. It is the only internal spiritual and psychological structure that remains from when we lived in pure soul. When we first live in our soul child, before the ego supersedes the soul, our only way of being in the world is to express our Holy Idea and the other spiritual qualities particular to us.

The Holy Ideas and the Soul Child

As a young boy, I attended catechism classes to learn about the teachings of the church and to be baptized into the faith. When the topic of God's three aspects came up, the minister explained it with an example I'll never forget. He said, "God is like an oyster with its three parts: the oyster itself and both its shells. All three are 'oyster.' Likewise, God is the Father, the Son, and the Holy Spirit." All three are God.

This example can be applied to the Holy Ideas as well. The Divine is the one pure light of love but when shone through a prism, that single light is broken into multiple color components. There are seven colors on the visible spectrum, and nine when we include infrared and ultraviolet. Likewise, there are nine Holy Ideas, all emanating from the one white light. Each Holy Idea is a specific component of divine love. In the same way as the oyster, some of the Holy Ideas consist of two or even three elements that complement and intertwine with each other.

In their totality, the nine Holy Ideas compose the wholeness of the Divine. The Holy Idea is our first understanding of reality and is integral to our purpose. Although all nine Holy Ideas contribute to the totality of the soul, one, in particular, best expresses the Divine within each of us. As I mentioned earlier, our Holy Idea is the foundation of our soul child and, ultimately, our soul.

Oscar Ichazo spoke of the almost magical way the Holy Idea works:

> The nine Holy Ideas have the innate power of transforming and transmuting our entire self through meditation and contemplation or as the way of the "theoretical life" or contemplative life and its actualization. . . . [T]he transformative power of the Holy Ideas receives the technical name Psycho-catalyzers that function in the same way as simple chemical elements known as catalyzers, which produce chemical alterations by their presence without being altered themselves. The Holy Ideas have to be envisioned as nine rays projected by the Divine One and

Holy Mind, and when they are present together, the pleroma is produced and their original, natural, unborn, and immortal state is unveiled and realized.[5]

Below is a complete list of the Holy Ideas of each ego type, along with descriptions of each corresponding soul child.

Ego Type One: Holy Perfection

There is an inherent perfection in everything because all is part of a divine process, which is perfect and whole. By aligning with Holy Perfection, Type Ones find the joy that was missing when they were fixated on keeping themselves and others in line.

Holy perfection does not crusade for continuous correction; it does not jump to fix each perceived flaw. It does not resent those who don't do the right thing. Nor is it attached to anger. Type One's Holy Idea of Holy Perfection includes the *acceptance* of imperfections. When embracing their Holy Idea and in touch with the natural progression of the universe, a Type One trusts that divine activity will eventually bring about healing and wholeness. This type, when conscious of their Holy Idea, discerns the best solution by aligning with divine purpose. Resentment and negativity are soon replaced by inherent optimism and joy.

This Holy Idea carries the Ego Type One against the arrow to their Soul Point at Seven. At Point Seven, Holy Perfection manifests as the ability to bask in the joy of abundance, maintain positive thoughts, and rejoice in the aliveness of the present. Because of Seven's optimism, they accept their own and others' flaws as areas for growth and perceive all as works in progress. Every moment is related to the ultimate fruition of divine purpose.

Who Is Ego Type One's Soul Child?

When living in their soul child, an Ego Type One is grounded in Holy Perfection, which they experience as joy in living, optimism, and the acceptance of all that is—just as it is. They accept flaws as a natural part of human existence. Their life is full of unconstrained laughter and anticipation of the next adventure. This outlook melts away their would-be

---

5. Oscar Ichazo, foreword to Almaas, *Facets of Unity*, vii.

agitation or worry. The Type One soul was born as a Seven. In that energy, they uphold everyone as worthy of being cherished. They have a bright disposition that thrives in the sunshine and doesn't dwell on the darker aspects of life. There is a contagious aliveness about them and a forward momentum that allows them to take action on their plans. They revel in the fun we find in everything. They are content in knowing that all is exactly as it should be. This is Sacred Righteousness.

Ego Type Two: Holy Will and Holy Freedom

Divine will shapes life according to a higher plan; by moving along with it, Twos have the Holy Freedom to be themselves without having to constantly serve to prove their value and identity.

When their soul child aligns with Holy Will, a Two is no longer a separate entity with a will independent of the whole. Alignment with Holy Will gives them the Holy Freedom to be part of the bigger picture, meaning they are not compelled to assume responsibility for meeting everyone else's needs.

This Holy Idea is their bridge to their Soul Point at Point Four. By reaching that destination, they are subject to Holy Will and have the Holy Freedom to express their true nature. As a result, they are not trapped in service as they are when governed by their ego fixation. They are secure in the knowledge that they are loved, and therefore do not have to ignore their own needs or coerce others into loving them for their gifts or services. Their soul's purpose, according to this Holy Idea, is to flow with the cosmic forces and their underlying natural laws. In attunement with these laws, they combine Holy Will and Holy Freedom with the conscious Four's awareness that we are true being. Grounded in this identity, they allow Holy Will to lead them to the particular needs that are theirs to meet in themselves and others. Their soul's foundational purpose, therefore, is to be a conduit of divine will and to freely express it, having self-remembered that their worth is independent of compulsive service and the pride they derive from it.

Who Is Ego Type Two's Soul Child?

The Two's soul child is characterized by an openness to divine will. They are intuitive about where and to whom their giving should flow. They are very aware of their needs and can meet them now that they are no longer compelled by obligatory giving. They are certain they are loved because—in expressing Holy Will and Holy Freedom—they are connected to their true nature and its inherent lovableness. They live from that consciousness, free from self-doubt and the prison of service. Their creativity thrives as they perform for others, make beautiful things, and present new ways to look at a situation or person. Their presence exudes both self-love and love for others.

Ego Type Three: Holy Harmony, Holy Law, and Holy Hope

Everything is ruled by the natural law of the cosmos, which operates as a unifying and harmonious force. Belief in this unalterable force brings hope. Threes who remember they are created out of this composite Holy Idea can receive love on their own merit as a person whose essence speaks for itself. No longer do they live behind a false image designed to win people's love.

In the natural order, there is an interconnection between all life and the planet. The natural order of the universe is constantly evolving. The soul of the Ego Type Three is conscious of this and that it, too, is part of the evolutionary process. The Three's ego, however, is unable to see this forward movement and instead assumes that progress is at a standstill—both inside and around them. Under this illusion of stagnation, they have no hope that things will move forward unaided.

Instead, because they have disconnected from the wholeness of natural law (Holy Law) and the harmony it brings, they accomplish their self-imposed goals in isolation. Disconnected from their essence, they want recognition and hope their accomplishments and competencies will bring the love they want. They equate how much they are loved with such things as their self-made image, their symbols of accomplishment, and their perceived status.

As an Ego Type Three enters into consciousness, they must work to overrule their ego's incongruous "me first" system. Eventually, they learn to operate under these higher laws, and, in doing so, find both Holy Harmony and Holy Hope in the knowledge that reality is progressively unfolding on multiple levels.

By going against the arrow from Ego Type Three to Point Six (their Soul Point), the Three embodies their true nature as they reconnect to the group and work for the welfare of all.

Who Is the Ego Type Three's Soul Child?

This child contains Holy Harmony, Holy Law, and Holy Hope. They understand the importance of harmony and foster it within both their family and the world containing it. The Three's soul child appeared on earth with Six energy, very connected to family, community, and others who share their life. This soul child gathers loved ones together for games and group activities. They live in sync with the natural order and relax in the knowledge that all is proceeding in a positive direction. The conscious Three feels no compulsion to take on projects or actions apart from the group so they can focus attention on just themselves. This Three soul child is sure that they are loved and so they exude hopefulness.

Ego Type Four: Holy Origin

All of nature has its beginnings in the Divine. As our holy parent, the Divine created each of us uniquely to serve a special purpose. Fours are inextricably part of all being and their originality and true nature spring from their intimate connection with that source. If they are disconnected from that Holy Origin, however, they are compelled to use their own brand of uniqueness to create an identity that gives them a sense of significance.

The same fixed laws of being that apply to the rest of the living world also operate within each soul child and each person. Like the soul, these laws stem from the Divine. Therefore, each individual is ultimately and uniquely connected to the Source, the Absolute—the Divine. This is their inalienable birthright, their true nature, and their Holy Origin. Their unique individual purpose is to express their connection to divine purpose.

At Point One, their Soul Point on the Enneagram's inner flow, Ego Type Four settles into their identity. They are transparent to the divine mind and can easily discern what is real, right, and authentic.

Who Is Ego Type Four's Soul Child?

The Four's soul child started at Point One. By returning to that energy, they renew their natural propensity for knowing the best path forward. Their wisdom is palpable from childhood: adults who ask their opinion remark, "Out of the mouths of babes...." The conscious Four knows their purpose as a discerner of truth and can see others as works in progress rather than problems to be solved. Most striking is their presence, a solidly confident embodiment of true being.

Ego Type Five: Holy Omniscience and Holy Transparency

The universe is made of divine intelligence, which permeates everything. True being is transparency and continual access to the Divine's omnipresent knowledge. When the Five remembers that they once lived in—and can reconnect to—this state, they relax and release their fixation on taking in and hoarding as much information as possible.

The Five's soul acknowledges that we are all interlinked, subject to the unalterable laws of the cosmos, which govern even the body itself. As such, they do not think about themselves as a separate entity, who is limited within the confines of their own knowledge. They are open to the Divine and understand that It is everywhere and knows everything. Holy Omniscience assures them that all knowledge is available to them when needed if they are open to it. Holy Transparency consists of face-to-face involvement with divine knowledge, without the barrier of the ego. This soul's purpose is to be receptive to all information and to use it in alignment with divine intention. This cannot be done from the isolated vantage point the Five's ego advocates.

For Ego Type Five to reach full consciousness of their Holy Idea, they must return to their soul child's origin at Soul Point Eight. There, they rebuild the state of empowerment and strength into which they were born. Giving up on the ego's quest for information and its proclivity for withdrawal, they assume their primary identity of compassionate, empowered movement in the world.

Who Is the Ego Type Five's Soul Child?

This soul child embodies an openness to information and the trust that the knowledge they seek will reach them when they require it. This confidence lets them abandon the frantic search for more and more information upon which to build their identity. They are children born into Eight energy, meaning that they carry innate power and mastery of their surroundings. In this energy, they are natural leaders. Even on their first day of school, they acted as if they knew what to do and others readily followed suit. Their strong will and ability to influence others are balanced by their compassion and drive to protect the weak. Their strength gives them a commanding presence, even if it is subtle or understated.

Ego Type Six: Holy Strength and Holy Faith

Strength and faith are present in all life. They allow plants to grow and forests to expand, despite potential restrictions. Inherent in that strength to surpass limitations is an inner intelligence and faith that we will continue to develop and to have access to what we need, despite appearances to the contrary.

The Six contains a wellspring of strength, which stems from the Divine. When they trust that strength and act in faith, they live in and are supported by the interconnectedness all around them. If they forget this, they feel weak and doubt others and themselves.

The universe is in continuous physical and spiritual self-regulation to facilitate the progress that its inherent intelligence wills. A Six's alignment with (and trust in) the laws of the cosmos brings harmony and fullness to their being and engenders confidence and Holy Strength. Holy Faith embodies the certainty of their spiritual nature. It ascertains that their essence as a spiritual being comes from and is inseparable from the greater Essence, the Absolute—the Divine. As an expression of this Holy Idea, their soul brings harmony and balance wherever it goes. In harmony with the self-regulating aspect of the universe, this soul uses Holy Strength and Holy Faith to stabilize all entities around them.

By flowing against their arrow to their Soul Point at Nine, the Ego Type Six can move in the world without fear or anxiety. The pure peacefulness at Point Nine reconnects them to their true nature of trust and strength. They can see that, even when there is a temporary feeling of imbalance, on a larger scale, everything is in harmony.

Who Is the Soul Child of Ego Type Six?

This soul child is a relaxed soul, built on the foundation of Holy Strength and Holy Faith. They feel supported by loved ones and connected to the world at large. They were born into Point Nine, embodying deep peace and love. As a young Nine, their soul expressed balance, fairness, and harmony. A precocious soul child of strength, they rejoice in their interconnectedness with both the Divine and those around them. They are willing to work past discomfort and tend to take on tough tasks and assume authority. However, this is not the entirety of their true nature; they are equally comfortable on their back looking at the clouds, listening to the buzz of bees, and making chains of clover. This soul child's sense of faith permeates everything with the knowledge that the divine forces of the world work together to bring about the present.

Ego Type Seven: Holy Wisdom, Holy Work, and Holy Plan

Before anything came into existence, it started as a divine idea, which later became part of a larger Holy Plan—both for the collective evolution of the cosmos and for each individual. Holy Wisdom understood that Holy Work was needed to bring this idea to fruition. When Sevens lose their connection to this purpose, their egos react by unsuccessfully imitating Holy Wisdom, Holy Work, and the Holy Plan. They replace Holy Wisdom with the belief that they can use pleasure and distraction to avoid feeling pain. They imitate Holy Work through their daily efforts to establish happiness through continuous consumption of such pleasure. Finally, in the absence of the Holy Plan, the ego does the planning. The ego's plan, fueled by the avoidance of pain through seeking pleasure, becomes a fixation. Thus, Seven's fixation is the frenetic mental activity designed to keep their minds on immediate and future gratification, rather than in the present moment where the realities of deprivation and pain may surface.

Reality is composed of an infinite number of moments, one after another. Human existence is brief and only by stopping their frenetic activity and their ego planning can they exist in the present and perceive the divine blueprint: the Holy Plan for them and the universe as a whole.

As they comprehend and are in harmony with each moment, they can accomplish their real work: Holy Work. Holy Wisdom provides the foundation from which their Holy Work comes and informs the substantive intention of that work. Both of these are in harmony with and follow the larger design, called the Holy Plan. The soul's purpose in this arena is to co-create with the Divine, in keeping with the ever-unfolding Holy Plan. Carrying this out is a return to bliss.

This ego type goes to their Soul Point at Five to return to their soul child. There, the soul contemplates, reflects, and processes. Once again, they become an observer and a categorizer. They are a font of wisdom, which they apply to concrete projects.

Who Is the Ego Type Seven's Soul Child?

This soul child is quiet, reflective, and contemplative, born into Five energy of introspectiveness and receptivity to information. They can be seen looking into the creek in the park, spellbound by the flow of the water over the rocks, by the small creatures living about the stream, and by the ways in which the world all fits together. This soul child soaks in every possible lesson from each experience. They reflect upon and process what they reveal. Grounded in this wisdom, they find their work in alignment with the greater Holy Plan.

Ego Type Eight: Holy Truth

Objective reality operates within its own laws, whether or not one agrees with them; we can experience and perceive this truth when we set aside our ego's version of the world around us. When they forget this Holy Truth, Eights react by making a facsimile of truth, creating their own laws of reality. They build a self-image of strength. They attempt to make the world conform to their perception of truth, rather than the opposite. Their essence, at Point Two, is a vivacious and compassionate heart. Their disconnection from compassion leaves a tremendous void and they search constantly to regain that vitality. Eventually, they find Holy Truth, which heals that emptiness by recognizing and accepting reality as it is. They acknowledge their own vulnerability and remember the compassion at their core, using it to build empathy and strength.

The ego's insistence that it can dictate how we experience the world and how each moment should unfold is an illusion. It is impossible to both accept Holy Truth and continue living in your ego. The ego operates under a misapprehension of duality that divides the world into "me" and "everything else." The soul, however, understands that we are all united. There is real power in seeking truth. This Holy Idea prompts the Eight to shift from egoic duality to the universality of true being.

The original identity of Ego Type Eight is tied to the Holy Idea of Holy Truth. They express their divine nature at Soul Point Two, where they bring people together in compassion, asserting truth, and providing validation by creating unification.

Who Is the Ego Type Eight's Soul Child?

The soul child of Ego Type Eight is born into the energy of Point Two, making them innately compassionate and giving, protective and nurturing. They are also easily moved to emotional responses; others' pains and needs capture their hearts. They want to take in strays and bandage others' wounds. They do not mind being vulnerable, nor are they wary of being the first to initiate a relationship. Indeed, they find both excitement and completion in developing close relationships.

Ego Type Nine: Holy Love

Everything comes from God; all serve a cosmic purpose of creating. Holy Love is the substance of the Divine and the energy behind all creative activity. When we contemplate creation and express thanks for its goodness, we begin to love ourselves and others. Nines lose this memory of how much they are loved and cherished. In the ensuing absence of confidence, they seek to ensure external tranquility by suppressing their individuality—merging with others, de-valuing themselves, and going to sleep on their lives. Once they remember the power of Holy Love, Nines can move in the world with renewed self-esteem and purpose.

The soul is aware of the positive, life-giving nature of existence. Though there is pain and difficulty, the universe and its laws are life-sustaining and benevolent. The light of Love is the creative force of the cosmos, which brought being, itself, into existence and continues the self-perpetuating cycle of life. Love is the unconditioned state of the human mind. Thankfulness to the Divine affirms a Nine's relationship with the Creator, and, in realizing that they come from love, itself, they are connected to all. This Holy Idea, the mother of all the others, strikes the deepest chords of love and bids them to make its expression their purpose.

The Holy Idea of Love sends them from Ego Type Nine to their origin at Soul Point Three, where they embrace their true nature as lovable champions whose actions serve the greater good. There, Nines are action-oriented and motivated by the common good rather than automatically moving to take the path of least resistance.

Who Is the Ego Type Nine's Soul Child?

This soul child has their beginnings in Point Three, where they live in love of the family, the group, and the common effort that goes into getting things done. They have a sense of what must be done in the larger scheme. They don't act for the sake of admiration or to receive love, but rather to smooth the way for everybody around them. They may build a Lego airplane or castle, but instead of bragging about their accomplishment, they will teach a smaller child how to do the same. When they win, it is collective—not a personal victory but one for the team. They lead well but do not seek attention for doing so.

How Do I Identify My Soul Child?

To answer the question posed near the beginning of this section, "How do I find the foundational qualities of my soul?" you must first be sure which of the nine ego types reflects you (you can find the test in my book *Becoming Conscious: The Enneagram's Forgotten Passageways*, or take the test online at The Institute for Conscious Being: theicb.org). Each ego type has a corresponding Holy Idea. Remembering, understanding, and re-embracing your Holy Idea equips you to re-connect to and re-identify with your soul child. By using the arrows, you can find the Enneagram point that contains your essence: your soul child. This is called your Soul Point.

The Essential Aspects and the Soul Child

My mother was understandably annoyed with me when I cut off that hank of hair. When I would not tell her what happened, she sentenced me to an inquisition by my father when he came home from work. My father was angered by my refusal to admit what I had done, yet, even after repeated chances to come clean, I kept quiet for fear of the consequences. Finally, exasperated, my father told me that if I didn't tell the truth, he would spank "the living daylights out of me." I had no idea of what my living daylights were, but I felt deep down they must be something valuable, essential. Little did I know that the Enneagram would one day reveal Living Daylight to be my Essential Aspect of the Divine. On a soul level, maybe I knew that phrase referred to my soul child's essential expression of God. Could that be why I guarded them so? I shut down completely and resolved never to speak of my actions that day, convinced that my silence would protect me. I remember this instance as the tipping point, a wound to my soul child that prompted its subsequent suppression. I was desperate for safety and my ego stepped up, promising to protect me.

The Soul's Essential and Ego's Idealized Aspects

There are many qualities of being that make up our essence. These qualities, called our Essential Aspects, are facets of the Divine that are expressed through all of us. However, each of the nine types of soul children has one specific Essential Aspect at its core. At the end of our soul child era, we disconnect from our essence and core Essential Aspect, after which our egos suppress any traces of them. Now, in our quest to rediscover our truest self, we must aim to re-embody the core Essential Aspect found at our Soul Point. By reconnecting to it, and specifically to our soul child, we can return to a state of consciousness that best expresses our true nature, our essence—our soul.

Because we are disconnected from our own core Essential Aspect, we experience much suffering. In response, our ego is drawn to and embraces another one of the nine Essential Aspects that seems as if it will end our suffering, cure our deficiencies, and return us to the bliss that we once inhabited. The ego romanticizes this alluring aspect, which is why we refer to it as the Idealized Aspect. To the ego's dismay, however, its version of this aspect only imitates the soul's life, rather than embodying it.

However, at its base, the Idealized Aspect is still a soul quality. Once we embody our true nature and live from our depths instead of from the mental structure called our ego, we understand our Idealized Aspect without needing to idealize it. We see it and live from it as the authentic quality of being it is. Our ego's Idealized Aspect sleepwalks, unconsciously going through necessary motions to maintain a distorted imitation of life. Only the lifeblood of essence can bring us back to awareness. After such a transfusion of essence, the ego's once "Idealized" Aspect becomes an Authenticated Idealized Aspect of Essence.

For example, as an Ego Type Six, my truest identity and soul qualities live at my Soul Point, Nine. Therefore, that is also where we find my Essential Aspect, called Living Daylight, which tells us that all being is an expression of the Divine that creates and sustains everything. We are supported by the power of love. As an Ego Type Six, I am part of the entire cosmos which—made of love—surrounds and holds me. But when I disconnected from my soul child who lived in this state of being, I fell into my ego, a mental construct that is a state of consciousness all unto itself.

My ego reacted to this disconnection by seizing a different Essential Aspect, then idealizing it as the answer to all my problems and challenges. In my case, my ego idealized the Essential Aspect of Will to reestablish the bliss of my soul child. As my Idealized Aspect, my ego distorted Will so that I depended upon attachments to authority figures or a group for strength, security, and direction. Following others' wills or, counterintuitively, imposing my will upon others, I imitated the safety, love, and support of my core Essential Aspect, Living Daylight. My ego believed it could regain bliss through sheer willpower. Life, however, taught me this did not work.

What *did* work? The transformation of my Idealized Aspect from an egoic imitation to an authentic state of consciousness. In the process of traveling around the Enneagram of Soul, we first go to our Soul Point, then continue to each of the other Soul Points, absorbing their qualities as we move in the direction of integration. Because of the amazing amalgamation process of our egos and souls (see chapter 7), our egos come to blend with and serve our souls instead of overriding them as they have for decades. My ego's Idealized Aspect of Will used to be characterized by my stubborn focus on the security authorities could grant me and my group's promise of others' love. Now, as I travel around the Enneagram of Soul and embody the Essential Aspects, my understanding of Will is becoming something far different: it is an inner strength and self-sufficiency. My community and I are increasingly anchored in self-reliance, meeting challenges with confidence, inner support, and unending courage. Will is now becoming an aspect of the Divine and an embodiment of love within my soul: I experience that everything, including me, is made of love.

My experience of this process is similar to that of many others with whom I have talked. The simple schema for many of us is that our ego type goes to its Soul Point's Essential Aspect, which is our core state of being. From there, we travel around the Enneagram of Soul until it comes back to our ego point. But with each trip around the Enneagram, the soul qualities gradually replace the ego's distorted expression of the Idealized Aspect. In time, the Idealized Aspect transforms into a pure aspect of the divine ideal and sheds the ego's imitation of it.

These terms started with Oscar Ichazo, who instructed that each ego type loses its original connection to one of nine Divine Aspects or Essential Aspects, that holds their life's purpose. From there, A. H. Almaas developed and continues to teach the Diamond Approach, which describes both Essential Aspects and their counterparts, Idealized Aspects.[6] Sandra Maitri further expands upon the Diamond Approach, teaching that Essential Aspects—like Holy Ideas—describe the ways each soul child directly expresses the Divine. My descriptions are from my personal experience, as well as my interpretations and syntheses of Sandra Maitri's and A. H. Almaas' writings.

Each aspect is both essential to the soul and idealized by the ego, depending on the ego type encountering it, meaning that the two aspects share names. At their Soul Point, an ego type accesses their soul's core Essential Aspect; however, an ego type at their Ego Point, who has not made contact with their soul child, can only reach a distorted version of an aspect: their ego's Idealized Aspect. Therefore, one person's soul's Essential Aspect and another's ego's Idealized Aspect represent a true and twisted version of the same concept.

Point One: Brilliancy

Soul's Essential Aspect of Ego Type Four, found at Soul Point One: the crystal-clear perception of reality in its totality. Out of reality's divine perfection emanates bright and vivid discernment.

"I contain the penetrating insight which emanates from the Divine."

Ego's Idealized Aspect of Ego Type One: clarity comes from doing the right thing and making sure everyone else is doing so as well.

"I demand perfection and reject all that is not impeccable. For me, Brilliancy means flawlessness and precision."

Point Two: Merging Gold

Soul's Essential Aspect of Ego Type Eight, found at Soul Point Two: the blissful state of togetherness with others, the beloved, and the divine beloved. Love creates a harmonious union between souls.

"I bring people together in compassion."

---

6. Almaas, *Keys to the Enneagram*.

Ego's Idealized Aspect of Ego Type Two: personal belief in being the source of abundance for people: profuse giving and goodness foster intimacy with others in exchange for love.

"I give in relationships to ensure that I am both indispensable and loved."

Point Three: The Pearl

Soul's Essential Aspect of Ego Type Nine, found at Soul Point Three: freedom from being anything except our purest, personal, and essential self—being in our soul's consciousness without relying on personality or ego identifications.

"I am an embodiment of essence, made in the image of the Divine."

Ego's Idealized Aspect of Ego Type Three: the establishment of identity and individual significance through enhancing personality and building an image of the separate self.

"I am a prototype of the ideal; I construct my own identity around my winnings and accomplishments."

Point Four: The Point

Soul's Essential Aspect of Ego Type Two, found at Soul Point Four: living out of true being and our inestimable uniqueness. The self-realization here and now that we are essence and no other expression of essence is like ours.

"I am true being, essence. My identity is certain and is rooted in the divine source."

Ego's Idealized Aspect of Ego Type Four: striving to create a significance, the recognition of which substantiates our worth and identity.

"I am different and special. Therefore, I am the original—the one and only, and the source of my own being."

Point Five: Diamond Guidance

Soul's Essential Aspect of Ego Type Seven, found at Soul Point Five: the embodiment of wisdom, which comprehends everything in its entirety. Past, present, and future are understood as a unity of knowledge that lights the way.

"I am in union with divine guidance as I understand and experience the present and the past simultaneously."

Ego's Idealized Aspect of Ego Type Five: the overwhelming desire for knowledge that—in and of itself—will provide the fullness of life.

"I continuously seek and store information to fill my emptiness; I use it to comfort, protect, and guide me."

Point Six: Will

Soul's Essential Aspect of Ego Type Three, found at Soul Point Six: inner strength and self-sufficiency. The community is anchored in self-reliance. All challenges are met with confidence that inner support is always there.

"I am solid ground of being, the rock."[7]

Ego's Idealized Aspect of Ego Type Six: an attachment to authority figures or a group who can provide strength and direction. Following others' wills or, counter-intuitively, imposing our will upon others.

"I have audacity, guts, and an authority figure who protects me from all that threatens me."

Point Seven: The Yellow

Soul's Essential Aspect of Ego Type One, found at Soul Point Seven: pure joy—both effervescent and quiet—is informed by the wisdom of our depths.

"I am Joy, which emanates from appreciation, delight, and simple happiness."

Ego's Idealized Aspect of Ego Type Seven: the constant search for happiness and the denial of deeper aspects of being; using fantasy and continuous consumption to distract from pain.

"My over-the-top consumption brings me joy and distracts me from deprivation and pain."

Point Eight: The Red

Soul's Essential Aspect of Ego Type Five, found at Soul Point Eight: power in aliveness and in the sheer magnitude of our capability.

---

7. Tillich, *Systematic Theology*, 1:235.

Directed by an inner core of compassion, The Red acts decisively in transforming the world.

"I am strength: vital, alive, and full of power and capacity."

Ego's Idealized Aspect of Ego Type Eight: the aggressive enforcement of a personal idea of what is best. The appearance of strength and denial of weakness drives action instead of our core of compassion.

"I lust for absolute control so that I am never seen as weak or powerless."

Figure Seven
Soul's Essential and Ego's Idealized Aspects

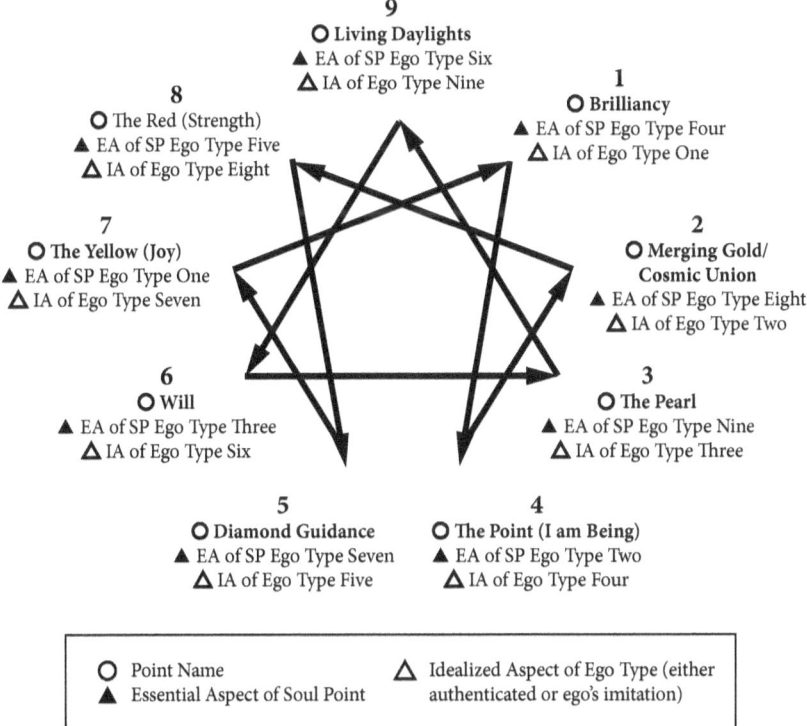

Soul's Essential and Ego's Idealized Aspects

Point Nine: Living Daylight

Soul's Essential Aspect of Ego Type Six, found at Soul Point Nine: we are all held in a container of love and are cared for, needed, and wanted. The entire world is a manifestation of divine love, from which we are never separated. "Everything in the cosmos, including me, is made of and held in pure love."

Ego's Idealized Aspect of Ego Type Nine: the avoidance of conflict and anything that might upset the harmony we have fabricated by relinquishing our will, significance, and separate identity.

"To maintain external harmony and the sense of well-being, I turn my anger inward, devalue my own existence, and avoid conflict."

Aspects by Ego Type

Ego Type	Soul's Essential Aspect	Ego's Idealized Aspect
Type One	The Yellow (Joy)	Brilliancy
Type Two	The Point	Merging Gold
Type Three	Will	The Pearl
Type Four	Brilliancy	The Point
Type Five	The Red (Power/Strength)	Diamond Guidance
Type Six	Living Daylight	Will
Type Seven	Diamond Guidance	The Yellow (Joy)
Type Eight	Merging Gold	The Red (Power/Strength)
Type Nine	The Pearl	Living Daylight

Mischief and Naughtiness in the Soul Child

I recall the mischief of my two-, three-, and four-year-old soul child. Over and over, I tried to ride the neighbor's German Shepherd like a horse. My friend's father spanked me for entering their apartment next door without permission. When my visiting grandmother held me down and forced me to take medicine, I retaliated by dragging her corset and suitcase into the living room and demanding that she go home now! I found solace in food and ate my mother's whole stash of chocolate.

I resisted putting away my toys, making countless excuses. I sold sticks to people for a penny and told them the sticks would make their plants grow. I was slow to get going and frequently languished for hours on the sofa, watching cartoons. I am sure that I did many other naughty things but as I recall each of these I do not sense they were from my ego. Indeed, my ego type had not yet fully formed. I was living from my Living Daylight.

The soul child is a human psychological structure. In life, they exhibit the human vulnerabilities, frailties, and foibles that are part and parcel of our essence. A key point here is that one's personal essence is not a product of the ego; therefore, the pure soul child is not a reaction to shame, anger, or fear. That's the ego's job.

For example, the soul child who later becomes an Ego Type Six has their essence at Soul Point Nine. This child may have some of Ego Type Nine's behaviors that we view as negative, such as laziness, apathy, lethargy, self-neglectfulness, self-debasement, and generally "sleeping through" life. Because of these and many other "Nine-ish" characteristics of the Six's soul child, we could easily assume that all soul children are born as an ego type—but this assumption could not be further from the truth. As soul children, we are in an early stage of development and operate primarily from our innate instincts, libidinal drives, impulses, and the pleasure principle.[8] These do not proceed from a developed ego. Instead, in the absence of a developed ego, each soul child lives from their primitive instincts, along with their Holy Idea, Essential Aspect, and other soul qualities. With this dynamic in mind, let us explore each soul child's impulsive, naughty, and socially inappropriate characteristics according to ego type and soul point.

Type Six's soul child, at Soul Point Nine, is simply at one with the slow but sure timing of the universe. In experiencing being part of all, their skill at merging with others is not an ego adaptation but a pure expression of oneness with everything. As a soul, they may be more self-neglectful than fastidious, less nimble than sluggish, more apt to downplay than to tout themselves, and more given to escaping life's turmoil by self-anesthetizing than by seeking protection. We may judge these to be examples of laziness, detachment, devaluing of oneself to avoid conflict, and self-narcotization to reality. Before the onset of ego, however, these behaviors stem from directly experiencing the energy of our Soul Point. For example, for the Six's soul child at Nine, laziness may not be defiance but part and parcel with relaxing into the divine flow; detachment is not

---

8. Moccia et al., "Experience of Pleasure."

an ego function but rather a sign of entering the dream world. Likewise, de-emphasizing ourselves may not be manipulation but a method of energy conservation. Avoiding conflict may simply be about staying calm, and self-narcotization could signify a natural willingness to enter other states of bliss. None of these natural human qualities of the soul child originate in the ego structure or stem from an ego narrative.

The Wounding of the Soul Child

The soul child's inherent modes of expression proceed from its libidinal drives, genetic factors, innate reflexes, and the pleasure principle. Yet, there is another source of the soul child's behavior that some hold to be even more fundamental to this little being than any other force: the Divine. I have drawn from several integral sources about the soul child: the literature, the re-experiencing of my own soul child, the observations of our two children, the spoken memories of hundreds of adult patients and students, and my one-on-one clinical interactions with hundreds of soul children since 1975.

For me, the soul child's most essential elements are their soul qualities, which as a group comprise their identity. Each small child has their own uncontaminated presence, posture, and way of interpreting the world. They express their soul through their voice, their eyes, their gestures, their play, and their uncensored observations, questions, and statements. They express their souls in unrestrained movements and spontaneous actions. Their touch, too, leaves an impression of their essence via the Body Center. Soul children do not have egoic agendas but freely express from the energy they were born with. Their motivations spring from their natural curiosity and the simple need to give and receive love. Their particular perception of the world can be linked to what will become their ego type's Holy Idea, soul's Essential Aspect, and Idealized Essential Aspect.

In my experience, a soul child in the throes of being wounded has a particular look in their eyes. Some of these little ones are thought to be depressed, others have tantrums and behavior disorders. (I am not speaking here of extreme cases of mental, physical, or sexual abuse. Presentations of such issues in children of this age are far more serious than presentations of "normal" wounding.) The soul child in the wounding process seems to know on a deep level that they will soon have to give way to the ego and retreat under a crust. There is inherent grief for the slow death of their natural selves. The changes necessary to become a "big boy" or "big girl" or to join the ranks of older siblings may be daunting. Roles transform, as does their self-image.

A soul child is green, unconditioned. When we were soul children, we were the personification of our inherent qualities, living in the assurance that we were held by the universe. Barring unusual circumstances, there is no reason to question our safety or existence—no reason, that is, until we receive the message that we are not "OK" in our current state. A soul child cannot understand the expectations of the world or the resulting rejection and punishment for being themselves. Gradually, our parents and others teach us that we are not acceptable the way we are. This message hurts as bad as a physical injury and we are forced to protect ourselves from the pain. All good parents use rewards and punishments to help their children conform to what is expected. This constant correction and shaping eventually creates a more socially palatable personage and the barrage of criticisms against our most natural selves decreases. This is when, for most of us, the ego takes command and our soul child goes undercover.

The unconditioned soul child was innocent. They could, for instance, proudly appear naked without shame. As we grow older, because society deems our innocent instincts to be taboo, we shift to the ego as our identity and trust it to keep our shame at bay as we move through the world. In response, the soul child isolates itself from our conscious awareness.

We develop a crust, a scab over our wound that hides our soul child beneath it. Like the earth's crust that tempers the release of magma and underground water, this crust seals away the soul child's energy. It protects our vulnerable soul child from future wounds. Unfortunately, the crust also obstructs ready access to the exuberant and beautiful qualities of our soul child, including its Holy Idea and other soul states of being.

Like geysers and volcanoes, however, the soul child sometimes erupts from beneath its crust. It bubbles up when we are least controlled: when we are under pressure or our defenses are down. It spurts out through the crust's fissures in an entirely natural but "out of our character" way. Our soul child surfaces as bouts of spontaneous playfulness, impulsive purchases, unexpected tantrums, and stubborn resistance to finishing work before we take leisure time. It can manifest as road rage, impatience in the grocery store line, and self-indulgence. We grab selfishly for immediate gratification and may shove others aside to get it.

Likewise, a reversion to the soul child may be responsible for our messy desk, bedroom, office, car, or home.

On the other hand, the soul child also appears in an unexpected display of empathy for a person or situation we had every "right" to resent. The soul child produces a sudden, brilliant flash of insight that reduces everyone to tears with its unalterable truth. Our soul child's unconditional love comes forward when we might otherwise make conditions. Gifts from the heart are pure, with no strings attached.

Our soul child is that extra piece of energy that comes from a long-ago time; it empowers us to move a mountain, the sight of which would have caused our adult self to crumple in defeat.

The soul child appears when there's something fresh in us: a twinkling gleam in our eye, an expectant aura—not from striking it rich, winning the tournament, or becoming a star—but because of inestimable spiritual treasures like trusting the outcome, being held, and feeling assured of our connection to all life. It's the soul child bubbling up when we stop and notice the light playing on the leaves while our better judgment bids us move on and stay on schedule. It is the soul child who'd rather play with the dog or cat than do anything else right now, and it's the soul child who yearns for the tenderness and closeness of yesteryear. Our soul child revels in embarrassing us with its naked truthfulness.

The Soul Child's Journey

The soul child is a powerful psychological structure. It is the internalized experience of our truest nature before our ego conditioned us: the link to our soul and its divine qualities. Sadly, for its own protection, it becomes concealed from our consciousness and the ego takes charge. We live in the ego from later childhood until it can no longer sustain us. During these years, for the most part, the soul child remains unacknowledged under its crusty barrier.

This hidden aspect of our identity is our only psychological structure that once lived every day as our personal essence without a developed ego. Indeed, in our childhood, it did not feel separate in any way from the direct experience of being held by the universe—by the Divine. The soul child is therefore possibly the most powerful part of our psyche in terms of its contribution to our spiritual formation. Its journey is part and parcel of the integrative process that relieves us of ego suffering and transforms us to soul consciousness. We have already discussed the earliest steps in the journey of the soul child. Below is a full list of the soul child's steps in its vital journey toward helping us reach spiritual realization.

Stages of the Soul Child's Journey

1. The soul is part of the Essence of All Being and enters the person at their creation, as the soul child.

2. The soul child is born into one of the nine sacred energies depicted on the Enneagram of Soul.

3. The soul child progresses through the developmental stages of childhood until a gradual or sudden emotional wounding sends the message that they are not OK the way they are. The result is a shift in identity away from the soul child/soul type to the ego type, which protects the inner child and creates a persona with which to move through the world.

4. The ego becomes the primary identity and contact with the Holy Idea, the soul's Essential Aspect, and the Authenticated Idealized Aspect is lost. The ego creates a facsimile of the Idealized Aspect and the soul child is protected under a hard crust to prevent its re-appearance.

5. The ego type is a reaction to the rejection of the soul child. Our ego reacts by setting up a new "fail-safe" strategy for facing the world. This strategy aims to imitate and reconstruct the bliss that our soul child experienced. The ego's perspective is built on irrational ideas and distortions of reality and can never attain that lost bliss.

6. The soul child remains concealed, piercing the crust only for brief periods when it expresses its divine qualities and/or foibles.

7. The ego's protective strategy also causes suffering, which finally reaches a critical mass. This suffering and its difficulties cannot be solved on the level of the ego. We begin to look for another method to ease our pain. The soul child remains under the crust but it resurfaces in the form of flashbacks of earlier times of bliss.

8. We continue to search for relief from our suffering and yearn for the bliss of our soul child. Our Holy Idea serves as a bridge from our ego

type to our truest nature. Through self-remembering,[9] we cross the gap between the ego and the essence and we arrive at the Point of Integration, where our soul child has been all along. The hard crust that sealed our soul child off from our consciousness is removed and we directly experience life in our soul once more.

9. The process of healing and wholeness includes the alchemical combination of the ego's acquired wisdom amalgamating with the soul child's qualities. This intermingling creates a new consciousness. We travel repeatedly through the successive life-giving energies at each of the nine points, in the Enneagram's inner flow. Each healthy, conscious expression of the nine Enneagram energies takes us on an upward spiral toward spiritual restoration. Remembering and re-embodying the soul child is a gateway to this inner flow. Without an upward spiral and the amalgamation of ego and soul, we stagnate or travel downward in a spiral of disintegration, during which we lose consciousness of the soul child once again.

The Inner Flow of the Enneagram

To see how the Enneagram's integrative process works, we will use the example of Ego Type Three. The Three ego's efficiency, status, and continuous accomplishments do not give them hope that they and the rest of the world are progressing. Indeed, their ego's activity fails to bring the love from others they most desire. Feeling unloved and unlovable creates in them an intolerable hopelessness that triggers a search for relief. In their wanderings, they imagine what life was like before all this suffering. They have flashbacks to times when, as children, they were connected, supported, fulfilled, and loved. Their heart remembers once having lived in harmony, trust, and hope. These remembrances spark their composite Holy Idea: Holy Harmony, Holy Law, and Holy Hope, which, when embraced, leads the Three to their Soul Point Six, where their soul child lives.

At Point Six, the Three enters their true nature, where they perceive that there is harmony in loving communities and that natural laws govern the progression of the world, alleviating them of that burden. They realize when living in these states of consciousness that there is inestimable hope. In this place, the soul qualities (Essential Aspects and Idealized Aspects, etc.) also amalgamate into the being.

9. Ouspensky, *In Search of the Miraculous*, 119.

Next, the Three travels against their arrow from Point Six to Point Nine, where they absorb the Holy Idea of Holy Love. At Nine, the Three becomes conscious that authentic love happens not because of their successes but because of their ability to recognize their own soul qualities and those of others. The Three returns to themselves at Point Three in a much higher state of consciousness and self-realization. This traveling against the arrows continues, with each round taking them higher and higher on the spiral of consciousness.

Given this inner flow, it is, in a sense, a misnomer to call someone a "Four" or a "Two"—these numbers are labels associated with the fixations of egos, whether in their healthy, average, or unhealthy states of consciousness. It may be limiting to refer to someone by their number on the Enneagram of Personality, since it cannot possibly describe the person in the process of integration.

Those of us who are integrating beyond our personality, into our depths are continuously making the return to our essence. This is a journey into wholeness, in which eventually all of the Holy Ideas are expressed in us to some degree. This expression increases with spiritual practice. Such persons are no longer readily identifiable by ego fixations because their soul qualities are much more prominent. In this state of being, they are much like their soul child, including its natural and unconditioned foibles. This truest identity, also called "our true nature," eventually amalgamates the ego and soul, transforming the ego into a servant of the soul.

Integration of the Soul Child into Our Consciousness

Re-embodying the soul child is a process that lasts for years; most people don't begin it until the second half of their lives—after their ego strategies have collapsed. Returning to the past in terms of reliving one's childhood is a familiar archetypal journey but is not necessarily an altogether pleasant one. Classic works such as *The Iliad* and *The Odyssey*, as well as more modern creations such as *The Trip to Bountiful*, address this paradigm.

Now, due to the plethora of studies on the human mind and the resurgence of ancient spiritual processes, we have more access to the subconscious than ever before. Practices such as mindfulness, yoga, dream interpretation, meditation, journaling, guided imagery, self-remembering, etc., reveal our depths. Professionally guided imagery can help re-awaken someone's soul child in just minutes. Such progress is contingent upon an experienced guide who takes one back to the beginnings of life by way of carefully designed mental pathways.

Conclusion

The soul child is a quintessential entity that has been known, in some form, since the beginning of recorded history. It is part of the life force of every human being and its power is vast. Imagine the potential we have today that goes untapped while we ignore this energy inside us! On the road to self-remembering, self-discovery, and self-realization, we can reach back to our beginning to answer the Zen question, "What did your face look like before you were born?"[10]

---

10. Pine, *Platform Sutra*.

4
Who Is Your Soul Child?

Now that we know our soul child contains our specific soul qualities, the best way to consciously re-embody these sacred qualities is to get back in touch with that inner child of ours. The earlier-mentioned process of "reaching back" opens up many memories of our earliest experiences. To trigger such memories, we may ponder a photograph of ourselves from when we were very young. After we get the sense of that little being, we may try to recall the context of the photograph and the situation or the people around us at the time. By far, the most important aspect of viewing this photo is to observe the eyes of our soul child. As you look into those eyes, consider: What emotion is conveyed? What type of thought does the picture indicate might be going through the child's mind? What does the child's body language seem to be saying?

Most of us do not stop to think about our soul and the specific qualities that compose it. If you list some qualities of the child that you observe in the photo, however, you will begin to identify some specifics about this soul child of yours. After you make your list, ask yourself whether you identify with these qualities or if they seem far away from the person you are now. In this section, you will learn various methods to experience and re-embody your soul child.

One remarkably effective way to trigger memories is to visit the places where you lived as a very young child. Some time ago, I made such a trip to the home in which I lived from ages four to seventeen.

Nervous but resolute, I knocked on the door of my childhood home. Over fifty years earlier, I had watched as this house was built on a vacant lot. Although I had passed by it several times over the decades since my parents had moved farther outside of the city, I had never gathered the nerve to go up to the door and ask to see inside. Something about this day lent me that strength. When the front door opened, I introduced myself to the lady behind the screen door. She smiled and greeted me without hesitation, "You must be one of the two little boys who grew up here! I knew this day would come—and here you are! Would you like to see the house?" Surprised and grateful, I immediately entered my earliest years as I passed the threshold. Her sweet narration about what they had done to update the house fell on deaf ears; I was in another world, transfixed by the experience of each re-lived moment.

My mind's eye saw none of the remodeling she was pointing out to me. I saw only my home of yesteryear, with its soft green plaster walls, hardwood floors, and the fringed drapes that my mother had made and hung. I pictured my mother, father, little brother, and myself in every room and on every occasion: sitting around the Christmas tree, celebrating birthdays, and—most often—eating at the dining room table or getting ready for work and school. In my bedroom, I could see myself awakening every morning to the breeze coming through my window and playing with toys like my electric train. I looked at the back of my door and watched myself making the mark of Zorro with my plastic sword. In my parents' room, I saw myself creeping into their bed after a bad dream and slipping in between them for comfort. When I glimpsed the kitchen, I saw myself helping my mother set the table and recalled having to eat vegetables I didn't like. In the yard, I saw the places where I played endlessly with my brother and picked up fallen birds and squirrels, either to nurse back to health or bury. I saw the very spot where—while planting azalea bushes—my father and I dug up an ancient horseshoe, which I still have.

Being in this environment for even that small amount of time put me in contact with my soul child in a very real way. Even today, when I play back my memory of that visit, I perceive many qualities that my soul child expressed before I had any identity but my soul. If you arrange such a visit in your mind's eye—or for real—be sure to make a voice recording or journal of your impressions while they are still fresh. Pay special attention to your soul child's demeanor, behavior, words, and expressions. You can extract descriptions of your soul child from your voice recording or notes. List these.

Another way to bring back our soul child is by talking to family or friends who knew us in those early years. They add tidbits about us that we would not have known otherwise. For instance, my mother left me in the apartment alone while she popped over to the market across the street to buy me an orange for my lunch bag. While she was gone, the kindergarten bus rolled up outside our door to pick me up as usual, but my mother was not there and I did not know what to do. I had never boarded that bus alone. I was paralyzed. Finally, something came over me; I opened the screen door and slowly made my way to the bus. As we drove away, I looked back from my window to see my mother running after the bus with an orange held high in her hand. She was too late; the bus wouldn't stop. I recall being overwhelmed with sympathy for my mother. I broke into tears and had to be comforted by the lady on the bus. My mother tells me that when she came to the kindergarten later, I had calmed down but I needed reassurance that she too, was alright.

I can identify certain qualities of my soul within this story. Namely, as a soul child, I had immense courage, empathy, and a strong connection to others. My mother highlighted that courage with another anecdote from when I was nine months old. She held me by my arms in a standing position in a hotel elevator. When the doors opened, even though I had never been able to before, I suddenly broke away from her and walked straight out as if I had been walking all my life. As you check with family members and friends who knew you "way back when," you will accumulate a variety of stories that illustrate characteristics from when you were in the state of being called your soul child. Make a list of all these qualities.

Of course, home videos are excellent primary sources for observing our soul child. In these animated time capsules, we can watch our interactions with others, our behavior, and our bearing as a baby and small child. We notice the changes in our body language and voice as we get older. What soul aspects are expressed by our soul child in these tender years? Again, as you watch the videos, take time to list the characteristics and qualities you observe about your soul child. These are the qualities that defined your life before your ego and personality took control of your identity.

Writing down or voice recording our earliest memories are two other ways to tap into the memories beneath and on the surface of our mind. Begin by writing or narrating your very first memory, then let yourself enter a stream of consciousness and write or say whatever comes to mind. You will likely find that memories and images, stories and impressions will flow—first slowly, then bountifully—into your recollection. You may want a family photo album or a set of loose photos to jog your memory.

From the stories that come forward, look for your characteristics as a young child and baby. Distill and then list your early behavior, verbalizations, or reactions that each story illustrates.

Meeting Our Soul Child

Guided meditation is another, specialized method to reconnect us with our soul child. Facilitated by a guide who helps us reach a calm, relaxed, and meditative state, we visualize ourselves at a particular time in our childhood. This technique can be amazingly successful in helping us reach the child who is still inside us. Even more impressively, through a Jungian process called active imagination—written about extensively by Jungian analyst Robert Johnson[1]—many of us can actually hear and/or imagine our soul child speaking to us. What the child says can be extremely important when reconstructing our soul qualities.

Word of Caution and Informed Consent

Please be aware that this exercise may bring back long-concealed memories or impressions that may not be positive. In fact, in such a meditation you might remember an instance of trauma or abuse and run the risk of experiencing some of those same feelings again. This is why a trusted person—a trained and accomplished guide—is essential. The guide can assist you in carefully detaching from the exercise and processing any disturbing material. Together, you can decide whether or not professional counseling would be beneficial. It is rare for someone to encounter such severely distressing memories but it is a possibility to bear in mind.

The Process

The first step in the guided imagery process is to clear the time and space for this activity—that is, no cell phones or other interruptions. The guide may work with you solo or as part of a larger group.

The second step is a preliminary interactive exercise conducted by the person guiding you. Take five minutes to draw a map of the back yard in which you grew up. If you prefer, you may draw a map of your room,

---

1. Johnson, *Inner Work*.

your house, or your apartment as you remember it. If you had many places in which you grew up, just pick the most familiar one. Now, with your guide or another person present, review your map and explain the different areas and features of the space. Share any memories you have of this space, especially any significant spots or activities.

The guide will then facilitate a meditative state, using a variation of the following directions:

> *Remain sitting upright with a relaxed posture. Breathe in deeply through your nose and exhale through your mouth three times. Have a photo of yourself as a baby or small child that you can focus on. If you do not have a photo available, just imagine yourself at the age of two, three, or four. Pay particular attention to this child's eyes and look into them deeply. Now, refer to the map that you have just drawn. Where in that yard or house was that little person most likely to be? What were they likely to be doing?*

Next, the guide will help you conduct a mental scan of your body to release any tense areas. They will instruct you to:

> *Begin by closing your eyes and releasing any tension in your head, eyes, mouth, face, neck, and shoulders. Let the relaxation extend down your arms to each finger and thumb. Notice the difference between the relaxed areas and those which are still tense. Breathe in from and out into those places. Now, relax your chest, lungs, and rib cage. Pay attention to the rhythm of your heart and let your breathing sync with it, breathing in and out in time with your heart's beating. Relax the rest of your torso and all the internal organs, all the way to your pelvic floor. Notice any remaining tension and then let it slacken. Relax your hips, thighs, and knees. Let go of any strain in your lower legs, calves, shins, and ankles. Now, release any stiffness or tension in your feet and toes. Notice your entire body is calm and at rest. If you quickly scan your body again now and find an area that requires more relaxation, take the time to give it.*

With your eyes closed, listen to the guide's words:

> *Stay fully relaxed and visualize your back yard. As the person you are now, enter that yard through a door from the house, by an outside gate, or simply by walking freely into the space. Look around and notice all the familiar things. Take in the smells. Are there fragrances from home cooking or flowers? Is the air humid, dry, breezy, or chilly? What sounds do you hear: dogs barking?*

children playing in other yards? music? What draws your focus? Is there a swing set, a favorite tree, a patio, a vegetable garden or gazebo, a barbecue, a sprinkler, a garden, or a dog house? Notice the things which make this yard uniquely yours.

Now, locate your favorite place in the yard. Walk around the space and pay attention to which emotions you feel: happiness, peacefulness, excitement, wonder, concern, hesitancy? Now, look for your childhood self, the one whose photo you just saw. Where are they? What are they doing? What mood does your soul child seem to be in? What could they possibly be thinking? Note your observations so that you can list them later.

Now, approach your soul child, make eye contact, and ask, "May I sit with you?" Listen to your soul child's answer, then ask the following:

Ask, "What are you doing now?" Listen to their answer.
Ask, "Where have you been for so long?" Listen.
Ask, "What is your favorite thing to do?" Listen.
Ask, "Why is it your favorite?" Listen.
Ask, "What is your best toy?" Listen.
Ask, "What's the best thing to think about?" Listen.
Ask, "What's your favorite color? How about your favorite animal?" Listen.
Ask, "Who do you love?" Listen.
Ask, "Who loves you?" Listen.
Ask, "Why were you born?" Listen.
Ask, "What do you need?" Listen.
Ask, "What makes you happy?" Listen.
Ask, "What makes you sad?" Listen.
Ask, "Who is God?" Listen.
Ask, "Where is God?" Listen.
Ask, "Where do we come from?" Listen.
Now, it's your turn to answer your soul child's questions.
Your soul child asks:
"Why did you leave me?" Listen to your answer.
"Where did you go?" Listen to your answer.
"What do you think about?" Listen to your answer.
"What do you feel in your heart?" Listen to your answer.
"Why do you live?" Listen to your answer.
"Who do you love?" Listen to your answer.
"Who loves you?" Listen to your answer.
"Who has helped you come into being?" Listen to your answer.
"Will you leave me again?" Listen to your answer.
"Will you stay with me?" Listen to your answer.

You may want to embrace your child, and/or hold them on your lap. You may simply want to be present and share a space with this soul child of yours.

Now, it is time to return from this meditation. Let the scene fade away unhurriedly, leaving your soul child in the yard. Slowly return to the here and now in the room where we began this exercise. As you breathe deeply, open your eyes gradually, and, with a soft gaze, come back to yourself. As you sit here, be aware of all that surrounds you. Notice your emotions, your thoughts, and your body's physical sensations. Upon return from this deep meditation, some of us may see colors more vividly, identify shapes more distinctly, and sense the presence of others more intensely. This is because, in returning to our soul child's state of being, the ego is no longer imposing its perceptions on what we experience. In this lingering state, you are more likely to be transparent to reality.

After this exercise, it is best to debrief with the guide and/or someone else who has just experienced the same journey. Record or journal your observations about your soul child.

From the list of questions and answers above and based on your observations, which qualities, expressions, behaviors, and verbalizations describe your soul child? Be sure to pay attention to your reactions—both to your soul child's answers to your questions and to the answers you gave to your soul child. Write a brief character sketch or "soul sketch" of your soul child, based on the qualities you recorded.

Listing the Qualities of Our Soul Child

Some qualities to note among others you may experience in the above exercises are:

Heart/Emotional Qualities

- Affection: Generously expressing your heart's love in words and/or touches
- Awe: Amazement at the reality of things witnessed or finally comprehended
- Charm: Expressing a genuine sweetness magnetic to others
- Compassion: Joining others in their pain and bearing it with them

Drama: Passionately acting out your feelings

Empathy: Feeling the pain of others

Extroversion: Generously and openly sharing emotions with others

Faith: Trusting that everything will be OK

Forcefulness: Putting forth emotions and opinions with strong energy

Generosity: Giving freely from the heart, without expectation of compensation

Gratitude: Giving continuous thanks for all that you are given

Happiness: A sunny disposition emanating from a carefree and positive take on life

Hope: Looking to the future with optimism

Humility: Perceiving yourself as a fallible human being who sometimes makes mistakes; i.e., no better than anyone else

Introversion: Keeping matters of the heart close and sharing them only in intimate settings

Joy: Overflowing with deep and ongoing happiness

Loving-kindness: Caring for others through sensitivity and empathic support

Mercy: Extending compassionate grace to those who have trespassed against you

Patience: Understanding that divine timing does not always match our concept of timing

Peace: Manifesting serenity from your depths

Presence: Being right here, right now in mind, heart, and body

Reticence: Wariness of sharing emotions

Tolerance: Being able to endure that which cannot be changed

Mind Qualities

Attunement: Oneness with the now, yourself, and others

Clarity: Perceiving reality sharply and accurately

Contemplation: Taking in and processing reality

Detachment: Ability to stay away from all that confuses and confabulates

Discernment: Using skill to break down problems and mysteries

Expressiveness: The ability to convey thought, emotion, or meaning

Faceted: Having many aspects of thought

Freedom: Ability to think outside the box, unconfined by external pressures

Imagination: Creating (or "discovering") mental concepts

Inquisitiveness: Curiosity about that which you do not understand

Introspection: The thoughtfully reflective examination of your own thoughts and feelings

Intuition: Knowing or understanding something to be true without definite proof

Logic: Objectivity in thinking through and solving problems

Memory: The storage of information, impressions, reflections, and concepts

Observation: Ability to survey situations

Openness: Ability to consider all information and concepts

Presence: Being in the moment, attuned to your own thoughts and those of others

Quick-wittedness: Adaptability and ease of making decisions on the spot

Reasonableness: Using plain sense to work things out

Receptiveness: Non-judgmental openness to other people and ideas

Searching: Looking for that missing piece, whatever that may be

Serenity: Maintaining an ongoing tranquility of mind

Tentativeness: Reticence to share thoughts

Transmitting: Ability to convey thoughts well

Transparency: The practice of sharing your actions in a visible, accessible manner

Wisdom: Knowing and applying one's knowledge of the nature of things

Wonder: Immersion in awe and curiosity

Body Qualities

Acting as conduit: Channeling energies from beyond yourself

Action-orientedness: Expressing the soul through action

Adaptiveness: Ability to adjust to new norms and morph into whatever a situation calls for

Affection: Expressing love through the senses in addition to body movement and action

Animation: Energizing life with expression and movement

Balance/Relaxation: Removing tension and renewing equilibrium

Demureness: Modesty and reserve

Dissent: Using one's full body energy to lean against that which must be opposed

Ebbing and flowing: Having alternate bursts of energy and rest

Energy: Exuding life force

Expressiveness: Physically demonstrating your soul qualities

Formidability: Possessing large, strong energy that commands attention

Fragility: Tenderness or weakness in certain spots or circumstances

Groundedness: Aligning with reality on a gut level that invites the heart and head to join

Interaction: Physical engagement with others

Luminosity: Having a soul so bright that it shines forth through your physical presence

Merging/Suppression of individuality: Merging easily with others and relying on group strength over your own

Palpability: Spiritual presence so strong that others experience its presence in profoundly impactful ways

Perception: Using all body senses to comprehend reality

Poise: Readiness for whatever action is called for at the moment

Presence: Full awareness of and engagement of all sensations

Strength: Physical power

Substantivity: Having a solid stance

Vitality: Energized aliveness

Your Soul Child's Emerging Profile

After completing any of the exercises explained above, take time to compile a list of your soul child's characteristics and soul qualities.

Find your ego type's Holy Idea and Essential Aspect. List them beside the description of your soul child. Are your Ego Type's Holy Idea and Essential Aspect compatible with the nature of the child whose description you have just written?

When you consolidate your lists, your Holy Idea, and your Essential Qualities, a profile of your soul emerges. This profile will likely be quite different from the profile of your Enneagram Personality Type because the soul child is the person we were before the ego and the personality predominated. Therefore, as a soul child, we essentially expressed our "being" in terms of the inherent, unconditioned true nature within us at our making.

Part Two

Exploring Your Soul

5

The Enneagram of Soul

By age four, I had witnessed many kind and loving interchanges between my little friends Patsy and Deborah Linthicum and the three generations of their family who lived in our post-WWII apartment complex. One day, I accompanied my mother up the apartment stairwell to their home, where their grandmother was bed-bound with an illness. Standing with my mother at the bedside, I was too young to understand much about illness or the end of life. I just recall the solemn feeling in the room, the sadness on my friends' faces, and Mrs. Linthicum's heavy breathing as she spoke from her bed.

A few days after our visit, Mrs. Linthicum passed away. I distinctly remember watching men carry her draped body out and place her in a large black car parked on the street. This was not my first contact with death; our paperboy had been killed in a terrible motorcycle accident the year before. Now, a bit older and further along in my understanding of the world, I asked my mother a slew of questions. Among other things, I learned that Mrs. Linthicum's body was to be buried in the ground. I came to understand that my parents—and even I—would one day be put into the ground as well. This shocked me so much that I felt queasy and troubled for days. It was more than my little mind could handle.

My mother noticed my change in behavior and asked me what was wrong. I told her how sad I was that we would all eventually be buried. She took a deep breath and said, "It is just the body that's put in the ground; remember, our souls are still alive."

I have to give my mother an "A" for the way she handled such a tough topic. She provided me with a ray of optimism amid all the gloom in the air that day. From that period of my young life until today, I have pondered and studied the idea of the soul. More than that, I have sought to be aware of my own soul throughout the various stages of my life. My mother's simple explanation of the soul was understandable and comforting, and her reminder of its eternal nature was encouraging. Yet, as life's difficulties appeared, I searched to know more about this truest identity of ours. Many of the answers I found came from the Enneagram, which, as a map of hope, beautifully reflects our essential and infinite identity.

Knowing Our Soul

To know our soul is to know our depths and to experience our true nature: our essence. No other soul that has ever lived, or will ever live, is the same as ours. It connects us to our source and holds our spiritual purpose. In shifting our attention to our soul, we cease living only from mental structures like our ego and superego and we access our "spiritual personality," which I have termed "soulality." As I explained earlier, our soulality is the array of spiritual characteristics unique to our particular soul. We can reconnect to these characteristics by re-contacting our soul child. The soul child was born expressing our soulality and—as the soul grows—more aspects of our soulality develop. Our personality, on the other hand, is the expression of our ego, superego, and other psychological constructions. When we manage to live from our soul, our surface personality and ego submit to and reflect our soulality. In this state, we live from our depths and experience life in spiritual consciousness.

Delving into our personality is fine, and even supremely satisfying, for some of us. Others of us may find it intriguing but still long to explore beneath and beyond that personality—we know intuitively that we are more than our body, mind, emotions, and personality. For that reason, we sense the magnitude of our soul. Those of us who know the soul hear it calling us to our deepest meaning.

To ignore our soul is to be disconnected from our truest nature and, therefore, our spiritual attachments to others and to being itself. To be sure, plenty of us live satisfying lives on the surface level of existence. Indeed, many brilliant people—some of whom have made substantial sacrifices for and contributions to the world—are never able to connect their life experiences to the soul, much less, manage to live from it. By the same token, those on the spiritual path to consciousness may have numerous inadequacies and regressions in moral, spiritual, and consciousness development—all of which can make for a life that could very well be judged as deficient. The essential difference between these two groups, including the points on the continuum between them, comes down to whether or not they interpret meaning and purpose in light of the soul. In other words, are we living primarily from the soul or the egoic mind? These are two very different understandings of being, and they follow different paths.

The journey of the ego differs from the journey of the soul in a couple of major ways. The ego has many ideas and ideals, which do not necessarily reflect reality. The journey of the soul, then, is one toward an acceptance of reality. The journey of the ego seeks to manifest the ego's idea of happiness—which frequently includes the pursuit of enjoyment, the assumption of various roles and statuses, the search for freedom from pain, and the consumption and accumulation of both material goods and information. By the end of life, this quest may indeed have been accomplished very successfully.

The soul, meanwhile, seeks to fulfill its divine purpose while progressing spiritually. In this realm, joy has more value than enjoyment; freedom from pain is considered an impossibility. Consumerism is replaced by the desire to fulfill spiritual needs. Making soul relationships (i.e., being aware of and receptive to the soul qualities of others) is superior to achieving high status or simply amassing goods; likewise, developing wisdom is preferable to accruing information. Our soul's objective is to create more and more consciousness and, thereby, express our divine nature.

The Progression of Our Soul

Our soul transforms and grows throughout life, continually collecting truths and spiritual aspects, one point at a time, from all nine energy points on the Enneagram. This spiral of growth is an upward trajectory. Each loop of the spiral consists of a complete passage through all points of the Enneagram, gathering the essence energy and higher truths from each of the nine soul types along the way (more on that in the next chapter). In becoming conscious, we understand that burning away the veils of ego is vital to realizing the wholeness of our soul. Therefore, the upward spiral of consciousness and the diminishment of the unhealthy ego are essential to the progression of our souls.

Our soul's progression includes the phenomenon of shock points that are built into our journeys around the Enneagram. A shock point is an occurrence—oftentimes an abrupt loss—that disrupts our life as we know it, affecting our sense of reality, our inner balance, and our perceptions. Suddenly, our established understanding of how the world works explodes and all the pieces fly up in the air. When they finally fall to earth, we experience reality very differently from before. The new knowledge we receive from the loss may shape our outlook in a way that immediately propels us to a higher level of consciousness. Some of us, on the other hand, react to the shock point by regressing, and our ability to function declines as our fixations increase in intensity. Many of us emerge from this deterioration; others regress.

As with most other people, I have had many shock points. The one that placed me into a completely different state of consciousness—regarding both life and the Enneagram—was the death of our son, Ben. I got the call from Lark in the morning at my office, in the middle of a session with a patient. The first thing Lark said in a raised and trembling voice was, "Joe, Ben is dead." My world—and time itself—seemed to stop. Lark explained that she was with Ben at his apartment and had found him there, non-responsive. She had called the paramedics at once but he was already gone. He had slipped into a diabetic coma and his heart had stopped. I couldn't believe my ears—and yet, on another level, Ben had been drastically declining physically and mentally and part of me had been anticipating this. I rushed to his apartment, three blocks away. Lark and I sat for a time, with our son's body still in his bed as if he were asleep. I was shaken to my foundations. The little life we had loved and nurtured—the person who had delighted us and enriched our entire being—was gone. Ben was in my heart; I had devoted my life to him and his little sister, Lauren. It was unfathomable that we would no longer be able to hear his voice or experience his presence again. Eventually, the hearse pulled up outside his apartment and they brought a stretcher for my little boy's body.

It was then I had a flashback to when I was four years old and Mrs. Linthicum had just died. I recalled her stretcher being taken to the hearse and what my mother had told me about the soul. In this recollection, I remembered Mother spoke to me about the aliveness of the soul even after we die. Though a suffocating grief came over me, I held on to hope because I believed Ben's lifeless body was *not* Ben or the essence of Ben. I knew in my depths that he was more—far more—than his body and that his soul continues.

This shock point thrust me into a new realm of perception and reality. The best way to describe it is that I finally understood that, regardless of how strong my ego is, reality always wins. Therefore, I stopped following my ego mind's predetermined expectations as if they were reality. Now, I knew beyond the shadow of a doubt that any plans, even those about how life would unfold, could be smashed in an instant. The shock sent me into the realm of my soul because my ego alone lacked the capacity to navigate this devastating event. The shock point awakened me to a reality far greater than my self-made one. Intellectually, I had known it existed long before this shock point but now it was so real that my ego had to submit to it.

Integration, Higher Consciousness, and the Enneagram of Personality

The Enneagram of Personality depicts nine ego types. Each ego type (and its personality) progresses to higher levels of development by moving against its arrow, toward another point on the Enneagram, called its Point of Integration. There, we absorb that point's healthy and conscious characteristics (see chapter 1 for a full list). Then, we travel to each of the other points of the hexad or the primary triangle, embracing their conscious and healthy traits.

The propulsion upward to the next rung on the spiral of consciousness culminates in a more complete integration of the personality and the ego. In a higher state of self-awareness, we can recognize that the conscious and healthy aspects of our point of integration are the exact antidotes to the fixations and passions of our ego type. With each journey around the Enneagram, our personalities develop along with our ego. The spiral goes both ways, however; rather than growth, we may, instead, follow the path of disintegration.

Figure Eight
The Spiral of Consciousness

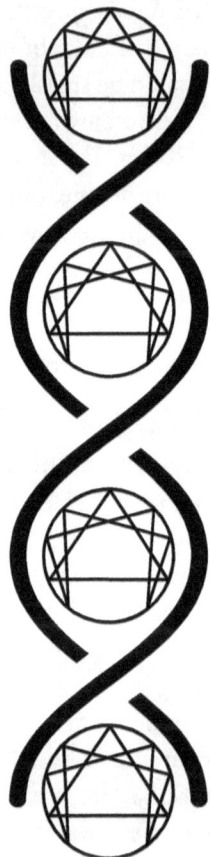

Diagram of the Spiral of Consciousness (Howell, *Becoming Conscious*, 201)

    A person whom I will call Jeremy is a great example of the upward spiral of personality growth depicted on the Enneagram of Personality. Jeremy has a great sense of humor and was constantly bringing people to tears with laughter. His ego identified him as an entertainer and he'd even considered a career in stand-up comedy early in life. His delightful personality shone through in his "performances." He made people clap with delight, double over with laughter, and beg for more. Most of Jeremy's jokes and stories were in good taste but some skirted the edge of decency, targeting racial, sexual, and gender differences.

In his studies of spirituality and the Enneagram, Jeremy's consciousness grew. In integrating from his Ego Point at Two, he journeyed around the Enneagram, picking up the healthy/conscious characteristics of his own soul type (Four) and the other five on the hexad. At the same time, his two wings (see chapter 1 of this work or my *Becoming Conscious*), the One and the Three, were also making the journey around the Enneagram of Soul; therefore, he was simultaneously integrating on the inner triangle and the hexad. With a greater awareness of both his own and others' needs, Jeremy became sensitized to those who are marginalized and rejected by mainstream society. He became viscerally aware, for the first time, of the harm he had likely caused those who bore the brunt of his jokes.

He realized he had been trying to find love by pandering to his audiences, sometimes at the expense of other groups and individuals. His jokes poked fun at the underprivileged and those with disabilities, as well as people of various races, sexual identities, and gender orientations. The growth that the Enneagram afforded him completely changed his style of humor. He realized that certain stories that had delighted him in the past were no longer funny to him as he now saw plainly how they belittled other people.

Jeremy continues to integrate and grow in consciousness. He has become aware of his fixations, traps, and avoidances, and—most of all—his passion of pride. His ego type's virtue of humility increased his empathy, while his Holy Idea of Holy Freedom and Holy Will has brought him into another realm of being. He has slowly changed. His playfulness is still palpable and his audiences still split their sides laughing, but the brash recklessness of his personality has been tempered by empathic sensitivity. No longer is his personality fixated on pleasing some at the expense of others. Jeremy now honors those whom society frequently rejects.

At the same time as his ego and personality are transforming, Jeremy's soul is also growing. There is another spiral that runs in concert with the spiral of ego and personality development: that of the soul.

The Enneagram of Soul

Picture the structure of DNA, found in every cell of all living things. It is composed of two intertwining spirals (helixes) that hold the substances of our genetic code. The spirals work in tandem to determine our characteristics.

We can compare the two spirals of the Enneagram of Personality and the Enneagram of Soul to the double helix of DNA. One determines the progression and regression of our ego and its personality; the other controls the progression and regression of our soul. Like their biological counterparts, the two Enneagram helixes are connected at every rung, meaning that we navigate them together, journeying up or down both at the same time. (See illustration.) The link between the two spirals also means that a shock point felt on the Enneagram of Personality is echoed on the Enneagram of Soul, and vice versa.

A shock on the Enneagram of Personality could lead us to integrate into a higher-developed ego/personality and ascend to a higher rung of the spiral. At the same time, we would experience the shock on the Enneagram of Soul and our soul would also develop in consciousness. Therefore, because of the shock point experienced by our ego/personality, we integrate into that realm as well as the realm of the soul.

For example, I believe I was operating at Ego Point Three during much of Ben's illness because I was relying on my own strategies to keep him alive and functioning. I had gone in the direction of my arrow to the unhealthy part of Ego Three (my Point of Disintegration, also referred to as the Stress Point). When all of my Herculean efforts failed, I felt guilt and shame for being a father and psychologist who was unsuccessful in saving his own son. On the level of personality, I noticed the problems and patterns that my unhealthy Three was causing.

This shock point could either have led me to spiral down further into the disintegrated aspects of the Three and then those of the Nine and so on, or, conversely, to spiral up to my Soul Point. Fortunately, it did the latter, which bumped me to a new level of personality integration. At the healthy part of my Soul Point, Nine, I finally relaxed into the truth that I hadn't possessed the power to heal my son, regardless of how much I loved him. To understand this, I had to relinquish my ego's preconceptions of the meaning of life and its concept of my purpose. At this point of surrender, my Soul Point Nine's peace displaced my Ego Type Six's anxiety.

My stubborn ego, which had always resisted surrender, now willingly let go of control. This surrender led to others, which allowed peace and acceptance in unexpected circumstances and outcomes. Now, my ego and personality express a degree of trust in the unknown that I'd never experienced before.

In concert with the shock to my personality, my soul received a violent shock the moment I learned of Ben's death. All the limitless hopes and possibilities of a lifetime were decimated in a single second. I imploded; a person sacred to me, whom I loved dearly, and whose life had embodied hope, was no more.

This shock shattered the meaning of my very existence and immediately thrust me to a higher realm of consciousness. On this next higher rung on the spiral of soul, I realized, existentially, that—regardless of the length of Ben's life—I had nurtured, loved, and guided him the very best I knew. On a soul level, I had indeed given my all. His passing didn't negate the love he gave me or that I gave him. The things I realized because of Ben's illness and death served to push my soul in the direction of integration. Things that I could never have comprehended before became crystal clear. I even received an expanded perspective of life's meaning: regardless of the length of time we have on earth, our souls learn what they need to learn in order to progress on their own unique trajectories.

Our Ego Type's Active Holy Idea

We learned in chapter 3 about the Holy Ideas of each of the ego types on the Enneagram of Personality. Sandra Maitri explains[1] that "the Holy Ideas are nine different direct perceptions of reality when it is perceived without the filter of personality, so they are nine different enlightened perspectives." Therefore, the Holy Ideas reflect our understanding of reality, from the perspective of our true nature. We utilized our Holy Idea in early childhood but disconnected from it at the end of that period. The Holy Idea is a facet of the Divine, a part of our soul embedded in the ego that leads us back to our original and divine perspective of our experiences. The Holy Idea is integral because once we regain and reactivate the soul's original perspective, the stage is set for further spiritual transformation.

On the Enneagram of Personality, our Holy Idea acts as a bridge to our Soul Point. In the same way that an idea is not the same as an action,

---

1. Maitri, *Spiritual Dimension of the Enneagram*, 10.

a Holy Idea cannot be a soul quality until we remember it and then activate it or take it "live."

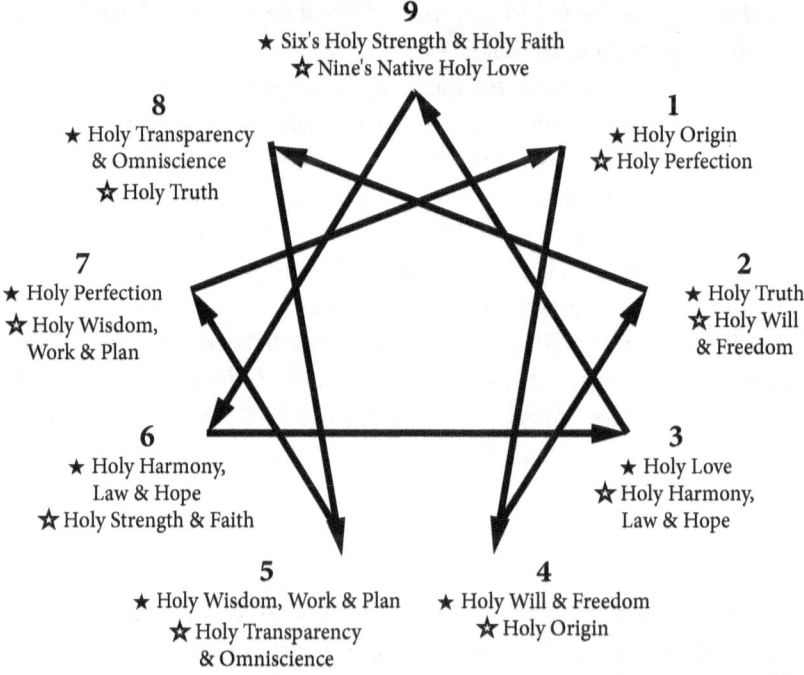

Figure Nine
Expressed and Activated Holy Ideas

★ Ego's Expressed HI at Soul Point   ☆ Activated native HI of Soul Point

Each Ego Type's Activated Holy Idea (see chapter 3 for detailed descriptions)

Another person, whom I will call Sasha, is an Ego Type Nine, whose Holy Idea is Holy Love. Like all Holy Ideas, Holy Love is a bridge to the soul child or essence of all Nines. Sasha's soul child was unquestioningly a living manifestation of love and she perceived reality through the lens of love. The thought that she was unloved or unlovable wasn't a consideration—until her wounding, when her ego took over. Like everyone else, Sasha's soul child disconnected from her Holy Idea of Holy Love and she instead adopted her ego's way of moving in the world. As an Ego Type Nine, who'd separated from her truest identity and the love it is made of, Sasha became angry but could not express it; she reacted by shutting down not only her anger but her participation in life itself. Sleepwalking through life, she just went through the motions. Life was spiritless, to say the least, and clinical depression with anxiety paralyzed her.

The Holy Idea at her ego point was only an idea, but remembering Holy Love was the bridge to finally re-embodying it. At her Soul Point, Three, Sasha re-membered, re-embodied, and actively expressed her lovableness, self-love, and love for every other person and creature. In her regained consciousness, Sasha's Holy Idea had now gone "live." She reached out with that love and gave it freely, becoming a living expression of love for herself and others. Her life went back into action at Soul Point Three and her paralyzing depression and anxiety lifted. Like Sasha, when we remember our Holy Idea and activate it, we shed our ego's distorted sense of reality, reconnect to the reality of our essence, and *embody and express* it once again.

The Activated Holy Idea of Our Soul Point

Sasha activates Holy Love at her Soul Point, Three, but Point Three also carries the Holy Idea of Holy Harmony, Holy Law, and Holy Hope. This Holy Idea is native to Soul Point Three: it is what leads Ego Type Three out of its ego and into its essence at Point Six. At our Soul Point, we not only activate our ego type's Holy Idea but also the Holy Idea native to that Soul Point: Sasha amalgamated her ego type's Holy Idea (Holy Love) with the Holy Idea at her Soul Point (Holy Harmony, Holy Law, and Holy Hope). Here, she puts action into her life by being in harmony with herself and others. In Holy Law, she relaxes into the natural order, and in Holy Hope, she involves herself in the continuous and upward unfoldment of reality. This example illustrates the interwoven elements of the Holy Ideas. They stand separately but are part and parcel of one another because in their totality, they are the Divine perspective within each of us.

The Inner Triangle

When Ego Type Three reaches its Soul Point, Six, in addition to its own Holy Idea: Holy Harmony, Holy Law, and Holy Hope, it activates the Holy Idea of Point Six: Holy Strength and Holy Trust.

When Ego type Six reaches its Soul Point, Nine, in addition to activating its own Holy Idea: Holy Strength and Holy Faith, it activates the Holy Idea of Point Nine: Holy Love.

When Ego type Nine reaches its Soul Point, Three, in addition to activating its own Holy Idea: Holy Love, it activates the Holy Idea of Point Three: Holy Harmony, Holy Law, and Holy Hope.

The Hexad

When Ego Type One reaches its Soul Point, Seven, in addition to its own Holy Idea: Holy Perfection, it activates the Holy Idea of Point Seven: Holy Wisdom, Holy Work, and Holy Plan.

When Ego Type Two reaches its Soul Point, Four, in addition to its own Holy Idea: Holy Will and Holy Freedom, it activates the Holy Idea of Point Four: Holy Origin.

When Ego type Four reaches its Soul Point, One, in addition to its own Holy Idea: Holy Origin, it activates the Holy Idea of Point One: Holy Perfection.

When Ego type Five reaches its Soul Point, Eight, in addition to activating its own Holy Idea: Holy Transparency and Holy Omniscience, it activates the Holy Idea of Point Eight: Holy Truth.

When Ego Type Seven reaches its Soul Point, Five, in addition to its own Holy Idea: Holy Wisdom, Holy Work, and Holy Plan, it activates the Holy Idea of Point Five: Holy Transparency and Holy Omniscience.

When Ego Type Eight reaches its Soul Point, Two, in addition to activating its own Holy Idea: Holy Truth, it activates the Holy Idea of Point Two: Holy Will and Holy Freedom.

After reaching our Soul Point and expressing our ego type's Holy Idea and the Holy Idea native to our Soul Point, we continue our journey around the Enneagram to every other Soul Point, collecting and remembering those points' Holy Ideas. We hold all the Holy Ideas within us, but there is one with which we most identify. That is the Holy Idea associated with our ego type because it expresses our particular perspective of reality from the standpoint of our soul's expression of the Divine.

Our Virtues

Each ego type has a virtue that takes the place of our ego fixation, replaces our passion, and diminishes our avoidances and traps. Realizing and activating our virtues lets us move smoothly around or transform the ego barriers that block us from our soul.

Our virtue is the key to expressing our Authenticated Idealized Aspect (see chapter 3), the state of being that is our soul's full expression. The ego devises its own strategy to express the Idealized Aspect, but this is only an imitation of the Idealized Aspect's full, genuine, and authentic expression. For example, when the ego of Type One simulates its Idealized Aspect, Brilliancy, it does so by demanding rightness, keeping tabs, and correcting everything in its world. These kinds of behaviors are pale echoes of the true aspect's shining clarity. Brilliancy, to be authentically expressed, requires the virtue of serenity. Serenity, when activated, is the very energy that unveils Ego Type One's frenzied compulsion to correct the world and opens space to discern reality more clearly: without the blocks of fixations, avoidances, traps, and passions.

The virtues are also qualities of the soul that require activation in order to be expressed. We have all the virtues inside us but each type has two major, interrelated virtues: that of its ego type on the Enneagram of Personality and that of its soul type on the Enneagram of Soul. For example, when Ego Type One expresses their virtue of serenity, they express their soul's true state of being: Brilliancy (Authenticated Idealized Aspect). From Brilliancy and their Holy Idea of Holy Perfection, Ones absorb their Soul Point's virtue of sobriety. In sobriety, Ones are free of their ego's addictive patterns of the false self's roles, status, relationships, egoic perceptions, narcotization, etc. Therefore, our virtues—along with our Holy Ideas, Essential Aspects, and Authenticated Idealized Aspects—transcend the barriers to our soul child and we perceive reality with growing clarity.

The embodied and expressed virtue of our ego type facilitates the expression of our soul type and the genuine state of being our soul was created to express. Once we return to our soul, we more fully experience its virtue as well as that of our ego type. We each contain all the virtues to some degree, and as we journey from our own Soul Point to all the others, we collect, express, and build their qualities into our soul. The ego's distortions create our passions from what used to be the original soul quality of our virtue. It is by shifting back to our virtue that our passions are healed.

I refer to Sandra Maitri in her book *The Enneagram of Passions and Virtues*: "So we are seeing that the virtues depict attitudes and orientations that are not only the expression of our realization of our deepest nature, but they are attitudes and orientations that help make that realization possible."[2]

Our Soul Child

(For a more in-depth discussion of the importance of our soul child as a property of our essence, and of the unobstructed soul, please refer to chapter 3.)

Barriers to Soul and Components of the Unobstructed Soul

Point One

Barriers to Soul of Ego Type Four

Avoidance:	Despair/Loss of true self
Passion:	Envy
Fixation:	Melancholy
Trap:	Authenticity

Components of the Unobstructed Soul Type One

Holy Idea:	Origin
SP Native HI:	Perfection
Soul's Essential Aspect:	Brilliancy

---

2. Maitri, *Enneagram of Passions and Virtues*, 9.

Authenticated Idealized Aspect:	The Point
Ego Virtue activated at Soul Point:	Equanimity
Soul Virtue native to Soul Point:	Serenity
Soul child	

Point Two

BARRIERS TO SOUL OF EGO TYPE EIGHT

Avoidance:	Weakness
Passion:	Arrogance
Fixation:	Vengeance
Trap:	Justice

COMPONENTS OF THE UNOBSTRUCTED SOUL

Holy Idea:	Truth
SP Native HI:	Will and Freedom
Point of Disintegration: Five:	Intellectual Proprietorship
Soul's Essential Aspect:	Merging Gold
Idealized Aspect:	The Red
Ego Virtue activated at Soul Point:	Innocence/Simplicity
Soul Virtue native to Soul Point:	Humility
Soul child	

Point Three

BARRIERS TO SOUL OF EGO TYPE NINE

Avoidance:	Conflict
Passion:	Arrogance
Fixation:	Indolence
Trap:	Seeker of others

Components of the Unobstructed Soul

Holy Idea:	Love
SP Native HI:	Harmony, Law, Hope
Point of Disintegration: Six:	Individualism/Factionalism
Soul's Essential Aspect:	The Pearl
Idealized Aspect:	Living Daylights
Ego Virtue activated at Soul Point:	Action/Diligence
Soul Virtue native to Soul Point:	Veracity/Truthfulness
Soul child	

Point Four

Barriers to Soul of Ego Type Two

Avoidance:	Neediness
Passion:	Pride
Fixation:	Flattery
Trap:	Freedom

Components of the Unobstructed Soul

Holy Idea:	Will and Freedom
SP Native HI:	Origin
Soul's Essential Aspect:	The Point/I am being
Idealized Aspect:	Merging Gold
Ego Virtue activated at Soul Point:	Humility
Soul Virtue native to Soul Point:	Equanimity
Soul child	

Point Five

BARRIERS TO SOUL OF EGO TYPE SEVEN

Avoidance:	Pain
Passion:	Overindulgence
Fixation:	Planning
Trap:	Idealism

COMPONENTS OF THE UNOBSTRUCTED SOUL

Holy Idea:	Wisdom, Work, and Plan
SP Native HI:	Transparency and Omniscience
Soul's Essential Aspect:	Diamond Guidance
Idealized Aspect:	The Yellow
Ego Virtue activated at Soul Point:	Sobriety
Soul Virtue native to Soul Point:	Detachment
Soul child	

Point Six

BARRIERS TO SOUL OF EGO TYPE THREE

Avoidance:	Failure
Passion:	Deceit
Fixation:	Vanity
Trap:	Efficiency

COMPONENTS OF THE UNOBSTRUCTED SOUL

Holy Idea:	Harmony, Law, Hope
SP Native HI:	Strength and Faith
Soul's Essential Aspect:	Will
Idealized Aspect:	The Pearl

Ego Virtue activated at Soul Point: Veracity/Truthfulness
Soul Virtue native to Soul Point: Courage
Soul child

Point Seven

BARRIERS TO SOUL OF EGO TYPE ONE

Avoidance: Anger/Being wrong
Passion: Anger
Fixation: Resentment
Trap: Perfection

COMPONENTS OF THE UNOBSTRUCTED SOUL

Holy Idea: Perfection
SP Native HI: Wisdom, Work, Plan
Point of Disintegration: Four: Despair
Soul's Essential Aspect: The Yellow/Joy
Idealized Aspect: Brilliancy
Ego Virtue activated at Soul Point: Serenity
Soul Virtue native to Soul Point: Sobriety
Soul child

Point Eight

BARRIERS TO SOUL OF EGO TYPE FIVE

Avoidance: Emptiness
Passion: Stinginess
Fixation: Stinginess
Trap: Knowledge

Components of the Unobstructed Soul

Holy Idea:	Transparency and Omniscience
SP Native HI:	Truth
Soul's Essential Aspect:	The Red/Strength
Idealized Aspect:	Diamond Guidance
Ego Virtue activated at Soul Point:	Detachment
Soul Virtue native to Soul Point:	Innocence/Simplicity
Soul child	

Point Nine

Barriers to Soul of Ego Type Six

Avoidance:	Deviance
Passion:	Fear
Fixation:	Cowardice
Trap:	Security

Components of the Unobstructed Soul

Holy Idea:	Strength and Faith
SP Native HI:	Love
Point of Disintegration: Three:	Egocentric Action
Soul's Essential Aspect:	Living Daylights
Idealized Aspect:	Will
Ego Virtue activated at Soul Point:	Courage
Soul Virtue native to Soul Point:	Action/Diligence
Soul child	

The Enneagram is as complex as life itself. Because the life of the soul is such an ambiguous yet vital concept, it is helpful to consult a chart of each Soul Point's major components. Basic to the Soul Point is its corresponding ego type's Holy Idea: one of nine major divine perspectives. When we reach the end of early childhood, we disconnect from our Holy Idea along with our soul child. Without it, we lose consciousness of our soul's particular divine perspective and understanding of the world.

The ego type's Holy Idea is like a bridge to reach its Soul Point. It is embedded in the ego type on the Enneagram but fully manifests at its Soul Point. Once our ego type remembers its Holy Idea and re-connects to it, we perceive reality much as we did as small children. Each Soul Point activates the ego type's Holy Idea in addition to holding its own native Holy Idea.

The Soul Point also contains the soul's Essential Aspect: the part of our truest being that is our original expression of the Divine. Our Idealized Aspect is one of the essential qualities of Being that our ego embraces and identifies with. The ego idealizes this quality and thinks it will be the answer to all life's woes. However, the ego can only imitate this quality. In its purest, authenticated form, the Idealized Aspect is a major component of soul. Meanwhile, the Soul Point also contains the virtues of both the ego and soul types. These virtues counterbalance and transform the passions, avoidances, and traps. Finally, the Soul Point contains the soul child itself. The diagram below includes the following major components of the Soul Point:

- Our ego type's Holy Idea (HI)
- Our Soul Point's Holy Idea
- Our soul's Essential Aspect (EA)
- Our Idealized Aspect, whether in its authentic form or that of our ego's imitation
- Our ego type's virtue
- Our Soul Point's virtue
- Our soul child

Most of the time we show the Enneagram of Personality separately from the Enneagram of Soul, but for these purposes I want to demonstrate how your ego's characteristics interact with those of your soul at your Soul Point.

This is what each Soul Point contains, except for its beatitude:

Figure Ten
Contents of Each Soul Point

9
○ Sacred Loving Peace
★ Six's Holy Strength & Holy Faith
☆ Nine's native Holy Love
▲ Living Daylight
△ Six's IA: Will
◇ Six's Virtue of Courage activated at Nine
◆ Nine's native Virtue Action/Diligence
♥ SC Ego Type Six

8
○ Sacred Power
★ Holy Transparency & Omniscience
☆ Holy Truth
▲ The Red (Strength)
△ Diamond Guidance
◆ Detachment
◆ Innocence/Simplicity
♥ SC Ego Type Five

1
○ Sacred Righteousness
★ Holy Origin
☆ Holy Perfection
▲ Brilliancy
△ The Point
◆ Equanimity
◆ Serenity
♥ SC Ego Type Four

7
○ Sacred Joy
★ Holy Perfection
☆ Holy Wisdom, Work & Plan
▲ The Yellow (Joy)
△ Brilliancy
◆ Serenity
◆ Sobriety
♥ SC Ego Type One

2
○ Sacred Benevolence & Compassion
★ Holy Truth
☆ Holy Will & Freedom
▲ Merging Gold/Cosmic Union
△ The Red
◆ Innocence/Simplicity
◆ Humility
♥ SC Ego Type Eight

6
○ Sacred Kinship
★ Holy Harmony, Law & Hope
☆ Holy Strength & Faith
▲ Will
△ The Pearl
◆ Truthfulness
◆ Courage
♥ SC Ego Type Three

3
○ Sacred Action
★ Holy Love
☆ Holy Harmony, Law & Hope
▲ The Pearl
△ Living Daylight
◆ Diligence
◆ Truthfulness
♥ SC Ego Type Nine

5
○ Sacred Wisdom
★ Holy Wisdom, Work & Plan
☆ Holy Transparency & Omniscience
▲ Diamond Guidance
△ The Yellow
◆ Sobriety
◆ Detachment
♥ SC Ego Type Seven

4
○ Sacred Creativity
★ Holy Will & Freedom
☆ Holy Origin
▲ The Point (I Am Being)
△ Merging Gold
◆ Humility
◆ Equanimity
♥ SC Ego Type Two

○ Point Name
★ Ego's Expressed HI at Soul Point
☆ Activated native HI Of Soul Point
▲ Soul's Essential Aspect
△ Idealized Aspect (either authenticated or ego's imitation)
◇ Ego Virtue activated at Soul Point
◆ Soul Virtue native to Soul Point
♥ Soul Child

Contents of Each Soul Point

I am also including a written list of these qualities so that I can both explain the meaning of each point and clarify the elements that belong to our Ego Point vs. our Soul Point.

Point One: Sacred Righteousness: The sense of direct guidance through alignment with divine order

> Ego Type Four's Expressed Holy Origin; Point One's Activated Holy Perfection; Brilliancy; The Authenticated Point; ego's equanimity; soul's serenity; the soul child of Ego Type Four

Point Two: Sacred Benevolence and Sacred Compassion: The compassionate understanding of what is needed and the heart to give it, which spring naturally from a deep connection to divine abundance and grace

> Ego Type Eight's Expressed Holy Truth; Point Two's Activated Holy Will and Holy Freedom; Merging Gold; The Authenticated Red; ego's innocence/simplicity; soul's humility; the soul child of Ego Type Eight

Point Three: Sacred Action and Sacred Diligence: Divinely inspired activity and movements that animate an idea

> Ego Type Nine's Expressed Holy Love; Point Three's Activated Holy Strength and Holy Faith; The Pearl; Authenticated Living Daylights; ego's action/diligence; soul's truthfulness; the soul child of Ego Type Nine

Point Four: Sacred Creativity: Co-creation with the Divine in all aspects of being

> Ego Type Two's Expressed Holy Will and Holy Freedom; Point Four's Activated Holy Origin; The Point; Authenticated Merging Gold; ego's humility; soul's equanimity; the soul child of Ego Type Two

Point Five: Sacred Wisdom: Being a container for and living from divine wisdom

Ego Type Seven's Expressed Holy Wisdom, Holy Work, and Holy Plan; Point Five's Activated Holy Transparency and Holy Omniscience; Diamond Guidance; The Authenticated Yellow; ego's sobriety; soul's detachment; the soul child of Ego Type Seven

Point Six: Sacred Kinship: The deep spiritual connection to the divine, the community, and the planet that underlies and supports all being

Ego Type Three's Expressed Holy Harmony, Holy Law, and Holy Hope; Point Six's Activated Holy Strength and Faith; Will; The Authenticated Pearl; ego's truthfulness; soul's courage; the soul child of Ego Type Three

Point Seven: Sacred Joy: The direct experience of bliss in the divine connection

Ego Type One's Expressed Holy Perfection; Point Seven's Activated Holy Wisdom, Holy Work, and Holy Plan; The Yellow energy of joy; Authenticated Brilliancy; ego's serenity; soul's sobriety; and the soul child of Ego Type One

Point Eight: Sacred Power: Strength and force, empowered by divine energies, applied to all facets of being

Ego Type Five's Expressed Holy Transparency and Holy Omniscience; Point Eight's Activated Holy Truth; The Red energy of strength; Authenticated Diamond Guidance; ego's detachment; soul's innocence/simplicity; and the soul child of Ego Type Five

Point Nine: Sacred Loving Peace: The divine power of love, which creates, holds, motivates, and displaces chaos in all being.

Ego Type Six's Expressed Holy Strength and Holy Faith; Point Nine's Activated Holy Love; Living Daylights; Authenticated Will; ego's courage; soul's action/diligence; and the soul child of Ego Type Six

Each Ego Type's Disintegration into Their Stress Point

Though most of us aim for integration and living in the soul, the reality is that sometimes our ego regains control over our soul. When we integrate, we move from the Enneagram of Personality to the parallel Enneagram of Soul: the second spiral of the double helix. The opposite is true when we disintegrate. The Stress Point, also called the Point of Disintegration, is the number on the Enneagram whose unhealthy characteristics we exhibit when we deteriorate. Our ego is attracted to this number because it appears to solve our dilemmas; in reality, it tears us down.

Figure Eleven
The Stress Points on the Enneagram of Personality

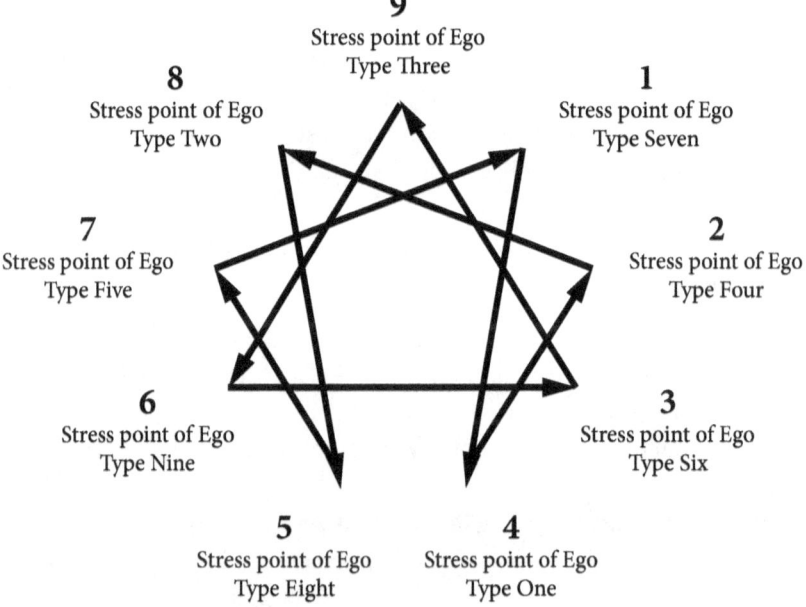

The Stress Points on the Enneagram of Personality

On the Enneagram of Personality, the disintegration/regression process for each ego type is as follows:

Ego Type Ones disintegrate when their desire for perfection implodes. Once they reach a critical mass of frustration with their own and others' imperfections, they deny their own mistakes and turn their anger inward or displace it onto others. By that time, they are already angry at others for their wrong choices. They say, "I know the right way to go, but no one will listen to me or do the right thing. That's why the whole world is going to hell in a handbasket." Finding it difficult to express their anger, they internalize it until they lose all control and erupt into a volcano of rage. At this point, Ego Type Ones go with their arrow to the despair of Point Four, where they sink into depression, withdrawal, and self-absorption.

Ego Type Twos give and over-give to feel loved, wanted, and needed. Out of touch with their lovableness, Twos work tirelessly to cultivate and maintain warm, intimate relationships that show them the love they want. Twos idealize these relationships, raising themselves in the eyes of others and imagining themselves to be indispensable. Sooner or later, however, their continuous service causes them emotional and physical exhaustion. Very prideful, Twos become indignant if they do not receive the love they desire and believe they deserve. They react by going with their arrow to Point Eight: "After all I have done for them, how can they disregard me like that? I am cutting them off." Their revenge takes the form of tyranny; therefore, they receive no praise or love, only an obligatory homage out of fear. Twos respond by seizing even tighter control, until they strangle the life out of the relationship.

Ego Type Threes are apt to confuse praise with love. However, they are convinced it takes constant accomplishment on their part to be praised and therefore loved. Like ants that build huge hills in a single day, Threes' perpetual motion does fantastic things efficiently. The more they produce, the more they believe, "The amazing things I produce win hearts and make people admire and love me." To receive even more acclaim, Threes leave behind established relationships to seek out additional opportunities for independent recognition. When they fail or fall behind and production is low, they maintain their self-image by presenting a façade of success. Disintegrating into the unhealthy Nine, Threes become narcotized by their self-image and lax with their standards: they start to believe their own hype. The once accomplished person goes to sleep on their own life, losing integrity as deceit takes over and they give up on innovation. Without their connection to community, they lack genuine support and guidance, so their once bright comet burns out in self-deception and narcotization.

Ego Type Fours are consummate creators and dreamers who rely on their talents to set them apart as special. Having lost the connection to their deepest identity and the lovability it carries, Fours do not know who they really are. So, they create an identity so unique that everyone is guaranteed to notice them. Unhealthy Fours get attention for their melancholic predispositions and think, "My unique suffering indicates I am real and someone of substance." Their focus on painful experiences spawns a tragic story that they hope will get them the recognition and love they crave. At the same time, they are envious of those who seem to receive love so naturally. Fours disintegrate by going to the unhealthy Two, where a relationship appears to promise the love, significance, and identity they passionately desire. The relationship is usually co-dependent, but unhealthy Fours manipulate their partners and vie for domination. By smothering, over-controlling, or in some cases, intimidating their beloved, Fours ultimately destroy their relationship. There is an unhealed existential dilemma for Fours that crops up in their relationship issues and fuels their despair: their disconnection from Being.

Ego Type Fives say to the world, "I am wise." They collect knowledge through reading, experience, and observation. Fearful of the inner emptiness left when they disconnected from their soul child who had access to everything it needed to know, Fives want their acquired knowledge to fill the void. Therefore, unhealthy Fives guard their knowledge, resources, and time. Anything they give away enlarges the emptiness within them. So, to secure their bounty of knowledge and the totems that represent it, they withdraw into a "cave" where—free from invasion—their greatest pleasure is to fill themselves with all they've amassed. Still, their greed for more is insatiable. Their avarice regresses them to the unhealthy Seven, where they live entirely in their heads, detached from reality. At unhealthy Seven, Ego Type Fives become gluttons for what they desire. Their hedonism is not the overdoing of sensual pleasure that the word typically implies. Rather, it applies to their all-encompassing delusion, which constitutes a form of overindulgence, and therefore a type of gluttony.

Trapped in their own fantasy world, Fives' thirst for more knowledge goes unquenched; more than that, they never reconnect to their true selves who had access to all knowledge all along.

Ego Type Sixes were once connected to a world where everything was made of love. This was a state of being where security and support were never even a question. But when they disconnect from that state of being, Ego Sixes experience the world as uncertain and dangerous. In reaction to the scary new world, they hide in groups as team players, loyally following the authority figures that protect them. An unhealthy state makes them hyper-vigilant, paranoid, and doubtful of themselves. In disintegration, Sixes follow their arrow to the unhealthy Three. Here they adopt the Three's fixation on perpetual activity and accomplishment but use it for a different goal. Rather than striving for acclaim and love, Sixes are in constant self-serving action to gain favor with their superiors and groups who provide their protection. Inevitably, however, their superiors and groups abandon them, demolishing their security. As a result, anxiety completely takes over; they lose their will to continue and the world eats them up.

Ego Type Sevens are joyous folks who know—or think they know—how to be happy. Sevens bring enjoyment and beauty into the world. Masters at creating fantastical realms of their own, Sevens have a contagious sense of excitement, stimulation, and happiness. As a soul-child, they live in a world of divine wholeness and perfection; when they disconnect from that and meet a world of unpleasantry and pain, they say to the world, "I will be happy, whatever it takes—regardless of reality." Fearing pain and deprivation, Sevens will go to all lengths to deny these. In disintegration, they go to the One's unhealthy fixation on perfection: they arrange a world perfectly free from suffering—or even discomfort. This means a continuous and excessive intake of all good things: food, drink, entertainment, shiny objects, and travel to distract from the real, the mundane, and the painful. When regressing to the unhealthy One, Ego Type Sevens become picky, fastidious, and rigid in maintaining their world of abundance and denial. By their strict maintenance of a life without pain and discomfort, unhealthy Sevens oppress those who do not adhere to their "rules" that perpetuate their unrealistic world of perfect happiness. When reality finally hits, they resent whomever or whatever popped their bubble and implode in anger.

Ego Type Eights are the power brokers of the world. Denying any weakness, they wield their authority with a heavy hand, bringing about seismic transformation. They are strong leaders of their worlds and respect strength in others, even those who oppose them. Fearless, they execute hard decisions and therefore intimidate many people. Eights administer justice, especially to those in their charge. They lust for an extension of their power and influence, although they already have a kingdom and castle. In disintegration, Eights are trapped in the compulsion to force the world's compliance with their own brand of justice. They are the ultimate authority and must control everything, including others' beliefs and—in extreme cases—the definition of truth, itself (Intellectual Ownership). By going with their arrow to Point Five's unhealthy aspects, Eights lose touch with others and reality. In wrath and revenge, they withdraw support from those who refuse to submit. When they raise their castle's drawbridge to seal others out, they also cut themselves off from the milk of human kindness they crave.

Ego Type Nines are peaceful people who see all sides of situations. Disconnected from the healthy self-love, and the love from others that they experienced as a soul child, they reconstruct that blissful state by avoiding all conflict. They find there is less conflict if they do not matter, so they are constantly and openly ingratiating and debasing themselves. They feel most comfortable when they express no opinion because it allows them to merge with a "faction" that carries them along. Opposition means conflict, which is a disruption to their all-important peace. Instead, their mantra is, "I am a good person; I don't ruffle any feathers and I get along with everyone. Life is OK." Nines pretend they don't matter, but the long-suppressed rage over denying their personhood eventually resurfaces. Caught between paying the consequences for releasing their anger or slinking back into the woodwork, Nines are caught like deer in headlights. They need to be an individual in their own right but are terrified they will be targeted for their point of view. They disintegrate into unhealthy Point Six, where anxiety and doubt overwhelm them.

6

The Soul Types of the Enneagram of Soul

JUST AS THE ENNEAGRAM of Personality contains nine personality types, there are nine soul types that comprise the Enneagram of Soul. Our soul type holds our most fundamental aspects, the qualities of our true nature; our personality type can only express the outer layers of our identities—a set of characteristics that, for the most part, developed in concert with our ego.

We find our soul type in the same place where we find our soul child: at our Point of Integration on the Enneagram of Personality (also called our Soul Point):

Ego Type One's soul type is at Point Seven

Ego Type Two's soul type is at Point Four

Ego Type Three's soul type is at Point Six

Ego Type Four's soul type is at Point One

Ego Type Five's soul type is at Point Eight

Ego Type Six's soul type is at Point Nine

Ego Type Seven's soul type is at Point Five

Ego Type Eight's soul type is at Point Two

Ego Type Nine's soul type is at Point Three

It is important to remember that the Enneagram of Soul is not made up of a set of personality characteristics but rather the most fundamental drives, purposes, and qualities at the depths of our true nature.

We were born into one of the nine soul energies of the Enneagram of Soul and we lived there for the first part of our childhood. Inevitably, our egos developed and took control and we lived our first few decades of life at the level of our personality. At some point (a shock point), we experience a crisis, an unexpected event, or a sudden realization that reminds us of the soul to which we were once connected. It is then we hear the call back to our soul, whose qualities we have long suppressed. When we finally reconnect with it, we feel like we have come home after a lengthy journey.

A Story of Coming Home

Like many, I struggled in childhood to create an acceptable personality—especially once I reached the storm and stress of adolescence. I wanted to make friends and be valued as a contributor, so I worked on accentuating my positive attributes and minimizing my negative ones. Still, I went through the inevitable rejections and hurts that most of us endure. All of these struggles were on the level of personality and ego. As an Ego Type Six, I was motivated to protect myself from harm and rejection, so, by age twelve, I had read Dale Carnegie's *How to Win Friends and Influence People*. My "defense" mechanism against fear and rejection was to become a leader in my own right. If I had stayed a follower, I felt I would have been taken advantage of: that others would have used me for their own agendas. After all, even an Ego Type Six has some pride to go along with their fear.

My soul, meanwhile, made itself known during the summer of 1969, when I had a job in construction with a college work team in northern Michigan. Right before I left for Michigan, the United States government conducted a lottery to determine which young men would be drafted into the armed services. My birthdate was one of the first to be drawn, meaning I would be drafted immediately after I graduated. The Vietnam War was raging and flag-draped coffins were coming off transporter planes by the thousands. I imagined being in a war I vehemently disagreed with and in situations that terrified me. Powerless against the massive gears of government, geopolitics, and the draft board, my life was shaken, threatened. Having just come from the structured life of a college kid, I was now plunged into extreme uncertainty. Regardless of how much my parents loved me, they could not extricate me; the challenges and consequences of my decisions were all mine. Daring to delve beneath my ego, a slew of existential questions stared me right in the face: What is my purpose? What value do I place on my life? What are my convictions and what are my fears? What do I want to live for? Do I want to die for a cause I think is wrong in order to be loyal to my nation? Do I have the courage to go to war and fight for my country? Do I have the courage not to? This new level of consciousness thrust me into an unfamiliar but essential part of my being. My newfound awareness and questions couldn't be dealt with on the level of ego or my personality. My soul called to me in a faraway voice but I felt paralyzed, as if in a dream.

The shock point of being drafted sent me into the depths of my soul. While in northern Michigan for that summer, I spent a lot of time apart from the work team in a secluded place on a hill among the towering firs. For me, that little clearing was a sacred space, though I didn't have a name for it at the time. There, I wrestled with my ego's fears, but my focus was on the essential questions of my existence. It was strangely peaceful, though I had no idea what this new reality was or the identity of the deeper me whom I was slowly unearthing. An inner strength I had not known I possessed was now practically blooming forth. I rediscovered many aspects of myself I had previously thought to be alien. I experienced courage, will, and love; they felt familiar but I did not remember having ever experienced them in these ways. Little did I know, I was returning to my truest nature, my inner home. Of course, as with most young adults, my ego and corresponding personality eventually returned and took control. That wasn't the only such occurrence, though; at various events throughout my life to come, my soul resurfaced in a similar manner. Each time I connected with my soul it moved me deeply.

Personality and Soulality

It is helpful to understand that our personality's passions, avoidances, traps, and fixations progressively lessen in intensity as the ego gradually submits to and amalgamates with our soul. Our personality transforms because the passion that once drove us no longer overpowers us. Its retirement helps us to escape our compulsive ego avoidances, gradually freeing us from our traps and fixations. As our egocentricity wanes and our soulality begins to predominate, our internal systems transform, our desires shift, and our outer personality naturally changes.

What specifically happens to our personality once we shift our focus from our ego to our soul? Do we suddenly disavow our personality's tastes, sense of humor, choices of entertainment, our attraction to certain friends, or our way of relating to others? For most of us, the shift to soulality is a gradual process in which we incrementally relinquish egoic patterns such as our passions, traps, fixations, and avoidances. In soulality, our personalities change when the soul is allowed to express itself directly. For example, after the shift to soulality, an explosive personality may begin to emulate their soul's tranquility; a personality that was fixated on being right may affirm opinions that differ from their own. Envious attitudes and a propensity for drama may transform into admiration for those we once saw as rivals. An introverted, hesitant personality may express a newly gregarious aspect of their soul, feeling supported rather than threatened by others. The flighty person who tries to please everyone may become grounded and reflective.

Our attraction to certain people, including friends—and even our beloved—may change as our soulality becomes primary. In soul, our priorities change as our true nature wins out over our ego. For example, a self-absorbed ego seeks out those who give it attention. In contrast, in soulality, as we become conscious of our interconnectedness with others, we begin to value reciprocal relationships over self-serving ones. The soul's truest nature is essentially love, which is not about the self. As a result, we become less self-absorbed.

That said, there are different types of love. Our spiritual growth can have a profound effect on our connections to all of the people in our life, especially those with whom we are closest. This means that in shifting to soulality, we may no longer fit with our beloved. If our beloved is not on a similar journey, then, sadly, the union may experience disequilibrium. One of the partners may change or they may grow in other directions on the level of ego. In these cases, unless there is an agreement to remain together in two different worlds, the initial relationship may dwindle. Others find in soulality that they no longer need a beloved, as such. Their journeys may lead them into relative isolation and/or their beloved may be replaced by their spiritual practice or their devotion to God or a spiritual entity. Many of us in soulality are fortunate to have beloveds and friends on journeys that are compatible with ours. Once our egos submit to our souls, our personalities, once propelled by our ego, naturally change their "shape" to fit our souls.

Not everyone in our lives will like our changes when we shift to soul. Our sense of humor may be different and some of our religious and political views may change. Some people will distrust the new amalgamation created by our inner spiritual work. Our outward presentation may have a different flavor and our reactions may not even resemble our egoic selves. Our old intentions may turn into new ones and our egoic prejudices may diminish or end. Some people may be confused by the changes; perhaps they will like the new you; perhaps they will drift away.

Once our soul is our primary identity, even simple things like our manner of speaking may reflect our change. Our ego talks in a manner consistent with its worldview. For example, if a person's ego is one of strength and power and lives according to those values, that person likely speaks a lot about issues of control and power, usually in a bold and decisive voice. A military retiree who held a high rank continues to speak to others as if she were still the officer she used to be. She thinks of how she can dominate and seize control of a situation. She has a naturally authoritative voice as well as an imposing demeanor.

If, on the other hand, someone's ego is about giving and helping, their voice is often friendly or even patronizing as they speak about meeting others' needs. All speech styles reinforce our ego's agenda and biases. In soul, however, there is no motivation to magnify, downplay ourselves, or propagandize our worldview. In soulality, our unblocked essence naturally comes through, loud and clear; our style of speech is instead fueled by our virtue, Holy Idea, or Essential Aspect. Our soualities are not in service to our ego but rather in service to love.

In soulality, certain external markers of personality, such as our voice, our distinct laugh, our gait, or even the twinkle in our eye, will remain but are intensified as we increasingly express our soul energy. The soul tends to relax an otherwise hypervigilant body and to rouse an otherwise somnolent one. In the shift to soulality, the beautiful soul is free to express itself without the encumbrances of the ego's fixations, avoidances, passions, etc.

For the soul, suffering—whether physical or emotional—is part of the sacred process of soul evolution. St. John of the Cross's poem "The Dark Night of the Soul" depicts the difficulties the soul must endure on its journey to be unified with God. We hold such challenges and hardships of our souls in sacred reverence. Our souls know that this suffering is meant to bring them into a higher expression of their soul qualities and is not to be confused with the suffering caused by our unhealthy egos. The soul experiences suffering primarily in terms of how it relates to the purging of all that prevents its spiritual evolution.

In soulality, a personality's taste in clothing may change. We usually see ourselves through the lenses of our egos. Therefore, we dress in coherence with our ego's message to the world. For example, those whose egos desire attention may dress in loud, flashy colors and patterns with exaggerated silhouettes. Alternatively, if we desire anonymity, we may camouflage ourselves with more muted colors and less tailored shapes. There are infinite arrays of sartorial ego expressions meant to signal that we are unusual, pious, witty, charming, innocent, mischievous, attractive, proper, trendy, novel, disheveled, powerful, etc. The soul, on the other hand, does not depend on others' perceptions; therefore, our choices of such things as clothing, cars, and homes are a reflection of our ego's choices or of our ego and our soul working together. Fortunately, those who are drawn to our soul's choices, including the external and material ones, are generally also drawn to our soul.

My personality changed substantively when I was nineteen, during the summer that I spent in northern Michigan doing construction work. Preoccupied with the looming draft and all the uncertainty around that pivotal issue, I became quieter and more serious. My speech grew less self-centered as I began to focus more on society, global affairs, beliefs, and the interconnection of all people. Though I was still my basic optimistic self, I was shaken and therefore less naïve and flighty than my old "normal." Now, I was willing to explore the realities of my situation rather than be paralyzed by them. I also became much more adventurous on the job; I found myself learning to operate large equipment that I would usually have left to others. I formed a powerful relationship with nature, becoming one with that unfamiliar and beautiful region.

Granted, many of my outer changes were caused by simple maturation and exposure to novel experiences. However, many of the personality changes were due to the shock my system underwent and the depths to which it took me—allowing me to become aware of my previously hidden unconscious and soul. I eventually recovered from the shock and—in the end—was not drafted. The realizations from that summer stayed with me, but after the crisis, my ego returned in full force. My soul would not appear again to any great extent for a long time, except in brief spurts and at times of crisis; I did not begin shifting to soul—and my soulality—until mid-life, when Lark and I faced the long illness of our son Ben.

Why Soul Types?

My short stint in soul during the summer of 1969 was new territory for me. I strongly believe, however, that if I had already known my soul prior to that summer, I might not have been quite so afraid of being drafted—I would already be in touch with my courage and consciousness of other spiritual qualities. I might have handled my sentiments and fears about the war in more productive ways. As the part of myself most closely connected to the Divine, my soul would have begun the process of healing my passion of cowardice as well as tempering my resentment toward what I considered a dubious war with needless untold losses. My entrenchment in ego, though age-appropriate, was the thing preventing me from reaching a higher level of consciousness. During this brief period, I learned that the soul increases our consciousness, our self-awareness, and our connection to the Divine.

Enneagram enthusiasts and students frequently ask me, "What is your type?" I don't actively avoid revealing my type but I feel somewhat disingenuous saying, "I am a Six." For me, it is like telling someone my middle name: while it *is* part of my name, it is not my *primary* identity and I feel awkward when someone uses it to address me. Though Point Six is my ego base and I return to it after every trip around the Enneagram, I spend much more time thinking and flowing into Point Nine. I am most grounded at Nine; it is where my soul child "lives and moves and has its being,"[1] where I feel comfortable and at home. Frankly, it is a relief to have come back "home," where I am afforded soulful alternatives to the futility and blind alleys of my Six ego. Now that I can recognize them for what they are, my shift to soul has mitigated my trap in addition to my fears and avoidances. For many who start with the Enneagram, the ego type becomes our primary descriptor—the way we describe ourselves to others. If we really do the spiritual work of the Enneagram, however, we amalgamate our ego with our soul to create a new, more conscious being. In soul work, we are becoming more than just a better version of our personality type.

---

1. Acts 17:28.

The following descriptions are realistic conceptualizations of each soul type, its energy, its components, and its purpose. So much of the literature that describes the soul leans toward the vague and the ethereal. Other, more concrete, explanations are spotty in describing the dimensions of the soul, much less, how to know it. This is why I am offering a starting place to flesh out our souls by presenting actual characteristics and components of the nine different types of souls. I draw these descriptions from Plato and other philosophers, from the leading Enneagram teachers such as Oscar Ichazo, Claudio Naranjo, Sandra Maitri, A. H. Almaas, Russ Hudson, Don Riso, Patrick O'Leary, and from my own observations over the past forty-five years of clinical practice and experience.

When we come to know our soul as well as our personality, we are on the road to higher consciousness. When, as a collective, we know our souls, we are all together on that same road. With collective consciousness, our species has the chance to survive. Therefore, I have put together portraits of each soul type, taken from the soul components I explained in the previous chapter. I hope that these descriptions help you imagine and reconnect with your deepest self; I hope that enough of us actually shift to soul awareness and consciousness so that as a collective we will come into a new era of depth, empathy, and peace.

The Nine Soul Types

In order to transition into the Enneagram's inner flow and begin to live from our soul type instead of our ego type, we must essentially shift to another realm of consciousness.

Soul qualities are divine qualities, which many of us may find ethereal and intangible. Due to their semi-amorphous form, soul qualities are best explained in stories, rather than charts and lists. Besides being elusive, the nine soul energies are also in such harmony with one another that their qualities tend to interlock and overlap, thus making them even harder to delineate.

We each have core qualities that compose our souls; when we come to identify these, we can help them flourish. What sparks us to know our soul? Our ego paints us into a corner where it seems we will suffer for the rest of our lives. Eventually, when we can no longer bear the pain, we search for relief. Then, we reach into our depths and find an entirely new set of qualities from which to live. Our soul qualities may seem alien to us at first, but once we can remember them, we can rediscover our true home.

In shifting to soul, we give up our quest for a better personality, otherwise known as "a better me." While striving for a well-integrated personality is a beneficial goal, it is not the endgame here. Awareness of our personality characteristics, compulsions, traps, avoidances, and passions certainly helps integrate our personality, as does knowledge of our virtues and Holy Ideas. However, simply knowing these aspects and behaving in accordance with our understanding of their roles in a personality's disintegration or integration is only a preliminary step toward developing our *being*.

Those of us on the road to spiritual development seek more than personality integration; we seek to *manifest* or *activate* our being and its soul's qualities. We achieve this manifestation by actively expressing our soul qualities in every facet of our lives—that means we must go further than simply knowing and imitating them. This we accomplish via a process of spiritual alchemy in which our ego is amalgamated with our soul. This new union, led by the soul, directs our heart, head, and mind.

Once we are on the Enneagram of Soul, we perceive every person and situation through the eyes of the soul, rather than those of our egoic mind. This new viewpoint redefines what is essential, allowing us to focus on what is true. When we look at another person, we don't see a meeting of two egos but two souls face to face. Sadly, if only one of the two parties sees with the eyes of the soul while the other remains in ego, the latter may briefly misunderstand or even resent the intentions of the person operating in souality. Fortunately, in this case, the soul always wins out and there is never any prolonged negative entanglement.

While it is best that both parties operate from soul, even if only one is in soul, there can still be peace and fruitful interaction between the two. The soul's issues and concerns are not about competition, judgments, mind chatter, or categorization of others as "with me or against me." The person in soul does not demand that anyone conform to their principles, but is always poised to witness what truths arise in each present moment—what Eckhart Tolle calls "the now." The soul transcends dissension and takes the conversation to what really matters. The person operating from soul does not speak to the ego of the other person but reaches out to the other person's soul. Issues relating to the ego alone are redundant to the soul and only pertinent when the ego is in concert with the soul. In speaking about and accomplishing what really matters, the soul and ego work together, with the soul leading. The soul is, in essence, an entity of love, so it understands love's power to unfold divine outcomes, despite any plans of the human ego.

Soul Type One: Sacred Righteousness

The soul of Ego Type Four resides at Point One. Such souls are rooted in the Divine, certain of their purpose and their sacred identity. They move in the world as true beings, championing causes for justice and reformation, based on their understanding of morality. Soul Type Ones become Ego Type Fours when the ego takes control. After early childhood, the ego disconnects from its soul and its true nature. Though it wrests control from the soul, the ego seeks to reinvent its forgotten true nature by fashioning a life that feels special, unique, and sensitive to the tragedy in life. In this way, it simulates the feeling of purpose and conviction that living in soul once provided. Regardless of these efforts, it retains a feeling of identity loss and insignificance. The resulting depression, anxiety, and self-absorption it experiences are torturous, as is its bottomless envy of those who seem to have everything together in life. While the ego loses touch with the soul's wisdom, the soul is there all along, even when it isn't acknowledged by the ego. The soul is the enduring identity. When the Ego Type Four returns to their soul at Point One, their true nature abounds once more.

Soul Type One is loved, needed, and wanted, just as they are. Their soul virtue is serenity and their ego virtue is equanimity. These are the perfect antidotes to their deeply unsettled ego and are the beautiful qualities that drive the Soul Type One. They manifest this truth by living for their specific divine purpose—one that they alone are created to fulfill. They involve themselves in just causes and determine the best paths to take. At every moment, they are actively discerning ways to promote healing and wholeness. If the ego forgets its sacred origin, it regresses and grabs back control, but if it is conscious, it remembers the soul and returns for guidance.

Soul Type One's Essential Aspect is Brilliancy. Spiritual brilliancy—not to be confused with intellectual brilliance—is the light of true connection to the divine origin (Holy Origin).

In Brilliancy, Soul Type One shines like a star. Pointed at others, Brilliancy illuminates the shadows into which the neglected have been cast aside. Meanwhile, it also illuminates the defective, unwanted, and unloved facets of Soul Type One's own ego. With Brilliancy, they embrace and learn to love the "unlovable," both in others and in themselves. Their powerful consciousness lets them empathize with and soothe the pain of the hurting and the helpless. Though the pain of human depravity is immense, it is their sacred privilege to bring about healing and wholeness. Ego Type Four's Holy Origin and Point One's native Holy Idea of Holy Perfection work in unison for this purpose.

Ego Type Four's beatitude is "Blessed are they who are persecuted for righteousness' sake, for theirs is the kingdom of heaven." They join just causes that champion children's hospitals, a clean environment, animal shelters, and saving endangered species. Their cause may even be a small one, such as advocating for their friend with disabilities who lives next door.

Regardless of the cause or its scale, unless their soul is in the lead, their ego's inner critic will persecute them by insisting, "You are never going to find your true place or have your significance recognized by helping others from the shadows. *Your* problems and *your* past are the most pressing concerns, and you can't waste your life on others. Figure out your own issues first!" In presence, Soul Type One silences these voices. In terms used by theologian and spiritual teacher Henri Nouwen, the soul listens to the voice of love.[2]

Soul Type One is "persecuted" by those who disapprove of their causes. They are shunned, called peculiar or eccentric, and accused of forcing others to adhere to their personal moral code. They face pushback for championing such causes as animal rescue or upgrades to the local animal shelter. Their opponents say, "Wake up, you fool, you aren't making a dent in these problems. Our public funds are better spent on sidewalks and parks than on animals. I'm not going to join your little crusade." As a soul, they often confront those whose decisions hurt their community, the helpless, and the environment. They may be derisively called a "do-gooder" and shut out of social groups because of their unpopular stances that challenge unjust social norms.

When a Soul Type One openly opposed a city official who was upgrading his own neighborhood with public funds, her life was threatened. However, in soul, she was able to move forward, sustained by the connection to her true source.

2. Nouwen and Bodo, *Inner Voice of Love*.

Soul Type One lives in equilibrium with their emotions, thoughts, and body sensations. They do not soar too high when seemingly good things happen nor fall too low when seemingly bad things happen. They are aware that positive occurrences always have drawbacks and vice versa. By balancing the tension between the positive and the negative, they stay centered and calm. They cry and they laugh; they grieve and they celebrate—these expressions are from their depths, not their surface. They move through the world with honest emotions rather than drama; they can be proud of others without feeling envious. Centered within their own deep presence, they can brush aside the sting of persecution.

They continually glean wisdom from the experiences that the ego acquired. They benefit from all the ego's strengths, especially its creativity and sensitivity. This is the way of the soul: always growing.

Soul Type Two: Sacred Benevolence

Soul Type Two is the compassionate and giving soul of Ego Type Eight. They are a soul of the virtues of humility and innocence. They embody Holy Truth and create sacred relationships. Early in life, the world tells them that they are not OK the way they are: a compassionate and vulnerable being. In response, their ego disconnects from their soul and they forget the abundant flow of giving and pure compassion of their true nature. When the ego draws away from the soul child, it furiously says, "I am strong and will fight off any threat; no one will ever hurt me again!" The disconnected ego tries to create a form of compassion and connection to others but can only imitate these soul qualities. They express relationships through domination of the other person. They promise to protect others, with the caveat that if the others do not toe the line, they will lose that support.

This angry ego rules its environment and administers its idea of justice. It imitates Soul Type Two's abundance by lusting for all that would increase its kingdom. It imitates altruistic giving and compassion but demands deference and dependence, protecting only the loyal who pay it homage. It divides the world into perceived allies and enemies, fighting for the former and against the latter. It thinks that by being larger than life, it can possess life. These poor facsimiles of abundance and compassion cause much suffering. The truth is that we are all alike and connected. Soul Type Two moves in a non-binary world.

When Ego Type Eight crosses the bridge of Holy Truth back to soul at Point Two, they remember that Soul Type Two manifests truth by seeing and acting on reality. Their clear-sighted vision dispels the ego's illusions, fears, and compulsions. Walking in truth, they are aware of and can embrace their weaknesses and their need for assistance. They see the reciprocity inherent in all relationships and the interconnection between all living things. They see the continuous cycle of giving and receiving. They see that their significance and power are not found in controlling others but in embracing their own vulnerability. Point Two's native Holy Idea is Holy Will and Holy Freedom. Combined, these facets form Soul Type Two's purpose. In returning to soul, the ego surrenders its self-made power to divine will, lessening its self-imposed burden and allowing it to live in freedom.

Soul Type Two's Essential Aspect is Merging Gold: the holy alchemy of joining others in sacred relationships. By connecting the golden essences of others, they are in the divine flow of their gift and their purpose. Their deepest work as a Soul Type Two is as a servant-leader: one who takes charge not due to their own desire for control but in Sacred Benevolence to others.

Mercy nourishes Soul Type Two's innate compassion. In this compassion, they manifest genuine strength rather than the false strength that Ego Type Eight projects. Their strength is wrought from their soul virtue of humility and their ego virtue of innocence or simplicity. There is true power in these, rather than the delusion of self-made power or greatness.

They exert strength through their virtues by opening their hearts to the needs of others. One Soul Type Two started children's sports leagues in her town. Another led efforts to build canals to give all families in his city and suburbs access to the ocean. A Soul Type Two began a neighborhood food bank that served the poor of that region. She was criticized for possibly "enticing undesirables" into the neighborhood. Residents started a petition in the area that stated the property values of the homeowners would decrease if the connection to indigent people continued. To deal with this, she held a gathering in the park for residents and families using the food bank to meet and mingle. Everyone came together to share music and favorite dishes. It was an event that promoted mercy and compassion.

Soul Type Twos manifest Ego Type Eight's beatitude of "Blessed are the merciful for they shall be shown mercy." Mercy is made of compassion—they suffer along with others in true empathy. They are in touch with and have accepted their ever-present weaknesses and they know that those—rather than their power—are the sources of their mercy. In being merciful, they receive mercy. This connects them with those to whom they grant mercy; it is an activation of their soul's Essential Aspect of Merging Gold.

Soul Type Twos continue to use the wonderful gifts learned by the ego. These supply them with a keener sense of benevolent power and a strengthening of life force.

Soul Type Three: Sacred Action

Ego Type Nine's soul is found at Point Three. Theirs is a soul of action, veracity, and accomplishment. Soul Type Three's diligence complements Ego Type Nine's natural abilities to mediate and arbitrate. Ego Type Nine's Holy Idea of Holy Love magnifies their Soul Point's native Holy Idea of Holy Harmony, Holy Law, and Holy Hope. These spiritual ideas are the building blocks of their purpose, which is to align with the power of love that undergirds everything and brings harmony and hope to all.

When their Three soul child buries itself under the crust for protection, the Ego Type Nine takes control and forgets the soul's essential value. Even so, the ego continues to hold in its core the Divine's ever-present gifts of vision, creation, and active accomplishment.

Because of their disconnection from Holy Love, the Ego Type Nine loses the connection to their soul's lovability and true identity as a child of the Divine. As a reaction to this loss, and the anger it produces, the ego shuts down and cedes independence. It lives slothfully and passively, diluting its individuality to merge with others and relying on them to do the work of moving everything along. It avoids conflict because taking a stand requires too much energy and might alienate people. Having ridden on the energy of others, the ego loses its sense of identity and says, "I don't have to be in conflict—if I pretend that I do not matter, no one will expect me to make any big decisions." To accomplish this avoidance, it lies down on the ground and goes to sleep—but the ground is soft like quicksand, so it slowly sinks.

When this ego is nearly smothered by the quicksand, it gasps for air, flailing its arms, and finally remembers its soul child. Soul Type Three is the action-oriented core of Ego Type Nine. When the Ego Type Nine comes back to Soul Type Three they emerge from the mire, regain their individuality, embody action, and reconnect to their life force.

Conscious Soul Type Threes do not discount themselves; they affirm their essence and that of everyone else. Because they live out of Ego Type Nine's Holy Idea of Holy Love, they recognize that they are lovable in their own right and they love themselves and others. They move in the world to accomplish for the good of the family, the group, or the larger collective. Soul Type Threes are one with their point's native Holy Idea: Holy Harmony, Holy Law, and Holy Hope. Together, these balance all the moving parts of the universe, so they are also aligned with the Holy Laws: the unchanging principles that guide and regulate the cosmos. They live in the truth that all that needs to be done is, in fact, already in motion. As part of this energy, they act as an individual force of accomplishment. They are also a living expression of Holy Hope: they know that—despite appearances to the contrary—everything is ultimately evolving according to divine order.

In life, Soul Type Threes bring people together for a common goal. For example, in his profession of manufacturing, one Soul Type Three was regularly presented with ongoing disputes. He formed a think tank to prepare a strategy for solving these problems. This diverse group identified the causes, saw all the angles, and instituted a dispute settlement process with just a few policy changes. The problems lessened considerably once the team built a system for making organic changes to the industry. He was an Ego Type Nine who had entered the Enneagram of Soul by going to Soul Point Three.

He took action at the expense of his own popularity and was willing to bite the bullet for the common good. Imbued with Sacred Action, the soul attribute of Point Three, he guided the underlying disaccord into harmony. He acknowledged that cooperative community brain power automatically increases potential for solving problems. The company and its employees now had hope for their future.

Their ego virtue of action or diligence joins with their soul virtue of truthfulness. This union puts Soul Type Threes in the position of accomplishing with transparency. Their soul virtue allows them to both accept their own honest opinion and identify others' perspectives, while their ego virtue provides them with the knowledge of what needs to be done to improve everyone's situation.

Soul Type Three's Essential Aspect is The Pearl, which means that this type is transparent to and rooted in Being. Their Sacred Action comes not from acting autonomously to build an image, but from true nature, which is free from dependency on others' concepts of its image.

The Pearl of personal essence is made of the realized self and has little to do with cultural, racial, economic, gender, or physical shaping of influence. This soul marks true success based on their ability to embody and fulfill their potential.

Ego Type Nine's beatitude is "Blessed are the peacemakers, for they shall be called the children of God." When the ego reaches its critical mass of suffering, it is mired in sloth, self-narcotization, and anxiety. In returning to soul, it receives the energy to rise out of the sinking sand. In addition, the natural mediation capacities found in the Ego Type Nine meld with Soul Type Three's nature to achieve, creating the ultimate peacemaker. This peacemaking is their purpose, an aspect of the Divine. While the ego says, "There will be no conflict if I lie down and play dead," the soul of Soul Type Three says, "All conflict is an opportunity to make peace." As a child of God, per their beatitude, Soul Type Three's personal essence comes from God's great essence.

Soul Type Four: Sacred Creativity

The essence of Ego Type Two is found in the soul qualities of Point Four. Soul Type Four's purpose is to discern the will of the Divine and align with and live out of it. By carrying out Holy Will, they live in Holy Freedom: freedom from their ego's will. They live in the creative flow of love and abundance. All that they need comes to them and flows through them to others through grace: the abundant flow is a natural phenomenon that does not need to be earned. The native Holy Idea at Point Four is Holy Origin, which, with Ego Type Two's Holy Will and Holy Freedom, roots Soul Type Fours to their divine source and provides their purpose.

When the ego disconnects from its soul child, it forgets its Holy Idea and its deepest spiritual purpose. It forgets its creative flow and that it is loved not because of what it does for others but because of who it is. In its drive to recover its purpose and love, the ego becomes a giver, a helper. Sadly, it confuses the abundance of love that the soul receives naturally with the need to earn love by compulsively serving others. Eventually, giving becomes the only way it can measure its worth and it fosters dependent relationships to perpetuate the cycle. The Ego Type Two requires more and more relationships to be satiated. While others certainly admire the ego's help, it cannot recognize that gratefulness. Urged on by the need to win more love, it denies its own needs and suffers accordingly.

Trapped in service, the ego's agony finally becomes unbearable until, finally, it returns to the soul.

In returning to the soul and living out of their Holy Idea of Holy Will and Holy Freedom, Ego Type Two becomes Soul Type Four, who is free to give time and energy as they wish, no longer bound by the ego's determination to gain love through the services it gives. In touch with their needs and sincere desires, they give to themselves and others from the ongoing flow of creativity and certainty of their true being. Ego Type Two's virtue of humility joins Soul Type Four's virtue of equanimity. Together, these create a balance of mind, heart, and body, allowing them to live in their true nature. Soul Type Fours are not the saviors of humanity; they do not have all the answers to everyone's troubles. Nor do they need to be worshiped for their contributions. They are serene and settled in their identity, their needs, and their purpose.

Soul Type Four's Essential Aspect is "The Point," which is the embodiment of true being in this very moment and all future moments. The surety of this identity frees them from working for love and affirmation. Being grounded in their true nature, and living out of The Point, they freely accept the grace the Ego Type Two could never come to know on their own: the realization that such love comes naturally and does not need to be earned.

Ego Type Two's beatitude is "Blessed are the meek, for they shall inherit the earth." The meek are the humble, those who have found and accepted their true place in society. They have let go of pride. They are not searching to be worshiped or placed on a pedestal for their contributions. The meek do not need a reward for their humility. They are patient and generous with others, never demanding or entitled; it is precisely because they ask for nothing that they eventually receive everything (they inherit the earth).

A Soul Type Four had an autistic child. Instead of bemoaning her fate as a mother of a special-needs child in an isolated community, she looked upon the needs of her child with humility. She said to herself, "What can I do for my child and what may I learn because he was given to me?" In Sacred Creativity, she studied educational programs designed for children on the spectrum and collated all the materials, from which she created individualized lesson plans for her child. At the state meeting for children on the spectrum, she presented her creation, which took off like wildfire. Soon, she was making videos and self-publishing her individualized lesson formats. She knew she was in her zone; she had found her purpose and embraced the Sacred Creativity of her true nature.

Once the Ego Type Two submits to Soul Type Four, they become fully conscious of their needs and those of the world around them. They activate their purpose by reaching beyond to re-include those whom the world has left behind.

Soul Type Five: Sacred Wisdom

The soul of Ego Type Seven is found at Soul Point Five. They are a soul of quiet contemplation, reflection, and observation. Their true nature, their bliss, is being one with divine wisdom. While the ego forgets all of these wonders when it separates from the soul child, it nevertheless creates a facsimile of them to fill the ensuing void. The ego thinks it can reconstitute the panoply of divine diversity by expressing interest in a wide variety of subjects. It uses traveling to recreate the exhilaration of discovering new information. Likewise, it simulates divine guidance by planning ever more activities and diversions. It mimics the abundance of the kingdom of God through material acquisition. None of these attempts to recreate the satisfaction it experienced in the soul state was successful.

The ego believes that overindulgence and fun are the greatest antidotes for pain, mistaking them for the spiritual bliss of soul. It uses unchecked gratification to avoid all unpleasantries. However, the ego is never satisfied, regardless of the amount it consumes. Fearful of not having enough and exhausted from their constant frenzy for gratification, the Ego Type Seven finally stops. They say to themselves, "I will never find the happiness I am looking for this way. Once the 'newness' of something wears off, I feel empty again. I need something real, something that nurtures me: something that puts me in touch with my soul." This ego finally gives up on its extensive plans, parties, and huge meals, its incessant traveling, constant home redecoration, and materialism. It begins to recall memories from its depths and yearns for the simple life of long ago. Embracing its Holy Idea of Holy Wisdom, Holy Work, and Holy Plan, the Ego Type Seven returns to the soul child.

When Ego Type Seven eventually remembers their soul child, they are gently taken back to all the wonders their soul held. In soul, the ego is transported to its true nature, returning to the stillness, contemplation, and reflection from which it had detached. It recognizes that what it sought in its constant gluttony was actually Sacred Wisdom—not just intellectual knowledge but the felt sense of being directly in the midst of all wisdom. Holy Wisdom is the understanding that anything we need to know in our body, heart, or mind is immediately at hand in the present moment. The second part of Ego Type Seven's Holy Idea is Holy Work: the action the ego takes, in unison with the guidance from Holy Wisdom, to accomplish its purpose. The third part of the Holy Idea in which Ego Type Seven lives as a soul child is Holy Plan: trusting that there is a divine plan for everything, which negates the need for ego planning.

Point Five's native Holy Idea is Holy Transparency and Holy Omniscience. These two components form the Soul Type Five's inherent purpose: to live in transparency to all wisdom and to realize that all aspects of the Divine are readily available to them everywhere at all times. Soul Type Five's Holy Idea displaces Ego Type Seven's fear of depravation and pain while supplying them with everything they need to move in the world.

Ego Type Seven's virtue of sobriety tempers their overindulgences, while Soul Type Five's virtue of detachment allows the soul to move in the world unburdened by the ego's affinities. The ego is drawn to material temptation, repeating, "Look what I could buy, where I could go. I could have so much more of what I love to eat and drink." The soul, however, is free from those desires. A Soul Type Five does not need to live an austere life but their gratification is in the form of spiritual abundance and wisdom rather than in material bounty. The soul lets the ego inhabit the present moment and notice the beauty and continuous flow of spiritual gifts around them.

Soul Type Five's Essential Aspect is Diamond Guidance in all of its many facets. They absorb this sacred direction by being fully transparent. They are spacious in mind, heart, and body. They are the ego's conduit to divine wisdom. To proceed in Diamond Guidance, Soul Type Fives often pause and silence themselves before they take action or answer questions. Being privy to the voice of the Divine calls for a third ear: the ear that always hears the emotion in the distant bird's song—the ear that hears the message in the whispers of the wind—the ear that listens as their body interprets the vibrations under their feet.

Ego Type Seven's beatitude is "Blessed are those who mourn, for they shall be comforted." Ego Type Seven's greatest fear is loss and pain, yet the soul of Seven understands that sacred stillness heals their pain. When the ego submits to the soul, it can finally stop distracting itself from a loss and mourn properly. Soul Type Five regularly walks into the pain of loss. In meditation, such souls perceive the meaning of that loss, and in contemplation, they make sense of its results. In stillness, their oneness with the Divine allows them to comprehend the cycle of life rather than resisting it.

Soul Type Fives are an amalgamation of wisdom and power. One such soul type understood the properties of uranium. He had studied with scientists from all over the world in understanding the reduction of uranium, its radioactive properties, where it is found, and how it is employed in nuclear power. He made this knowledge known to the government who used him to teach what he knew about the development of safe and clean energy. Various independent contractors begged him to sell his "wisdom" to them. This Soul Type Five never even thought of keeping his secrets and selling them to those who wanted to personally profit from this knowledge. He formed a committee that studied the motivations and whereabouts of global independent contractors within the industry.

Soul Type Six: Sacred Kinship

The soul of Ego Type Three is found at Point Six. They are a soul of integrity; they see what needs to be done and how each step benefits the family, the group, or the community. They are alert to the interconnectedness of all life and how all systems cooperate with each other, including government, culture, economy, the arts, and education. Such cooperation fosters well-being and harmony among individuals and their communities. They are pure of heart, and as such, view things without the cloud of personal protection and gain at the expense of the whole. They see the equation perfectly: our personal gains also profit the group, just as our personal losses have wider consequences. No one operates in a separate bubble; we exist in communities, in which we evolve in unison.

The ego loses touch with its soul. It wants to recapture the sense of shared accomplishment that it felt in the natural interconnection of souls. Unfortunately, it forgets the healthy exchanges of community and thinks that it alone is in charge of shaping any progress. The Ego Type Three becomes restless, believing that things are advancing too slowly. They lose hope that anything can be accomplished without their personal provocation. Ego Type Three sets out to earn the love that they are missing. They think that the more they can accomplish, the more they will be loved. In truth, all the love the Ego Type Three craves is, and always has been, accessible through their soul child. Sadly, since the Ego Type Three doesn't understand that they do not have to "wow" others to gain their love, they avoid all appearances of failure. In their quest to avoid failure, the Ego Type Three produces a façade, lying to themselves and others about their true identity.

The Holy Idea of Holy Harmony, Holy Law, and Holy Hope helps the ego recall the time when all was harmonious. Ego Type Three remembers their natural state of soul, in which they relied on Holy Law, which turns the wheels of God slowly but so finely. The Ego Type Three's desperation to build, accomplish, outshine others, and win the game vaporizes when they remember and align with Holy Law. They understand that all is in a state of growth and integration; even though there are occasional setbacks, these are corrections in a general upward trend. Their achievements and those of others' souls help the cosmos move forward. Relying on Holy Law relieves the Ego Type Three from taking on such heavy responsibility for accomplishing and attaining. The ego is finally subsumed by the soul and the natural flow of divine achievement selects, directs, and energizes their divine purpose. This manifests Holy Hope.

With their virtue of veracity or truthfulness, the Ego Type Three looks for a better and more authentic way of living. They get so tired of hiding their lies and trying to live up to the illusions they have built. The suffering becomes too great when they realize their house of cards is folding and they will be exposed for who they really are. The ego is terrified that it will be caught in its lies and lose its ill-gotten love and admiration.

When Ego Type Three accesses Soul Type Six's virtue of courage, it magnifies their truthfulness. This courage facilitates Point Six's native Holy Idea of Strength and Faith. These elements help the Ego Type Three understand that they do not need to perform grand acts or search outside of themselves to gain love.

Soul Type Six's Essential Aspect is Will. This inward commitment drives all of their intentions. The essential will is the inner strength that stands up against threat and challenge. This refers to both the ego's personal will and its attachment to divine will, which is both tenacious and longsuffering. Those of Ego Type Three manifest essential will when they dispense with the delusion that their achievements present their only value in life. With the accuracy of clear vision, Ego Type Threes perceive that inner commitment built on truth is much stronger than the appearance of success, with its trophies, awards, and other symbols, such as a perfect body, expensive car, or large house. The belief that they are the "center of the universe" is what drove the Ego Type Three into darkness. When the ego's will submits to its soul, however, it manifests intentional fortitude, unbendable strength, and divine intelligence.

Ego Type Three's beatitude is "Blessed are the poor in spirit for theirs is the kingdom of heaven." In their preoccupation with their ego's narrative, Ego Type Three cannot fully embrace their soul or the Divine. Ego Type Three is full of egocentricity, but when they are "poor" in this spirit, the ego's fixation on itself goes away and the soul is revealed. In this state, they possess the kingdom of heaven instead of the self.

The ego amalgamates with the soul where they live at Soul Point Six. Ego Type Three surrenders their fears and coping strategies and submits their all to the soul. The ego has suffered because of that fear, but it is redeemed in its service to the soul. The wisdom that the ego gains through the fire of love[3] is subsumed into the soul and all that is irrelevant burns away. Then, and only then, can we move up the Spiral Continuum of Being.

Soul Type Sixes bind people together in communities of cooperation and common purpose. One such Soul Type Six had a family that was full of dissension. The misuse of money, ill will, and a history of betrayal had plagued her extended family. Her presence radiated sacred kinship, however she was upset that her children were now being exposed to all the underlying friction and intrigue. She called a meeting at her home with her adult siblings and explained the cascading curse that was spilling from them onto their children. She asked for a family alliance to insulate the children from the toxic interactions and manipulations that had torn the family apart for generations. One of her four siblings said in the meeting that he would have nothing to do with her harebrained scheme and he left. The other three were invested in keeping the conversation going, if not for themselves, then in the interest of their children. A family dynamics expert was brought into this sibling alliance and devised strategies for the continuance of harmony. These included releasing ties with certain toxic family members. This Soul Type Six suffused her rebuilt family with love and concern and she got them the help they all needed to continue on in Sacred Kinship.

---

3. Tajadod and Bononno, *Rumi*.

Soul Type Seven: Sacred Joy

The soul of Ego Type One is found at their Soul Point, Seven. They are a happy soul, full of optimism and hopefulness. They possess an incredible wonder of and fascination with life. Rather than dousing Soul Type Seven's Essential Aspect of innate Joy (The Yellow), an awareness of the sad and terrible things that happen in life deepens their conviction that—regardless of what happens—we are supported by a force beyond ourselves that enables recovery. They live in the sacred cycle of life, able to walk both in darkness and in light.

Soul Type Sevens can be a beacon of joy—embodying it and modeling it for those who are filled with terror and sadness, they turn their heads in the direction of healing and hope. Their smile, their aura, and their laugh come from a deep place of inner contentment where imperfection is accepted, the depressed are healed, and the alienated are brought back into the totality.

When they detach from their soul child early in life, Ego Type Ones try to create a perfect world. Unfortunately, they confuse living in joy with working for perfection—in themselves and their environment. They develop an inner critic that keeps them in line and focused on all that is going wrong, jumping to correct those faults immediately. Ego Type Ones monitor others to make sure all is going according to rules and regulations. They resent those who are disorderly or who don't operate within the law, the standard, or the rulebook. They become angry at the imperfection everywhere but do not feel that it is appropriate to express their anger. Simmering in their own juices, they quietly break down and sink into the despair they have tried to suppress. Finally, they recall that there was once a day when things were much more blissful.

The Ego Type One recalls an all-embracing perfection that was not flawless but whole. The completeness and inclusivity of Holy Perfection are far superior to egoic flawlessness. This is the Holy Perfection in which this ego once lived but has forgotten. Holy Perfection opens the way for the Ego Type One to return to their soul child at Soul Point Seven. The native Holy Idea of Point Seven is Holy Wisdom, Holy Work, and Holy Plan. These combine powerfully with Holy Perfection, allowing Ego Type One to proceed with the knowledge and daily work guided by the divine plan, living in the container of Holy Perfection.

Ego Type One's virtue of serenity is the antidote to their anger and the suffering it causes. This virtue and Soul Type Seven's virtue of sobriety bond to form a bastion of tranquil clear-mindedness.

Ego Type One's beatitude is "Blessed are you when they revile and persecute you and say all kinds of evil against you falsely for my sake. Rejoice and be exceedingly glad, for great is your reward in heaven, for so they prosecuted the prophets who were before you." Standing for what is correct and just is a beautiful and essential gift; when paired with joy and optimism, it can be prophetic. A rejoicing soul endures persecution and false accusation because Sacred Joy transcends pain.

A Soul Type Seven inherited his father's funeral home business. Though he had avoided the business all his life and made a living as a stockbroker, he made the move to the funeral industry. His true nature was Sacred Joy but the funeral home was a palpable place of sorrow. His light-hearted nature and optimism were contagious but no one in the home was affected by his hopeful radiance. He saw that his employees were a major source of the gloom: they were depressed and tired. Not only did they have problems of their own but the ongoing environment of grief depleted them. It made them incapable of serving as sources of strength and sympathy for those who had lost loved ones. The Soul Type Seven implemented a restorative program for his employees. It included in-house counseling and support groups to help process their own feelings as well as the sadness of their clients. The staff was invited to regular social gatherings that helped nurture their relationships. The funeral home became a place of introspective Joy that contained hope, compassion, and emotional support.

Soul Type Eight: Sacred Power

Soul Type Eight is the soul of Ego Type Five. They are a soul of great strength and compassion. They see a larger vision of life than most because they both lead and serve. They realize that the many challenges we face require great strength as well as great vulnerability. Arising from wisdom, their stature is tall and their presence significant. Their voice is penetrating and their embrace is warm and strong. They move across the territory as a lioness who protects her young, surveying the land for food and threats. They embody strength that can move mountains and in so doing can change the shape of the terrain. Their energy is rooted in compassion for the world, especially for those who are defenseless.

When the ego takes over, it retreats to a solitary island, where it hopes to gain mastery over its world by gathering and hoarding information. Finally, Ego Type Five's passion of avarice causes increasing isolation until the ego is completely cuts off from reality, deteriorating into a mind of irrationality. When the suffering becomes too great to bear, the ego searches for relief and remembers the engagement, wisdom, and compassion of its soul child. Ego Type Five recalls their soul's strength, power, and determination. They remember that everything they need to move in the world arises as necessary.

Ego Type Five sees the promised land of their soul through the lens of their Holy Idea of Holy Transparency and Holy Omniscience and they journey there. Holy Transparency allows the ego to see the soul clearly and to comprehend divine intelligence: the source of all knowledge, overflowing love, and immortal spirit. With Holy Omniscience, the ego understands that—so long as we are transparent to it—all wisdom is available to us anywhere at any time. Point Eight's native Holy Idea is Holy Truth, which is not only clarity but also the acceptance of reality. These Holy Ideas combine to form Soul Type Eight's purpose: to be a conduit of divine wisdom and to move through the world manifesting truth.

Ego Type Five's virtue of detachment allows them to break the connection to all that obstructs their vision and their consciousness. This virtue frees the ego from the prison of its compulsive quest for infinite knowledge. Soul Type Eight's virtue of innocence or simplicity reduces everything to its essential nature, lending clarity to complications. Soul Type Eight's essential nature is one of simplicity, vulnerability, and generosity.

Soul Type Eight's Essential Aspect is Strength (The Red), as embodied by self-realization and empowered by vulnerability and commitment. Soul Type Eights make use of divine strength, in combination with the knowledge they have collected, to become successful leaders.

Ego Type Five's beatitude is "Blessed are those who hunger and thirst for righteousness, for they shall be filled." Righteousness is God's gift of morally correct thought and action. When the ego separates from its soul child, it disconnects from the righteousness at its core. This leaves a void, which the ego searches hungrily to fill with information. Ego Type Five's journey back to Soul Type Eight satiates that hunger and liberates them from the island where they hid, gathering and hoarding information and totems.

The amalgamation of Ego Type Five's hard-won knowledge and The Red's strength of their true nature allows Soul Type Eight to move forward on a righteous, divinely sanctioned path.

A Soul Type Eight had the power to love the unlovable. She went into all the schools in her area for the express purpose of teaching anti-bullying. She met one-on-one with students who had been victimized and set up a helpline for those who had been so traumatized they had thought of harming themselves. She empathized with each child and taught teachers in every school how to recognize trauma associated with abuse. In her talks to parents, teachers, and students, her overriding tone of compassion moved people to take action. Some members of the school boards resisted her entrance into the schools. She did not fight them but rather encouraged those who had benefited from her approach to appear at school board meetings. Hers became a well-known anti-bullying program adopted by her state.

Soul Type Nine: Sacred Loving Peace

The soul of Ego Type Six is found at Point Nine. They are a peaceful soul, upheld by their connection to the teeming life that surrounds them. They are one with nature and live in the awareness that they are made of the same substance as the trees, rocks, ocean, and animals. They rarely move or speak quickly; their pace is measured and their actions are intentional. Soul Type Nines are always aware that all life is composed of the love that they constantly feel surrounding and undergirding them.

Ego Type Six lives in doubt and fear but, once well-settled, Soul Type Nine takes comfort in the knowledge that all is unfolding according to divine will. They know this when they live in the soul child but promptly forget their inherent calmness once the ego takes over. The Ego Type Six forgets the absolute wonder of being one with all life and constantly blooming into their fullness. Instead, the ego creates a semblance of safety by continuously building security mechanisms of mind (alliances and beliefs), body (physical vigilance), and heart (anticipating and strategizing around others' emotional reactions). However, the usefulness of these mechanisms breaks down when the ego realizes that there is no fail-safe security strategy for mortals.

In its terror, the ego eventually remembers its Holy Idea of Holy Strength and Holy Faith. This leads the Ego Type Six across the bridge and back to their soul at Point Nine. There, they begin to manifest these two branches of their Holy Idea, allowing Ego Type Six to be conscious of but not overwhelmed by fear. Meanwhile, Point Nine's native Holy Idea of Holy Love naturally emerges and combines with Holy Strength and Holy Faith to create inner and communal peace.

Ego Type Six retains their virtue of courage even in their isolation; eventually, that courage provides them with the wherewithal to cross the bridge from Point Six to their Soul Point, Nine. Their soul virtue of diligence bonds with courage and helps them meet every challenge. Soul Type Nine's union of courage and action/diligence—two dynamic virtues—ensures that the peacefulness of Soul Type Nine never disintegrates into sloth.

Soul Type Nine's Essential Aspect is Living Daylight: the illuminated and spacious clarity of pure light. In Living Daylight, they witness the interwoven web of love that supports and connects us all.

Soul Type Nine's guidance dissolves Ego Type Six's fear of isolation as well as the over-compensatory tactics they have relied upon.

"Blessed are the pure in heart, for they shall see God" is Ego Type Six's beatitude. A heart full of fear is clouded with egoic strategies that promise security but only obscure the clear vision. Fear makes Ego Type Six cower in the shadows, where they cling to someone they appoint as their protector. But that person can't save them from danger. They must do that for themselves by embracing the love that connects them to everything. In the Living Daylight, they see God.

7
Spiritual Transformation and Amalgamation of Our Ego and Soul

OUR SOUL AND OUR ego originate at our creation. Our original identity, the soul, carries the seed of our ego within it. In our soul child, we operate from true nature, while our ego doesn't fully come into its own for several years. Living in soul is, for the most part, carefree because we are held and supported, and are free to express the love that makes up our being. Later in childhood, our soul child gets the sense that it is not acceptable to society as it is. It seals itself off from our conscious awareness for protection. Meanwhile, our ego emerges as the face we present to the world: our vehicle for moving through it. Later in our lifetime, when we become disillusioned with our ego because of the immense suffering it has caused, we search for relief. We desire the wholeness, bliss, and sense of being held once more.

The Enneagram maps the route from our ego back to our soul. In the spirituality of the Enneagram, when it reaches that destination, the ego *amalgamates* with the soul. Because the ego and its passions cannot be subsumed into the soul as they are, the ego must transform before it can finally yield to the soul. This is the fulfillment of our destiny: as the ego begins to serve the soul instead of itself, our soul gains wisdom from the suffering that our ego experienced. In this new partnership, our ego's pain is no longer contained in the ego structure, with the ego stuck in

Spiritual Transformation and Amalgamation of Our Ego and Soul

the eternal loop of trying to heal itself. Instead, this pain is processed by the soul, which simultaneously absorbs its wisdom and realizations. This process is called amalgamation.

Amalgamation cannot be accomplished overnight. In life, we experience wonderful periods of ecstasy as well as defeats, losses, struggles, and other life-changing events that transform us. Decades of life experiences burn away powerful ego components such as our passions, avoidances, fixations, and traps. Without these components, our ego is left with the wisdom it gained from these experiences. When our ego is subsumed by our soul, it serves the soul. This amalgamation process moves the soul upward on the spiral of consciousness, as depicted on the Enneagram of Soul.

The alchemical amalgamation of the ego and the soul can be difficult to achieve but the process itself is simple. We can compare it to the unification of two separate pieces of land. A farmer owns a property that is mostly rocky but has room for a smallish garden. He makes a fairly good living off this land for years. Eventually, he decides to expand his garden, so he purchases the fenced-in property next door. The new parcel of land is flat, without rocks: excellent for growing larger crops to improve his livelihood.

One day, the farmer learns that he could use his lands more wisely by focusing more on his original property instead of his newer purchase. The original land contained a prolific natural spring, a creek, and abounding rock formations that would be perfect terrain for raising sheep. He takes down the partition that separated his two pieces of land and the sheep thrive in their natural habitat. Now, he can use the land that he had planned to dedicate as cropland as additional space for the animals to feed and roam, giving him optimal conditions for a healthier, larger flock. The soul of the venture was the original property, with its natural spring, yet it took the seamless blending of the two parcels for new life to flourish.

The process of blending the ego and the soul is similar: though the two terrains and the soil may be different, they can become one again if the fence between them is dismantled. Their union is natural because they were both parts of the same ground before humans came and separated them arbitrarily.

In the case of the ego and the soul's amalgamation, the soul becomes the leader of the ego. Beforehand, while the soul may have surfaced from time to time to take control during a crisis or a major trauma, our ego operated practically independently of the soul as the center of our daily existence.

Our ego is indispensable; it's the vehicle that transports us through the world. Indeed, it serves us well once we allow it to take over and protect our soul child. For years, our ego negotiates the world according to its own view of reality. Because of its biases, the ego is prone to distort reality, proving to itself that its narrative is true, even in the face of contradicting facts. Despite these distortions of reality, our ego serves us by protecting, defending, and allowing us to accomplish our goals. Sometimes it inflates our self-concept and we rise to that new image, occasionally exceeding our former limitations. Ironically, while most people only know about those with a "big ego," it can also deflate our self-esteem.

The Enneagram describes many facets of both the ego and soul, including the ten major ones that I have included here. As you can see in the chart below, each aspect corresponds to one on the other structure (remember my explanation of the double helix of DNA), both of which must undergo a spiritual transformation before amalgamation can take place.

Major Ego Structures on the Enneagram of Personality	Major Soul Structures on the Enneagram of Soul
A. Holy Idea	A. Holy Idea Expressed at Soul Point
B. Avoidance	B. Soul type's Holy Idea
C. Virtue	C. Soul type's virtue
D. Passion	D. Activated ego virtue and soul type virtue
E. Fixation	E. True Being/True Nature
F. Ego's Idealized Aspect	F. Essential Aspect, Authentic Idealized Aspect
G. False self	G. Essence/True Nature
H. Trap	H. Individual qualities of our soul
I. Inner critic (Super Ego)	I. Soul child
J. The transformed ego	J. The transformed soul

Mechanics of Spiritual Amalgamation

Amalgamation is a process in which the two columns above are combined so that the ego serves the soul. This is a complicated mechanism that takes place when the ego meets the unconditional love of the soul. I will use my own experience to demonstrate how amalgamation worked in me.

Line A: Amalgamation of the Ego's Holy Idea and Its Activation at the Soul Point

Until I express it, my ego's Holy Idea of Holy Strength and Holy Faith is still just an idea. That said, even as a concept, it remains fundamental. It is by remembering it that we bridge the chasm between the ego and soul. Once we cross the bridge of our Holy Idea to our Soul Point, we reach a different state of awareness; the ego no longer has the hold on us that it once had. From there, we can *activate* our Holy Idea (see chapter 5). In my terrible grief about Ben's death, I was paralyzed with doubt and fear. When I remembered and called upon my strength and faith, these powerful forces diluted my fear. This gave way to a newly awakened knowledge that I was enough; though I had to penetrate my ego to feel it, I did have courage and conviction. Finally, now that I was directly experiencing my soul's inherent strength and faith, I could move through the day without incapacitating waves of grief.

Line B: Amalgamation of Avoidance and Our Soul Type's Holy Idea

One of the most problematic issues, when we deal with the ego is how to negotiate issues that disempower it. Each ego has a particular avoidance that pushes it further into fear. My Ego Type Six's avoidance is deviance: the feeling of being defective, impaired, unfit, or even twisted. It manifested especially forcefully during Ben's fight against addiction, pancreatitis, and diabetes. His functioning had declined to the point that he had to withdraw from his honors program at the university. My son's trail of false starts, failed attempts at rehabilitation, numerous car accidents, legal troubles, and overall inability to take care of himself were difficult for us all. As for me, I felt not only fear for Ben but shame for my family and myself. I recall my visits to him during his stay at the psychiatric unit where I had once been clinical director. All around us were the very staff members I had directed.

As a mental health professional, wasn't I supposed to know the warning signals and how to guide my child away from addiction? Shouldn't I have been able to model how a family successfully manages mental and physical illness? Humbling would not quite be the word to describe the process of confronting my deviance. It was more like losing my fear of owning something that I had been taught was shameful about me. I increasingly relinquished my fear of being deviant. Indeed, my soul began to heal when I realized that all of us are deviant in some way. Then I could accept my deviance shamelessly.

Once we arrive at our Soul Point (or Point of Integration), we can join with that point's native Holy Idea. For me, this is Point Nine's Holy Love. I embraced Ego Type Six's Holy Strength and Holy Faith in facing my deviance and shame, but I was surprised that—in going into soul—the Holy Idea native to Nine also swelled up inside me. Holy Strength, Holy Faith, and Holy Love combined as healing agents. My life-changing realization was that I am made love itself—therefore, how could I be irredeemably flawed? Holy Love allowed me to love myself like never before, even in my deviance. My guilt and self-loathing burned away.

Line C: Amalgamation of the Ego Type's Virtue and the Soul Type's Virtue

My virtue as an Ego Type Six is courage, which is most available to me when I have shifted to my Point of Integration, my Soul Point. Our virtue can be magnified when we experience a shock point that thrusts us into a higher level of consciousness. A life-changing event can push our consciousness beyond the realm of personality and onto the Enneagram of Soul. When we re-embody our soul type, we reconnect to our soul virtue. For me, this is Nine's virtue of action/diligence. My Ego Type Six's virtue of courage, when joined with my Soul Point's virtue of action/diligence, moves me into courageous action. I felt this alchemical union when I stood to deliver the eulogy for my son. I could never have imagined having the courage to stand before an assemblage of people and utter words regarding Ben and the wonderful person he was to us and how his loss will leave us forever incomplete. But I honored my son in the form of a prayer which was the eulogy. The virtue of Courage had been deepened and activated by my soul.

Line D: Amalgamation of the Ego's Passion and the Activated Ego and Soul Type's Virtues

As an Ego Type Six, my passion is fear. This means that, with great and small threats alike, my ego urges me to "tuck tail and run." Fear rears its ugly head when I sense threats to my self-esteem, health, or security, or those of a dear one. Unsurprisingly, fear gripped me each time Ben lay critically ill in the hospital. I kept waiting for the other shoe to drop. Our family was traumatized, living with the ever-present fear that Ben would fall ill again and die. I added an extra prayer to my everyday spiritual practice—one to grant me the courage to deal with this continuous fear. Slowly this virtue of Ego Type Six began to emerge.

The dreaded *did* happen; Ben went to sleep in his apartment and went into a diabetic coma. He passed away in his own bed. Seeing the lifeless body of my child took more courage than I thought was inside me. This shock point catapulted me onto the Enneagram of Soul. I had gone to my Point of Integration and was in the Holy Love of Point Nine. There, I absorbed my soul virtue of Courage more deeply.

Line E: Amalgamation of the Ego's Fixation and True Being

The ego's fixation is its repeated and compulsive maladaptive behavior. For the Six, this is cowardice: my ego urges me to hide or run away; it whispers messages of self-doubt and shame until they begin to resonate. To a certain extent, fear helps protect us but, in this instance, it paralyzes me. Fortunately, my cowardice burns away when I come into harmony with True Being. In Being, I am present in my existence and grounded in the alchemical prima materia of life. When we reach the Enneagram of Soul, the energy of the ego is transformed into the felt experience of True Being. True Being is more than our essence; it is the ground of being from which our essence springs. In realizing our True Being, we are connected to our divine nature. There is no reason to keep the fixation when True Being manifests in us.

Line F: Amalgamation of the Ego's Idealized Aspect, the Authenticated Idealized Aspect, and the Essential Aspect

My ego's Idealized Aspect is "Will," which leads me to believe that sheer determination can save me from the fears and doubts that plague me. However, when I am on the Enneagram of Soul, my ego's Idealized Aspect recognizes that it is a mere imitation and submits to my Essential Aspect: Living Daylight. In Living Daylight, I shine in the spaciousness of light and peace; I am one with and connected to all. My will no longer has free rein to divert all energy toward protection and defense—instead, it now submits to the reality of overriding peace. I have found that connecting to nature feeds my soul and diminishes my ego. I am a child of light and it fills me. After finding my Essential Aspect at my soul point, I continue around the Enneagram of Soul, picking up each point's Essential Aspect until I return to Point Six. This time, having integrated the other Essential Aspects, I can see my Idealized Aspect in its true, authenticated form rather than the ego's sad imitation. (See chapter 3 of this work or Sandra Maitri's book *The Spiritual Dimensions of the Enneagram* for more on Essential and Idealized Aspects.)

Line G: Amalgamation of the Ego's False Self and Essence

The false self is the persona that we present to the world: the version of us that we want others to see. Our persona is a superficial structure within our ego that helps us navigate society. We identify with our persona, thinking that it represents who we really are, but it is not our true self, our essence. We put so much of our energy into developing and portraying our false self yet it brings little satisfaction when we begin to hunger for our truest selves. When we reach the Enneagram of Soul, we realize our essence and the need for the false self fades away. Our essence is what is left; it is our unconditioned self, the purest manifestation of our individual being.

Even when we are firmly under the ego's control and are portraying our false self, there are moments when our essence appears. Often, these are times of either deep sobriety and loss or euphoria and meaningful celebration. We say to ourselves, "Oh, *this* is who I am, this is what it is all about. I am really living my real life. This is *me!*"

When I received the call that my son had died, it was as if the reality of this existence came sweeping over me like the wind from a tornado. I felt my essence rise out of the dream state. I was with a patient in my office and I recall sharing the news. She immediately rose from her seat and asked if she could drive me somewhere or if there was anything she could do. At that moment, I was no longer my professional self, my psychologist self, or even my exterior self—all those outer layers were pieces of my false self. Those trappings dissolved and I was in my essence. We were just two people: one in the middle of a life-changing circumstance, the other a concerned observer.

Line H: The Amalgamation of Our Trap and the Qualities of Our Soul

Each ego has a unique trap. For Sixes, this trap is security. Of course, it is impossible to obtain insurance against all loss, rejection, or physical danger, but the ego of the Six doesn't believe this. Instead, it traps us in the quest for security, insisting that we amass more and more protections against all possible threats. When we reach the consciousness of living in soul, we can release this desperate need for security and surrender to a power beyond ourselves.

The qualities of our soul vary from person to person. Such qualities include patience, mercy, presence, and grace, as well as our soul and ego virtues. In amalgamation, these soul qualities combine to counterbalance our traps. My trap of seeking security becomes inconsequential when I access the courage to accept reality.

There is nothing like the chronic, debilitating illness of a loved one to make us face the fact that the ego's version of safety is an illusion. I recall my many attempts to "save" Ben: to provide him with the treatment he required and to smooth his path to rehabilitation as best I could. I became so invested in Ben's recovery that I began to value it even more than he did. I found experts and recovery centers and participated in endless family sessions, but changes were few and far between. Things transformed for me when I relinquished Ben's treatment into his own hands and those of the Divine. My soul's qualities such as patience and trust won out over my need for security. I trusted my ability to deal with reality rather than my being tethered to a specific outcome. I could tell Ben felt the shift in me; it was a healthier mindset for both of us.

Line I: Amalgamation of the Inner Critic and the Soul Child

The inner critic is the voice within that tells us that we made a mistake: that we did something wrong or did not measure up to certain standards. The superego springs from our ego and the two collaborate in the role of the inner critic. This critic serves to keep us in line but it often goes to such an extreme that we buckle under its assaults of guilt and shame. When we become conscious of our inner critic, we transform its energy by accessing our soul child. The soul child is unselfconscious; it has no internal critic; its ego and superego are not evolved. The soul child ignores the developing inner critic until leaving the realm of the soul child. But in later childhood, the child no longer ignores it. The soul child offers self-compassion. It disarms the inner critic by replacing its rigid perfectionism with an overwhelmingly relaxed and unscripted presence.

I introduced my soul child into my life throughout much of Ben's illness. Though at that point, I did not know the full depth of the soul child, I invoked it by reviving as many memories as I could of the earliest parts of my life. I found my childhood toys, books, and even a favorite blanket. While I did not have words for it at the time, by bringing out these things that had long been stowed away, I was able to re-embody my soul. These items triggered a myriad of memories and emotions, which brought me back to my essence. As I re-embodied my essence regularly, I found myself journaling about my childhood and after-childhood experiences, many of which appear in this book. My inner critic could not survive in the presence of my soul. The ego energy of the inner critic strives to maintain our societal acceptability through constant criticism, but our soul qualities transform these negative thoughts into messages of self-affirmation.

Line J: The Transformed Ego and Soul

The transformed ego has ceded control to the soul. It gives over all of the wisdom it has gathered from life experience, including all that it has learned from its passion, avoidance, trap, false self, etc. In transformation, our ego relinquishes its pride and becomes receptive to the world, having also surrendered its anger, fear, and shame to a greater power. In receiving what the ego has learned from life's pain, suffering, and joy, our soul evolves. The soul amalgamates with the ego's hard-won wisdom.

My ego remains a constant part of my life. It has relinquished much of its power to my soul, yet many other facets continue to emerge and I regress regularly into my ego structures. I find that these lapses are best treated by incorporating these newly discovered ego structures into my daily spiritual practice: acknowledging them and working to use them as growth opportunities.

Spiritual Operations and Tools for Spiritual Transformation and Amalgamation

Now that we know the process, the following are some of the instruments we can use in our individual spiritual practice to transform, integrate, and amalgamate our egos and souls:

1. Self-remembrance
2. Self-compassion
3. Self-forgiveness
4. Acceptance of forgiveness
5. Shift to essence
6. Manifestation of the qualities of our individual soul
7. Relinquishment of the ego's narrative
8. Surrender of attachments
9. Physical resonance with our soul
10. Mental coherence with our soul
11. Emotional coherence with our soul
12. Presence
13. Prayer
14. Meditation
15. Self-inquiry
16. Spiritual direction/psychotherapy

Other Examples of Transformation and Amalgamation

Another example of ego type and spiritual amalgamation is a man whom I will call Arthur. He is an Ego Type Four who compensated for not being secure in his identity by becoming an outstanding guitarist. He distinguished himself as a musician, even topping the Billboard charts. Arthur became a contributor to the field of the musical arts; he reaped many gains and learned many lessons along the way. His life was successful by standard social measures, but his inner being was very dissatisfied—even despairing—as he slowly reached a critical mass of suffering. He didn't feel like he was living authentically as his true self, regardless of his many awards.

Arthur envied others who seemed to be living their "real" lives and he became depressed. After turning inward during his depression, he had a pivotal insight: he realized that he found more peace within his core self—his essence—than when he had chased applause. Once he came to know his wonderful soul and its worth, he no longer strove to make himself special to feel legitimate. He realized that the Divine created him as a unique creature from the beginning; that he is pure being. This new understanding broke the spell of the ego distortion brought about by his fixation of melancholia.

Arthur's trajectory of spiritual growth was prompted by the *combination* of his ego's hard-won love and wisdom and the qualities of his soul. In the new amalgam, the ego serves the soul: the soul and its qualities are squarely in the leadership position. This version of Arthur is now, first and foremost, True Being. His grounded nature expresses his true identity. He no longer compensates by proving himself special to feel genuine and deserving of love.

From this existential security, Arthur feels loved more than ever because he lives from the authentic self of his early childhood: his soul child. This self is obviously (and demonstrably) loved by others, regardless of how many of his albums reach the top of the charts. Now that Arthur has complete access to Holy Origin and Holy Perfection—the Holy Idea of his ego and that native to his Soul Point—he has amalgamated his soul and ego. Here's how he expressed the change:

> *I have come to a point of confidence in my identity. This confidence comes from nothing else but the fact that I am more than what I look like, more than my talents, and more than my feelings. I am now very aware that we come from a divine source. How do I know this? Well, it came to me when I got out of myself and discovered the big picture. As soon as I was no longer focused on myself, I realized that we are all connected to something greater. All my music comes from somewhere far beyond me. My Holy Idea of Holy Origin lets me live in the certainty of my purpose. Having gone from Four to One on the Enneagram, I also pick up another Holy Idea that gives me an important component. In Holy Perfection, I am lovable even in my weaknesses, mistakes, misperceptions, and flaws. I am no longer driven to achieve uniqueness to feel loved. I am loved and lovable even in all my failings and*

Spiritual Transformation and Amalgamation of Our Ego and Soul   175

> *my strong points. Holy Origin has mixed with Holy Perfection to provide an identity that is "perfect" for me. It is my true self.*

Arthur's ego/personality travels the Enneagram of Personality and, as various personality traits integrate, they amalgamate with the Enneagram of Soul. There, he activates his Holy Idea and that native to his Soul Point, then continues around the Enneagram of Soul and gathers the rest of the Holy Ideas.

Arthur has complete access to his virtues. His Ego Type Four's virtue of equanimity and his Soul Type One's virtue of serenity join with each other to manifest an emotional balance. This puts Arthur in the position of steadied peacefulness, a wonderful soul attribute that emerges in this spiritual alchemical process. These newly found virtues completely disarm the ego's passions.

Unearthing his virtues and Holy Ideas gives Arthur a new way to move in the world. By reconnecting to his soul child, Arthur experiences his soul. When the ego tries to regain control, Arthur is conscious of its power, but instead of conceding to it, he can remain present in soul.

The ego is charged with taking care of us, but when the shift to soul happens, the power balance changes. After the amalgamation of ego and soul, the ego serves the needs and goals of the soul. This requires constant communication between the two. Though they now work as one unit, they still have distinct areas of expertise. The soul supplies our purpose for moving through the world, while the ego understands the logistics of doing so.

Malala Yousafzai, a young Pakistani woman famous for championing girls' rights in her culture, is another great example of ego and soul amalgamation. At age fifteen, the Taliban shot her on her school bus in response to her vocal protests about her culture's discrimination against the education of girls. She survived the attempt on her life and became the youngest recipient of the Nobel Peace Prize. Now twenty-six, Malala travels to every country of the world, lecturing and raising consciousness about educational oppression, sexual abuse, trafficking, and the silencing of young women by religious and political systems. She writes that raising consciousness is the mission of her soul. Of course, Malala also has an ego. It is her ego that books her flights and hotels, buys her clothes, and learns the protocols for greeting dignitaries. It is Malala's ego that wrote several books, that sat for her official portrait for the Nobel Peace Prize, and that makes sure she has adequate security at all times.

Malala's ego is not what fuels and perpetuates her personal narrative; it works to accomplish the mission of her soul. In her speech before the United Nations on July 12, 2013, she said, "This is what my soul is telling me: be peaceful and love everyone."[1] Indeed, when the ego surrenders its narrative, it surrenders to the mystery of the soul and the Divine to which it is tethered. Then the ego serves the soul.

Our ego does not lose its individuality or its personality when it combines with the soul. Rather, the ego channels the soul's intentions and expresses them through our personality. That said, the flavor of our personality may change somewhat when we are no longer masked by a false self. Our personality is a transparent "face" that our soul shines through. Malala's personality has the tenacity to keep speaking out, even while there are continuous threats to her life. Her personality has many other qualities as well. She has stamina, resilience, and a gift for presenting her urgent message in a loving way. Her soul uses these personality characteristics like a megaphone: to amplify her voice.

The personality shares certain characteristics with the native qualities of our soul that make up our soulality. For example, if she is an Ego Type Three, Malala's tenacity may be a trait of her ego's personality alone, or it may be used to express her soul's purpose. Alternatively, that tenacity may be a *shared* characteristic of her ego and soul. If, say, it is a native quality of her soul, it may express her Essential Aspect. If her Essential Aspect is Will, then her soul might express it through her tenacity.

There is an area in between the two poles of egocentricity and soulcentricity where the soul and ego share certain qualities. Here, the ego's personality characteristics move closer to the soul and are transformed into expressions of the soul's purpose. In ego, personality characteristics channel the ego's narrative, trap, avoidances, and fixations. When they cross into the realm of the soul, however, they are transformed by the soul qualities that now fuel them.

At some point, as personality traits are refined on the Enneagram of Personality, they enter the Enneagram of Soul and are readied for amalgamation into the soul. As evidenced by Malala's behavior, spoken beliefs, and personal sacrifices, her personality characteristics are likely doing more than simply improving or integrating. She is advanced in consciousness, and clearly has been since an early age; her personality traits have likely entered the Enneagram of Soul and are thereby beyond

---

1. Yousafzai, "UN Speech on Youth Education."

the realm of mere personality. Malala is not likely to be using her energy to escape her ego's trap or to address her avoidances. It seems very likely that someone of her profile would have, despite her youth, experienced the transformation of the ego trap, avoidance, passion, and fixation of her personal narrative. At this point, her attention seems to have dramatically shifted from the level of ego to her greater and original being: her soul and its purpose.

Amalgamation and Transformation: A Synopsis

In alchemy, two or more substances are chemically combined to create another substance that contains its own properties. Before their combination, the farmer's two plots of land were ostensibly two separate entities. When combined, they took on a new identity as a sheep farm. The process of uniting the lands did not involve literally taking up and combining the soil from each side, but the *functions* were combined. We can identify this as an alchemical change in the function of the land. The "soul" of the newly formed farm was the original land, but it took the recombination of the two pieces of land for it to accomplish its objectives. This is much the same as our spiritual amalgamation. We do not change physically but we develop and follow new thought patterns. Again, our major transformation is in our function. These new capabilities thrust us upward on the spiral of consciousness and our soul progresses.

For most of us, before the amalgamation, our ego is our CEO and our soul is on furlough. It is quite normal for teens and young adults to be consumed by their egos. In fact, it is crucial that we experience the fullness of our ego and its personality. Developing these is the beginning of the amazing journey back to our original self: our soul. After all, you have to first lose something before you can crave it. Why would we want to return to our true selves if we had never been entranced by our false selves and suffered the consequences of their actions? Why would we search out our soul's purpose if we had not followed our ego's ambitions and found how empty they were? Why would we risk the unknowns living in soul if we had not experienced the excruciating collapse of our own narrative? How would our soul grow if it did not absorb the wisdom hidden in each loss, each heartache, each exhilarating adventure, each disruption, and each celebration? How would we embrace the miracle of our virtue if our passion had not first failed to set our world straight? Why would we want to reconnect with our Holy Idea and live from it, if we did not cry out for its forgotten bliss? Why would we yearn for our Essential Aspect if our ego had not failed us? Why would we travel the entire Enneagram of Soul for the authenticated version if our ego's interpretation of our Idealized Aspect really worked? Why would our soul child beckon us to find and embrace them if we already felt completed?

In no way is my soul in full command, but I am becoming more conscious of it as I grow. I, like many, am in the liminal space between ego and soul. We live at the confluence of the two. The Enneagram of Soul and the Enneagram of Personality are intertwined as the two strands of the DNA's helix and we travel them simultaneously. In journeying with the Enneagram, we encounter the truths and lies of life that the Enneagram merely reflects. This is why there can be no final portrait of our soul: we are always growing and transforming, so its composition is always changing.

Personally, I have learned to recognize the voice of my ego and the ways in which it differs from that of my soul. In liminal space, I witness their collaboration. In musing about the past, I can see clearly how many of my actions were motivated by my ego as it came into its fullest expression. I take note of and understand the reasons behind my many follies now.

Still, the ego is insistent, and when we are in crisis or exhausted, its imprinted patterns can seduce us back into its narrative. The now easily recognizable ego says, "I can bypass contemplation and centering before I speak and act." It says, "I am not worthy and I must compensate for all that I lack." It has great ideas and good intentions: it wants to fix what is wrong, hide from what is scary, deny what it doesn't believe, and connect to people it admires. The ego has the potential to improve our situation but it will not slow down, put its ear to Mother Earth, and listen to the Ground of Being.

There is an element of hubris to my ego's desire for autonomy. It wants to make its own plans and carry them out on its own terms and schedule, consulting only with itself. My ego will not settle for slowness in getting things done. This frenzy for productivity makes it feel more worthwhile, gives it a sense of indispensability. My ego may be threatened when others know far more than I do in the particular area I study and practice. It may even feel ownership over a certain body of knowledge and fear someone will hijack what it claims.

While my ego may want control of situations, it does not want to be perceived as such. Instead, it waits to be invited by others to take the lead, then is miffed when that invitation is not forthcoming. It may feel envious of the contributions others have made to life, which it lacked the means or talent to accomplish.

As I have mentioned, Ego Type Six is fear-motivated. My ego will always worry about physical and existential threats; these fears could paralyze me if my ego overtakes my emotional center. My ego has a concept of the ideal life, which it recalculates at every loss. It assumes responsibility for whatever may have gone wrong in past relationships, then fears the inevitable abandonment or betrayal of all those it trusts or loves. When I am under stress or am tired, my ego thinks there is a chance I'll buy into its latest narrative.

Now that I am more centered in my soul, however, my ego is less successful at convincing me of these false accounts. This is largely because its voice has become so recognizable that it is easier to guard against. After my ego failed repeatedly at achieving so many of my dreams, I eventually reached a critical mass of disappointment with it. The illness and death of my son did more than separate me from the Ben I knew; they presented enemies to my ego's idealized life and the future I had long envisioned. Ben's illness destroyed all hopes I had for him as his disease slowly rendered him almost unrecognizable.

Many of my dreams for Ben turned out to have more to do with the expectation that he would carry out my own legacy. In doing so, he would complete me and give my life more lasting meaning. It is difficult to face this truth, but it has made me challenge myself to find new dreams.

I grieved then for Ben and continue to do so. At his death, my ego died a thousand deaths, making space for the sacred to enter and transform me. This experience—and the many other very private ones that such a loss brings family members—brought me into consciousness, and that journey continues. We do not have Ben with us physically, but we have many people who have gifted us with love through their very presence. Had my unchecked ego fought for its chosen narrative, I am sure I would have lived in bitterness rather than in the realm of love.

The amalgamation of my ego and soul is part of my daily spiritual practice. In meditation, I see clearly what my heart, head, and body struggle with each day. I also take readings of how active my ego is by assessing the level of its passion, fear. I listen to its mind chatter and try to grasp its mood that day. At the same time, I read the level of my virtue of courage and my connection to Holy Strength and Holy Faith. I journey through a centering prayer to my soul's Essential Aspect of Living Daylight. I reconnect with my soul child, sometimes briefly—just to step outside and smell the fresh jasmine growing at my childhood door. These—my virtue, Holy Idea, Essential Aspect, and soul child—are facets of my soul. It is essential to know the structures of both our ego and our soul to consciously do the real inner work of transformation. Many days, I fail miserably in paying attention to my ego and soul. I sink into distractions and fall victim to my latest mood. I have wasted many hours battling fear instead of building the spirit of love inside myself. Yet, I continue in the spiritual practice that heals me.

Our spiritual practice is the workshop for the amalgamation of our ego and soul. There, in that sacred space, little by little every day, we review our lives, our tasks, and our soul's purpose. We inquire of ourselves: "How far am I on the journey? How much have I healed? How much mercy have I extended to others? To myself? How have I faced my fears and lived in courage?" I let my soul speak. In the stillness, I listen as it breathes hope and assurance into me, reminding me of my true nature as part of all being.

In the liminal space of meditation, my soul begs me to look outside my window and see the trees and sky, to notice the details, the light, and the colors. When I do so, I see past the branches of individual trees to the greater designs, symbols, and patterns that emerge from the vast configurations of limbs and leaves. These beautiful patterns have appeared throughout time and across many cultures, from Native American blankets to Renaissance architecture to whimsical storybook characters.

There is a symbolic message in those limbs—whether they are the bare silhouettes of winter or covered with the lacy buds of spring. Sometimes I understand the symbols, sometimes I simply enjoy them. Always, during meditation, I am lost in the state of soul consciousness. As I experience the power of my soul, it becomes easier for my ego to relinquish control. Increasingly, the two become one.

The ego has wisdom from its wonderings and its wanderings. It has learned many things that my soul wants to apply later. In the sacred space of spiritual practice, the ego also submits its hubris to the soul, whose humility transforms it. The ego's narrative transforms to follow the current chapter of the divine narrative. The quest for control submits to a greater authority: the soul's sincere desire and its connection to divine will. It is then that the ego's strength serves the soul. The ego's envy and resentment toward others who are "better" and who make greater contributions to life become support for and appreciation of those who strive to improve

Spiritual Transformation and Amalgamation of Our Ego and Soul

the world. It understands that any such minor good has positive effects on the rest of the world. Instead of continuing in its rush to accomplish, my ego is more inclined to yield to God's great timing than to insist on following my imagined schedule. When my ego meets my soul in the sacred space of transformation, I am restored.

8
Three Major Levels of Soul Development

Through trials, celebrations, losses, and ecstasies, our souls progress. The Spiral Continuum of Being (see chapter 2) depicts the vertical progression from our beginnings in the soul child to our eventual return to essence. In each of the five stages, the soul undergoes metaphysical changes that broaden its spiritual scope and capacities. We may be better able to forgive and more accepting of others—even our enemies. Three general levels of soul development run in parallel on the Continuum of Being as it spirals; each level has sublevels.

What are the major levels of soul development? Perhaps more importantly, where are we in our own soul's level of development? These questions are best answered on an individual basis. To provide some structure, I present to you the hallmarks of the three general levels of soul development (leaving aside any discussions about sublevels). Over the years, between my clinical practice and personal life, I have been in relationships with people who embody each of these levels. These descriptions may assist you in answering this all-important question for yourself.

Just as our ego type has levels of consciousness, our soul type has its own progressive levels of development. For example, an Ego Type Seven's soul type is found at Soul Point Five, where there are three possible levels of operation. These levels progress from Level One, "the Obscured Soul," who is barely recognized; to Level Two, "the Emerging Soul," who is in a dance with the ego for leadership; to Level Three, "the Palpable Soul," who, fully expressed, leads the ego.

Soul Level One: The Obscured Soul

At Soul Level One, our soul is hidden from us. We live exclusively in the ego while our soul dwells beneath a protective crust. This crust thickens as we increasingly live out of ego and become virtually unaware of any other parts of ourselves. Our ego may choose any of the three centers (mind, heart, or body) with which to help us move through the world.

We are all egocentric to different degrees, but this does not negate our positive characteristics such as sacrifice and benevolence. The litmus test for egocentric behavior is our motivation. In an ego-dominated person, behaviors that on the surface may seem to be noble or altruistic may actually be intended to serve the ego's desires and fears. This level likely comprises a majority of the population.

In egocentricity, the motivation is often to become the best personality possible: a "good" person, a successful person, etc. Accomplishing this brings many benefits, including popularity, acclaim, safety, and good self-esteem. The soul has a separate agenda. Its energy goes toward manifesting its purpose and seeking out spiritually significant relationships and circumstances.

At Soul Level One, though sealed beneath a protective crust, our soul is still very much alive. It is not inert but rather restless because it cannot easily express itself. It isn't flowing through our heart, mind, or body. When the soul's flow is blocked, it eventually rattles our cage to wake us up to the problem. At Soul Level One, although our soul is ignored by our ego mind, it can make itself known by appearing as the "trickster."

The soul is in contact with all of our aspects and works within each of their functions. It is not the enemy of our ego or our superego. Rather, because it desires healing and wholeness, the soul needs the ego and the superego as integral parts of transformation that move us through the world. Accordingly, the soul may use the shadow and its trickster to remind us that the soul—not our ego—is our essential nature, our truest self: our real identity.

To illustrate, let's look at a thirty-three-year-old restaurant owner we'll call Juan. Juan was at Soul Level One and had an active ego that totally ruled and preoccupied him. He was a husband and father of two who lived a fast-paced life marketing his restaurants and managing some of the finest chefs in the area. Even at a young age, Juan had become a successful entrepreneur, doggedly planning ahead for the next opportunity. He tasted fame when the regional gourmet magazine featured his handsome face on its cover. His wife, Margaret, warned him repeatedly that he was spending so much time away from the family that he was slowly losing them. Juan ignored both her and the stirrings in his soul that agreed with her.

The opening day of Juan's new restaurant coincided with his wedding anniversary, and after an immensely busy day, Juan's trickster sabotaged him. While staying late to finish clean up, he hurriedly walked across a newly waxed floor with a tray of wine glasses in one hand. His feet slipped from under him and he fell, the glass shattering around him. While the cuts from the jagged glass needed stitches, it was his broken leg that kept Juan at home for a few weeks During his compulsory vacation, he reconnected with his wife and children.

Juan's soul was at the forefront during this time and every day he was painfully reminded of what mattered most to him. Throughout this trying time, Juan reaffirmed his deepest wish to live in solidarity with all of his loved ones—a goal that aligned perfectly with divine will. He had grown up in a thoroughly interconnected family that supported and loved him. But Juan had lost contact with that deep part of his soul. Over these three weeks, Juan fostered his relationship with his wife and children. This period helped him realize that he had abandoned his fundamental desire for interconnection in favor of chasing wealth and achievement. Sadly, Juan soon returned to the rat race because his ego demanded it. Powerless against the entrenched ego he, like many of us, returned to his passion of self-promotion and his fixation of vanity. Yet, in reminding Juan of his essence and its fundamental values, the trickster had permanently weakened these ego-driven flaws.

The trickster serves the will of the repressed soul by orchestrating circumstances that force us to finally take notice of the soul's intentions that we have been actively ignoring.

At Soul Level One, our soul also utilizes our superego, otherwise known as our conscience, to awaken us. The obscured soul has many ways of making itself known. Our superego is our internalized parent and inner critic. Our superego often falls under the control of the ego, which silences or amplifies it to accomplish its narrative, but the obscured soul marshals the ignored superego to make its purposes known. The ignored superego leaks out in the form of the inner critic, who relentlessly chides, punishes, and criticizes us. When the inner critic's damage is done, we are left as fallen soldiers from the inner campaigns against ourselves. Out of pure self-preservation, we finally ask ourselves if we are really as hopeless as our inner critic claims we are. At this pivotal juncture, we are forced to look at ourselves more realistically and then naturally turn to our soul—at first, to compensate for our apparent depravity by reconnecting with our essential goodness. Balance is achieved by finally including the superego among the acknowledged aspects of ourselves. Once at the table, even if temporarily, the superego can be heard as the realistic, still, small voice of consciousness instead of as blaring condemnations from inner megaphones.

A woman we'll call Kaitlin, who worked as an industrial engineer, disparaged herself continuously. Her inner critic said that she was neither a good employee nor a good person. Though she was commended at work for her abilities and had successfully climbed the ladder to earn her position, she still tortured herself mercilessly. She considered herself an imposter and believed she was incompetent, deceitful, and patronizing of others. She was convinced that one day she would be exposed and have to pay for all the wrong decisions she had made. She second-guessed all of her choices and frequently sat up in the night going over all her rationales and planning for their failures. She eventually had to take time off work because her inner critic had beaten her up and left her for dead.

Just short of imagining that things would be better if she actually *were* dead, Kaitlin's heart broke through her inner critic's voice, crying from her depths, "If you are so bad and so wrong, why do you cry at television commercials that feature disabled children talking about their disabilities and how they were helped by their hospital? That's a small thing but doesn't that mean you have at least some heart, some soul, some goodness? Didn't you help injured animals on the farm when you were a child? Wasn't that the right and natural choice for you as a child?" With this one voice from her heart, her soul emerged from obscurity, never to retreat under the crust again. Instead, Kaitlin became a volunteer at the local children's hospital.

In the small amounts of time in communication with her soul, Kaitlin re-contacted her soul's joy, from which she had been disconnected. Though she did not know that "Joy" (The Yellow) was her essential aspect, she experienced something powerful as her times of joy were a relief from the inner critic. As an Ego Type One, she was overwhelmed with achieving perfection, yet, with her soul's joy and serenity, she saw glimpses of a new perfection that included failures, faults, and self-compassion. Even at this level of soul development, Kaitlin's ego was still the stronger force—the one that guided how she lived and made most of her life decisions. She remained in communication with her soul and eventually progressed from Soul Level One to Soul Level Two.

At Soul Level One, we are still focused on the Enneagram of Personality and, as such, while we experience a few brief snippets of living in soul, we have not lived in our soulality. Therefore, the ego's fixations fuel the mind, heart, and body. Our ego avoids the things that shame, scare, or anger us, and our ego's trap inevitably ensnares us. Our soul is present, though obscured most of the time. Yet, depending on the shock points we experience in life, our soul may emerge from beneath the crust, maybe staying with us for a season or longer. The more we live in soul, the less we operate in ego and the closer we get to the practice of living in soulality daily. When we finally acknowledge that our soul is our life force and our meaning, we progress to Soul Level Two, where it has an honored place at the table.

Soul Level Two: The Emerging Soul

At Soul Level Two, our soul and our ego operate alternatively. At this level, our soul expresses itself openly but naturally vies with our ego for leadership. This space is not always peaceful; it may consist of a tumultuous clash between the two. I call this place on the Continuum of Being the "Mixture." In Mixture, our ego remains on the Enneagram of Personality while our soul has shifted focus to the Enneagram of Soul. At this level of soul, whenever our ego predominates, we are focused on the Enneagram of Personality and go up and down the spiral of consciousness as our personality integrates or disintegrates. However, when we most inhabit our soul, we are focused on the Enneagram of Soul and travel this Enneagram as we spiral into higher consciousness. Some of us may not be able to stay in our soul. In this case, while we return to living from our personality, the memories of living in soul remain. The trickster and superego continue to jar us into consciousness, although perhaps less frequently. While at Level One the soul is eclipsed by the ego, in Soul Level Two, the soul is frequently our way of moving in the world. Indeed, some of us inhabit the soul for such lengthy periods that we are readied for the transition to Soul Level Three.

At Soul Level Two, although our soul is a "partial prisoner," our ego also has some conception that there is a deeper being (our soul). During times such as shock points, when the ego defenses break down under overwhelming circumstances, the ego submits to the soul; our survival hinges on it. Even though our soul is partially acknowledged and expressed at Soul Level Two, our ego stubbornly holds onto the illusion that it alone knows best. The ego really wants to keep the soul in a box and pull it out only when necessary. The problem is that the necessary times increase as our lives demand more than egoic solutions.

Level Two is the stage at which the soul is becoming our major identity. It is ready to fully express and fulfill the purpose for which it was born. It knows part of that purpose is to contend with its ego, yet now it is ready to lead the ego. The soul at Level Two has to wait for the ego to submit, which does not occur until the ego reaches its critical mass of suffering and releases its fixation.

A thirty-seven-year-old woman at Soul Level Two, whom we'll call Bethany, was a mother of three and very much in love with her husband Drake. Bethany's soul made itself known almost daily. Just the other evening, she was out on her run and reached a place with a spectacular view of the valley. Before, she had always passed this spot without pausing, not wanting to break her stride. But this evening she stopped and took in the miraculous view of a flame-orange sunset in a turquoise sky. She stood there in awe of the beautiful expanse before her. It may have been her endorphins, but she went into a euphoric state in which she felt one with the entire universe. She felt whole and free, part of everything.

During this waking dream, she saw a vision of one of her daughters, who'd just had open-heart surgery. Their daughter's congenital heart valve issue had dominated the lives and well-being of Bethany and her husband Drake. Bethany's way to cope was to figure out the statistics and the surgical procedures and to be "up" on as many of the facts as possible. She read medical journals compulsively, looking for anything that might be useful, then regularly and rigorously questioned the medical professionals about the latest findings. This approach to controlling her daughter's health was not working, though. Her anxiety had become so high that Bethany was having sleep problems and mood issues. At this particular sunset, however, she felt as if she were a little girl once more—when everything was right with the world.

Bethany became part of the sunset and had the felt experience that her daughter would recover well. The weight lifted. This comfort was not given by physicians but by the Divine. Bethany walked home and embraced what had just occurred. The feeling emanated from her soul and she kept it as long as it would last. She had made a brief shift to soul, but her ego wanted control again. A struggle ensued. Things went back and forth, with Bethany's terror fueling her ego while periods of peaceful comfort periodically sprang from her soul.

At Level Two of soul development, the inherent struggle between the ego and the soul causes immense pain. We rely most upon our ego in everyday operation—our emerging soul calls for a leap of faith to return to it, but it cannot coerce us. Therefore, the ego distracts us with its new ways to solve our problems. Like a teenager, it vacillates between being a know-it-all and being full of self-doubt. In doubt and pain, it relinquishes to the soul—but only for a little while. Then it comes up with another way to accomplish its purpose. Of course, its cocksure ways are not new. They only prevent us "one more time" from amalgamating with our soul. Many of us live in this tension for long periods—sometimes our entire lifetime.

But when the ego finally turns loose and capitulates to the soul, we begin to embody the soul. Not only partially but wholly; it manifests in dreams, synchronicities, signs, wonders, and people who undeniably take us to another realm beyond our ego. Once we surrender to this other realm, we focus on the Enneagram of Soul and progress to Soul Level Three.

Soul Level Two is where I find myself. Beginning with my spiritual practice each morning, I meditate and read. Before I head to the office, I pray and reflect. I plan my day and how I can make contact with those I love. The ego's voice is loud and clear even in the mornings when in contemplation. Nearly every morning I think of those I have lost, among them my son. The pain of my son's death is not as overwhelming as it used to be but I still miss Ben terribly and have flashbacks of all our times together. At any given time, I am always just one second away from tears, as is my wife, Lark. These reflections are my ego's way of still trying to sort out the unspeakable and deal with lifelong grief. Now, however, my soul is aware of what these flashbacks and tears signify, and it rushes to my rescue.

While there is an ongoing struggle between the two, my soul—as my consciousness—has dominion over my ego. My soul immediately returns me to my essence. This is most readily accomplished by re-embodying my soul child. Fear still grabs and tortures me at times, especially in moments of uncertainty or heartbreak. My skittish ego is always on guard against hurt and harm. My Ego Type Six has always lived in fear and is well-trained to be hyper-vigilant against dreaded hurts, rejections, failings, and regret. Indeed, by imagining worst-case scenarios, it makes actual life seem better in comparison. Now, these worst-case imaginings are short-lived, and I do not live in as much fear as I did when my ego dominated. My soul creates a sacred space in which I frequently live and move and have my being. Increasingly, I feel most at home in my soul and prefer to spend my time there.

Though my ego often wars with my soul, the fights between them are not as prolonged. It used to be that, when these fights were over with, my ego usually came out on top. However, now my ego has begun to submit to my soul. Alas, frequently it still wins out; even so, it actually serves the soul more than it ever did beforehand. Therefore, there is always some form of struggle, even if short-lived, over dominance and submission.

Medical issues preoccupy many of us in the second half of life and I too, as an Ego Type Six, am alarmed when something goes awry. The process of aging in and of itself is frequently frightening. There again, the ego could make mincemeat out of me during health scares and medical procedures, and it frequently tries. But my soul is gaining power over the fear factor. The soul is teaching me to surrender to and relinquish fear. In uncertain conditions, I tremble at first but when I remember myself as having lived in a state of peace for my first few years, I can re-center myself around my soul.

My Holy Idea of Strength and Faith has come to be my best friend along with my Essential Aspect of Living Daylight and my virtue of courage. Of all the Holy Ideas, Essential Aspects, and virtues that exist in this world, mine are the ones that make the most sense and the most difference in my life.

Soul Level Three: The Palpable Soul

At Soul Level Three, our soul fully manifests as the leader of our lives and our ego transforms to serve our soul; this is the level on which we are most enlightened and conscious. At this level, we have migrated from the mixture between ego and soul, and live completely in our souality. We have surrendered our negative passion and are finally convinced that it is made up of illusions that can only pretend to fill us at our depths. At this level, we constantly express our virtue, Essential Aspect, and Holy Idea.

By this point, the previously self-serving ego has been relegated to ensuring our physical survival. After all, it is the ego that helps keep food on the table and clothes on our backs. At Soul Level Three, rather than being driven by its passion, the ego serves the soul from the standpoint of our virtue, Essential Aspect, and Holy Idea. That is, the ego cooperates with the soul's intentions and purposes in the heart, mind, and body centers of intelligence.

Soul Level Three includes lauded personages such as Nelson Mandela, Mother Teresa, and St. Francis of Assisi, but we do not have to be well-known or sainted to attain this degree of soul development. In fact, many of those at Soul Level Three are everyday people who remain relatively inconspicuous; I have come to know that this is by preference. Up until now, I have known or directly interacted with only a handful of people at Soul Level Three. In short, the person at Soul Level Three fully manifests their soul. Many who come into contact with them may not realize that they are witnessing a highly developed soul. However, for those of us who are attuned to the soul to any degree, there is a palpable magnetic force that draws us toward these rare and beautiful people. That is why I refer to this stage of soul development as the "Palpable Soul."

Palpable Souls are fully present and alive. They come in all forms and sizes, from all walks of life and all states of wellness. Yet, for me, they have a special outward sign. They have a luminous glow on their faces—a bright aura or halo—even while they are asleep.

Those on this level of soul are unassuming and humble. They may have a strong personality but it is driven by soul qualities rather than by passions. This personality, when emptied of ego-driven self-interest, amalgamates with the soul; in turn, the soul expresses itself through the personality. The soul expressed through the personality is our souality. It is as if the person at this soul level has returned to the innocence of early childhood, awed by the world and not preoccupied with self. At Soul Level Three, there is less of a preoccupation with the outcome and more attention paid to the process. These souls understand that presence happens in the now of the process of living.

Souls at Level Three are not insistent on getting their own way but are poised to experience the divine way that is ultimately emerging in each now. They are not awkward in silence but can comfortably allow long periods of silence—even when it would be easily broken with a small comment. Out of the silence comes an even deeper level of response from people, and this soul is not going to stand in the way of that, even if such an act would temporarily relieve others' anxiety.

Often, souls of this level will nod in agreement with all opinions in a discussion, even if they do not necessarily agree. The nod does not indicate assent but rather affirmation of the person who is expressing the opinion. When these souls contribute to the conversation, it is frequently in the form of a question that prompts others to think about the subject from another viewpoint they may not have considered.

There are many other characteristics of Soul Level Three but I think they are best illustrated by a person I knew who lived at this level.

Eric Parkman Smith was born near the turn of the last century in Concord, Massachusetts—a village just outside of Boston. His mother and father were natives of Concord who married and lived in the town center. Eric was educated at Harvard and became comptroller of the Maine Central Railroad. He loved his hometown so much that he stayed there and became a civic leader, town historian, and an active parishioner of Concord's historical Unitarian Church—all while commuting from Concord to Portland, Maine. Though he never married, he had many interests, friends, and activities, and he traveled extensively.

From 1978–79, during my internship in clinical psychology in the Department of Psychiatry at Harvard Medical School, Lark and I lived in Concord. We rented a house next door to Eric, who became our landlord. During our time living there, we came to know him so well that we became like family.

I got the impression that Eric was an unusual man on our first meeting when he interviewed me as a prospective tenant. He was warm and personable, standing in the side yard of the cozy Cape Cod–style house that I wanted to rent. After a delightful chat, I asked, with a lump in my throat, what the rent would be. His reply took me aback. Having just lived in Charlottesville, Virginia, for several years, the rental fees in New England were staggering to me. I said, "Mr. Smith, I am so sorry, I know that it is rare to find this perfect little house of yours, but I just cannot afford it because I am still a student. Thank you for your time today."

Before I left the conversation, Mr. Smith did something unusual. He asked what I could comfortably afford. After I told him, he paused for a moment and finally decided, "It's a deal." I was ecstatic, but had to add, "Mr. Smith, I have one more thing to let you know: we have a dog." Then he smiled and asked, "What kind?" I replied, "A cocker spaniel named

Byron." Mr. Smith clapped his hands and announced, "I love cocker spaniels!" Lark, Eric, and I remained close friends until 2008, when Eric peacefully passed away at age ninety-seven. We traveled to and from Concord many times to visit him and he also traveled to our home in Alabama.

Little did we know that our biggest gift from Eric would not be the initial benevolence he extended to us, but rather his lifelong friendship. Eric was possibly an Ego Type One who had, long before, begun to live in his soulality at Soul Point Seven. His was a unique amalgamation of Ego Type One's sense of the right direction and Soul Type Seven's optimistic joy. He was not a St. Francis, nor did he ever claim to be anything but the man next door, yet for Lark and me, his soulality was unmistakable. Eric Smith had very little ego as such but a lot of willpower. His life force came not from the energy of personal ego but rather a higher source. For us, his life exemplified Soul Level Three.

When Eric entered a room, he brought a sense of peace and joy that spread to everyone in his presence, regardless of their prior indifferent, contrary, or sour mood.

Always present, Eric accepted the worlds of others and invited others into his—one of wonder, history, ecology, literature, organic foods, health, joy, and curiosity. He rarely spoke of God or made judgments about who was right and who was wrong.

He never judged others or the situation too quickly. He gave validity to others' opinions and, by doing so, gave everyone a place at the table. When anyone voiced an opinion that he did not understand or he disagreed with, he did not challenge the other person but listened to the reasons why they felt the way they did. He always affirmed their opinion before quietly speaking his view. He took a stand when he felt it necessary, but he did so in a respectful, non-confrontational tone.

When he learned of bad news or that someone had cheated him on rent or repair jobs, he would sigh and say, "That's OK." I came to understand that these words did not mean the circumstances or behavior were acceptable but that *he* would be OK. He did not hold grudges, which is why he could always channel joy.

Eric's self-affirming mantra was: "Every day, in every way, I'm getting better and better and better." He was eternally optimistic and he believed that positive attitudes could turn around the most disappointing circumstances and relationships. He encouraged the best in everyone.

He had a lot of resources but spent very little on himself. Eric was always well-dressed, often with a bow tie and suspenders, and always with polished shoes. But he wore his clothes until they could no longer be worn. He gave money regularly to charities and to programs that supported animal welfare and the environment. He never told me of this; I saw the envelopes on his entrance hall table regularly.

Though he was very well-educated and had been around the world, I never heard him spout off knowledge as if he were the authority. He simply contributed what he knew to the conversation.

All his interactions were conducted in a space of mutual respect and joy that he created. His laughter was the background "music" for most conversations. Eric's unmistakable joy meant that conversations rarely, if ever, took a downward turn or became dismal or depressing. When a conversation seemed to be going south, he interjected a positive viewpoint that lifted everyone's spirits. When the circumstance was obviously sad, he was fully present.

Eric never received a gift or meal without extending his hand in gratitude. He frequently made mention of what he was thankful for on any given day. If the weather was bad, he would think of something else for which he was grateful.

When it came to time, Eric paced himself, yet he was never frenzied. He was aligned with a rhythm beyond space and time. Just as his joy was contagious, so was Eric's sense of timing. We relaxed into his rhythm. He never complained or seemed thrown off if we were late or if plans had to change. Schedule adjustments were not problematic because his personal sense of time fell in with the giant flow of a higher timing.

Eric never interrupted conversations to speak about himself. When asked about a topic, his answer was usually an interesting story that had meaning beyond its face value. He understood that he did not have to blow his own horn—that, over time, his behavior would reveal who he was.

Eric had a reverence for all life. In the street, he'd smile at passersby. He addressed everyone, regardless of their station, as neighbors and friends. He loved animals and was kind to the elderly. He supported and cared for the Finnish lady who had been his nanny when he was a young child. When he learned that his beloved Lilly had lost her family and was ailing, he sent for her and became her caregiver until she passed away.

When a decision had to be made that affected an entire group, he did not demand that others bow to his preferences. He merely stated his opinion of the best path forward, then calmly acquiesced to the will of the group.

When he perceived that he had slipped and made a comment about someone that could be taken negatively, he would balance out his statement with positives about the person. He was never defensive, instead readily acknowledging his ego, as well as his foibles and mistakes.

Eric was a good listener who reveled in others' stories and never sought the spotlight. When someone was making a statement, commenting, or telling a story, he felt no need to interrupt or interject his opinion for the sake of being noticed or having a stake in the action.

Eric did not judge by economic status, race, ethnicity, religion, gender, beauty, or strength. I never heard him demean any other human being, yet I heard him affirm many.

Eric was not resistant to being alone. He was probably introverted, yet over the years had struck the balance between reaping the best from being alone and being with others.

He did not have a hidden agenda and was honest with his needs and wants. He enjoyed giving and he received graciously.

He lived until the age of ninety-seven. Lying in bed in the nursing home, Eric's face shone. In his last days, while he was aware that he would not live long, he remained joyful. He was still more interested in others than in himself—curious about friends, neighborhood news, and world happenings. When asked how he was doing, his constant refrain from that bed remained, "Every day, in every way, I'm getting better and better and better."

Eric Smith's only biological family when he died was one first cousin twice removed. In his will, Eric gave generously to the charities and institutions that he supported throughout his life.

He died a conscious death.

9
The Enneagram's Passageways to Inner and Outer Peace

IT WAS EIGHT MONTHS since the death of our son Ben. Lark and I had prayed for comfort but our prayers seemed to fall on deaf ears. It was as if we were hidden in a dark chamber of grief and even God did not know where we were. We went through the motions of life by rote, unsure if we could begin anew and doubtful that we would ever experience happiness again. Yet, something extraordinary happened on a visit to our dear friends Buddy and Charlotte in Tucson, Arizona, in May of 2009.

Charlotte and Buddy Mullis have been our close friends since 1980. They had lived near us in Anniston for decades and knew well our trials with Ben's illness and our ongoing grief. As usual, in their empathy and helpfulness, they opened their hearts and invited us to their new home in Arizona. It was a land beyond our imagination; we were struck by the Sonoran Desert's amazing terrain and vegetation, including its massive, iconic saguaro cacti. One day, while the four of us were driving through the desert, I asked Buddy to pull over so we could inspect one of these majestic cacti that grew like trees, sprouting arms and reaching up to forty-five or even fifty feet. At a random spot in the middle of nowhere, the four of us trudged across the rugged desert to stand in front of one of the thousands of these flowering saguaros. While examining it closely, I remarked that its long, pointed spines, arranged in neat rows of little clusters, resembled thousands and thousands of toothpicks.

For fun, I reached toward the spines above my head and with my thumb and forefinger dislodged one of the spines. To my astonishment, it came out easily, but in my fingers was an unbelievable surprise that I will never forget: a manufactured wooden toothpick. For a moment, my stunned mind told me that this must be where we get toothpicks, but I immediately realized that couldn't be true. I tried pulling on the other spines but they were all anchored to the cactus and wouldn't budge. Staring at the toothpick, I wondered, how could this be possible? Lark was incredulous as she watched it happen. I told the Mullises. Charlotte grinned and said, "Joe, you've got to be pulling a prank." I promised her that I wasn't. Charlotte and Buddy looked to Lark for confirmation and the astonishment still on her face told them all they needed to know.

The four of us imagined the day when a hiker had placed the toothpick in one of the cactus' thousands of prickly clusters instead of throwing it on the ground. We imagined them walking away from their "implantation," smiling to themselves that no one would discover it in a million years. Happening against such great odds, I asked myself what this experience could mean. After returning home to Alabama from our refreshing trip, and after much reflection, the significance finally dawned on me.

So many times, I had wondered if God knew where we were, but after contemplating the extraordinary incident, I was now certain that the Divine and the forces underlying the universe were assuring us, "I know exactly where you are, down to the tiniest detail, the words in your mouth, the reach of your fingers, and the emotions in your heart." The unusual find went from being a mystery to a positive shock point that totally reversed our downward cycle of sadness. The find gave us much-needed hope.

For me, the tedium of Ben's long illness and the pain of losing him were radical wastes. My son was gone and I not only missed him terribly on the soul level but in retrospect I recognize that my ego's plan for our family had come crashing down. My life's meaning, as my ego had conceptualized it, was obliterated; all that remained was the will to live and take care of Lark and our daughter Lauren. Fear set in and I recall that emotionally, spiritually, and physically we hunkered down like the English in bomb shelters during the Blitz. Metaphorically, we were in the fetal position, waiting for another bomb to drop. But with the toothpick experience, our frame of reference changed from viewing the world through our egos' lens of loss and despair to perceiving life through the eyes of hope that somehow God knew of our exact suffering and was with us. For the first time, I could be open to the possibility that all the suffering before and after Ben's death was part of a plan greater than our minds could ever fully comprehend.

The fears and the primal need for meaning led me back to the Enneagram in a much deeper way. In past difficult circumstances, I had gone from my ego at Point Six, to my Point of Integration at Point Nine. Healthy Nine's laissez-faire approach, peacefulness, and composure had indeed been medicine for me. Now, I asked myself, "Why don't the positives of Point Nine help me in my grief?" The answer came from an altogether higher realm of the Enneagram that I hadn't realized existed until that moment. It revealed the organic and somewhat hidden relationship between my ego and my soul. I came to understand that my unchecked ego is a mental component of my personal consciousness (my soul) and that when it consumes me, it suppresses the expression of my soul's pure qualities. I came to recognize that the suffering of the ego is what my soul required in its particular progression.

I began to realize that the larger and more pervasive our egoic energy, the more it dominates, and the less our soul can manifest its divine qualities. When I took a longer look at the Enneagram with newer and clearer eyes, I saw that the nine points were not just nine personality types, but nine types of egos. Then I realized that our suffering must be directly related to our ego type. For me, my current suffering was not just grief; it was injected with terror and hopelessness—and fear was my ego type's passion. Specifically, I was afraid that Lark and I would never again find contentment or happiness, and that other grueling things that loomed just around the corner would totally destroy us. Having been shell-shocked, my Ego Six's fear and cowardice had spiritually paralyzed me and blocked the healing. Coming to understand the Enneagram on a deeper level than ever before helped me resume that healing process.

I reflected on the nine ego-based personality types of the Enneagram and wondered, "If we know the nature of our particular ego, could we comprehend exactly how it distorts our perceptions of the world?" By studying each of the Centers of Intelligence, I saw not only how an ego of fear distorts the perceptions of the Mind Center but how anger distorts perceptions of the Body Center and how shame distorts the perceptions of the Heart Center. In reviewing the nine ego types, their Soul Points, and the arrows, I understood that the Enneagram was about revealing our true identity, beyond the level of personality. I also saw the movements we make around the Enneagram as we grow and become. I came to know that the Enneagram was not a personality improvement inventory; it was not something short-term that labels people and puts us into a spiritual cubby hole where we remain for the rest of our lives. The Enneagram is a spiritual tool that takes us to our depths and shows us our soul—our true nature.

Then I wondered, "What are we to do with our egos if they obscure our soul? How much of our suffering could we end if we could diminish the unhealthy ego?" I looked even closer into the Enneagram and found many answers in its inner flow.

Answers in the Enneagram's Inner Flow

The Enneagram's inner flow is composed of hidden passageways, depicted by arrows that lead to our Point of Integration or Soul Point. We integrate by flowing from our ego type against our arrow to our Soul Point. The prospect of living in my soul offered much, but I asked myself, "Who wants to be a soul in a long white robe, walking above the earth on a cloud? Don't we need an ego and its personality to move us through this world? Just who would we be if we were not our ego and its personality?" The answer to this stream of questions fell right into my lap: the Soul Point is not another set of personality characteristics but one of the nine energies depicted on the Enneagram, into which our soul child was born. It represents an entirely different state of being from our personality.

The soul child holds the qualities of our soul and naturally manifests one of the nine facets of the Divine that it was created to express. Our soul is our essential self and remains as we were before our personality fully developed. It never leaves us—even if we have lost our connection to it, we can soon reunite with it. Further, if we re-embody our souls, our personalities can combine with them to become our new outward expressions to the world. Every one of us has a unique personality as well as unique soul qualities. When the soul instead of the ego fuels our personality, we live in the world as a conscious being and as our most authentic self. The amalgamation of our ego and our soul constitutes what I call our unique *soulality*. Soulality is our personality fueled by the soul that has incorporated the ego into itself. After amalgamation, the ego serves the soul.

Our soulalities deepen in capacity as we flow from our Soul Point, against the arrows to each of the consecutive points of the hexad and the inner triangle, until we return to our starting place. When we again reach our Soul Point, we do so at a higher capacity. This is the spiral of consciousness.

Because they are connected to the Divine, the nature of our souls is infinite. Yet, this doesn't prevent us from experiencing and even embodying our souls here and now. Living in soul, we are given new eyes and ears that perceive reality without the ego's distortions. In our soulality, the felt sense of reality is vastly different from our ego's perceptions of it. Our ego's strivings, narrative, and lens become redundant when we adopt the overarching significance of our soul, with its divine purpose and its soul qualities. In our soulalities, we are beings of self-compassion and we experience others' essences instead of their surface personalities. This is possible because our ego is now in service to our soul. Without most of our energies invested in the ego, its passions, avoidances, etc., we can experience our true nature directly, along with the felt sense of peace that this brings.

Thanks to the Enneagram and the spiritual practices it inspires, my soul has also given me a sense of being home: a familiar zone of peace and presence. My life, like everyone else's, contains struggles and challenges, disappointments, shocks, hardships, betrayals, failures, and losses. However, my soulality deals with these in a different way from my personality under the control of my ego. In tune with its divine connection, my soul—in its palpable peace—is increasingly the decision-maker and the interpreter of circumstances and relationships. Unobstructed, my soul's eyes see all occurrences as part of a larger mystery that I may or may not understand. My soul trusts that it is strong and tethered to the Divine; it views life as an unfolding story in the hands of a cosmic force and power far greater than I am. In my soulality, I no longer concentrate on my ego's narrative but on the present moment, when, in the arisings of each now, my soul manifests. Still, in times of stress, my ego—even in its unhealthy aspects—frequently takes over. When I become conscious of this, I try to have self-compassion instead of allowing my ego to punish me for my failures.

There was such a dramatic change in me when my soulality began to form that I wanted to share my new consciousness with everyone; I could hardly hold myself back from doing so. It was as if I had just awoken and spied a new harmonious and beautiful world. I thought to myself, "Wow, losing the ego and living from soul is the answer to humanity's suffering. If we can teach this simple concept, then the planet and our species have a chance of surviving and even thriving. I could not see it until my egoic suffering reached a critical mass, but now it's as plain as the nose on my face."

Totally energized by this wonderful discovery of my soul, I revamped the teaching materials I had used for years in presenting the Enneagram—not that the courses were boring or unproductive, they just no longer taught what I now knew to be the true soul of the Enneagram. My enthusiasm practically made new handouts appear out of nowhere. Lark and I began going all over the Southeast as word got around that we were teaching an exciting new, deeper, concept: the spirituality of the Enneagram.

The core of my new presentation focused on the soul child inside every one of us. To facilitate each participant's experience of knowing their soul child, I employed guided imagery that I had been taught by Jerome Singer, PhD, while a graduate student at Yale. An authority in the use of guided imagery[1] and Jacobsonian relaxation techniques[2] in treatment for anxiety and phobias, Singer supervised each of us as students while we treated phobic patients by taking them into states of increasing relaxation and comfort. From there, we slowly introduced imaginal scenes of the things that triggered their phobia. In a state of supreme relaxation and pleasant comfort, it is impossible for most people to feel anxiety. The state of relaxation achieved is so powerful that it inhibits anxiety and the treatment effects last into normal waking states. All this is to say that when the egoic concerns that operate in our minds all day every day are suspended, we return to a more natural, relaxed way of being in the world. Most of the time, this was also the state of being for our inner child of the past—our soul child.

In my study of the inner child, whom I later understood to be the soul child, it became evident that: in the first few years of life, we do not have an expansive and fully functioning ego; therefore, we do not experience the ego suffering that would accompany it. The only identity we have as a baby and small child is that of our inner being, which I have labeled our soul child. If we focus on children with healthily involved mothers or caretakers, we note that such babies and small children have virtually all of their needs anticipated and met. The worst they experience are bodily discomforts and occasional fear responses. All in all, the inner child of the past is in a state of extreme awareness, comfort, or even bliss.

---

1. Singer, *Imagery and Daydream Methods in Psychotherapy and Behavior Modification*.
2. Jacobson, *Progressive Relaxation*.

My PhD studies in child and family clinical psychology and my theological studies began to dovetail in a much more profound way with my evolving understanding of the Enneagram and human development. At work in my daily clinical practice, I now not only saw an Enneagram personality type with each patient, as I had for years, but also the severity to which any given patient's ego blocked their wellness. I was also privileged to witness the divine qualities of the soul emerge in the treatment (usually slowly) and bring the patient freedom from dysfunction.

My special interest was in the inner child of the past and its seminal meaning to our lives. This concept was written about by many Neo-Freudian psychologists and analysts, but a book by Hugh Missildine, *Your Inner Child of the Past*, gave a comprehensive framework for understanding this phenomenon in our psyche. Our inner child is the little being who encapsulates our identity during the formative phases of psychological development, from birth until the age of about five or six. This inner child is our soul child, who operates from our true nature rather than from a fully conditioned ego. During this stage, the groundwork forms for many of our complexes as our libidinal drives—as well as the qualities of our souls—have to accommodate family and cultural structures.

As adults, our soul child is the undeniable source of ceaseless energy within each of us, as well as of boundless wonder, innocence, joy, and unashamed honesty. Missildine's work is a child-developmental and psychological description of the soul child in psychological terms. The early experiences of the inner child shape much of the substance of our personalities and behaviors. These experiences are fundamental in helping us to understand the soul child's reactions to the world and why it had to go underground to survive.

I so wanted people to contact their soul child because in my work with patients and in my own inner work, I witnessed it as a living entity inside everyone. In our healings, I witnessed it as an active expression of our soul. I felt like an archaeologist who had found ancient seeds that, when watered, grew into mature plants even after thousands of years of dormancy.[3]

I witnessed that, through imaginal exploration of the soul child, we unearthed a long-hidden part of our vital nature and our original blessings. Through the power of our imaginations—visually, kinesthetically, and through all the senses—we observe, relive, listen to, and talk with the person we once were. That person, regardless of their unconditioned

---

3. Katz, "Scientists Grew Palm Trees."

foibles, is an amazing bundle of our uncontaminated soul qualities, just waiting to be discovered and re-embodied. By remembering our soul child, we self-remember and re-embody our very essence. We have something to *be* other than just an ego and its personality—something that far surpasses the ego's false self: we can be our true nature.

This implied that—with access to our essential identity—we could take great leaps in spiritual development. We could actually make an internal shift from the unchecked ego, who we thought was our only self, to our soul and the self we are when living primarily from the qualities of our soul: our soulality. So, with this deeper awareness of the power of the Enneagram, I started to offer conferences that not only taught about the Enneagram's basics but also provided a method by which the participants experienced their own soul child. This blew the roof off the concept of mere personality integration that I had understood previously to be the meat of the Enneagram. By actually experiencing our soul child, the Point of Integration transformed into a personal point where our soul came alive and where we could explore our depths. With the guided imagery exercises, the Soul Point was no longer a cognitive concept that we only read about in a book. It was a conscious state of being that involved the direct experience of the emotions, mind, and body that express our soul.

Meanwhile, my own consciousness was expanding and jumping beyond the limited framework from which I had operated. I could not keep up with all I was assimilating through these new eyes and ears of mine: the new energy I had discovered inside, the absolutely new awareness of life's purpose, and the realization that we are our souls, were overwhelming. I wrote down everything that was coming through to me. I had many, many childhood and adult experiences that I had not yet fully processed despite my years of personal therapy and inner work. I processed these incidents in light of my new understandings. They validated that my soul was indeed progressing all along, even in the darkest moments. I saw this only in the light of my new consciousness. These stories of my life flowed from me like a fountain and I wrote them down over a period of years; I tell them at conferences and in my teachings at The Institute for Conscious Being because they illustrate the progression of soul from my depths.

I remember that when my soul overtook my unhealthy ego, my entire consciousness changed and insights flashed before me continually. This still occurs, although less frequently than when the initial aftershock thrust me toward a new rung on the spiral of consciousness. It was an unfamiliar but welcome feeling to live without the fear of others' imminent judgment and condemnation. In my unhealthy ego states, I was apprehensive about speaking to audiences. I was uncertain of my ability to bring forth the truths I sought to teach and feared that I might be misperceived. Those fears, however, were rooted in the erroneous belief that truth depended upon the audience seeing me in a certain way.

Now, I realize that the truth is always making itself known and that when I teach, it does so *through me*, rather than the image I project. I learned that I can be a conduit for truth, even when I cannot see or measure the results. I also learned that the expression of truth is not dependent on how I am perceived but rather whether my image and ego are able to get out of the way for truth to express itself through me. I realized that the substance of the message to audiences is what really matters. When I tell a story from my personal life, I am sharing from my depths, and truth shines through in amazing ways I could never before have imagined. Regardless of my role as the teacher, I learn from my own stories every time I teach. My previous fears and doubts were born from my ego; now they have been replaced by an overriding enthusiasm for the truth to make itself known through me. I interpret this enthusiasm as a quality of my soul.

During these paradigm shifts, it dawned on me I was no longer inflating or deflating myself to fit the occasion or situation. All my life I had held certain people in unrealistic admiration. They were golden to me. When with them, I felt very inferior and "faded." Similarly, I unconsciously assumed that some people were lesser than me. When I became conscious that such hierarchy is nonsense—that no one is superior or inferior in terms of the soul—I said to myself, "If I were to meet even Abraham Lincoln or Jane Goodall, I would not be nervous in the least. Though I admire them greatly, I would be more fascinated in having an honest conversation with them than in wasting energy thinking about how they were taking time with little old me." On the other hand, I said to myself, "I would also be able to talk with the man in our city who buys liquor for underage children and gets away with it. Regardless of his behavior, he is a soul like me; I can speak with his soul." The concept of the soul is so freeing; it puts every human on an even playing field in terms of our inherent worth.

Living out of soul means everything in our lives that we had previously built around our ego changes. Sadly, it is the natural order of things to don an ego to protect our little essences—our soul children. We live that way for the first half or so of our lives until we realize we are the most grounded and true to ourselves when we return to who we were as a soul child but forgot; then we can amalgamate our ego's hard-won wisdom with our soul. The individuals who remain in their ego state suffer terribly, as does the collective that they belong to. Becoming conscious of our ego entails much more than meets the eye. The ego will not give up. For example, the distortions of the unhealthy ego would have us believe that we should be granted all our desires and be able to avoid all our fears at all costs, even if it means estrangement or going so far as to destroy one another. In soulality, however, the "other" is also a soul, and in this "I/ thou" relationship, other souls are held in sacred reverence. This may seem like a "no brainer" for us "good" people, but I am constantly reminded of it when someone intrudes upon my territory or takes something I possess and my unhealthy ego immediately sweeps in to take control. If I become conscious, it is then up to me to dismiss its control.

Consciousness gives us the best chance to subsume the ego and find solutions that preserve our interests but do not throw us into the darkness of retaliation. Yet, for consciousness to arise we have to be very familiar with the workings of our egos. When the unhealthy ego rears its head, we have to be aware of our body's feelings and its mental and emotional states. We can do this only by having a spiritual practice that helps us embrace our soul qualities that are stronger than the ego. These qualities are a *replacement* for the unhealthy ego's natural inclinations.

Of course, there are hundreds of pervasive changes in our entire being when we become conscious. Newly acquired values and insights allow us to experience almost everything in spaciousness instead of the tightly pieced together jigsaw puzzle of our ego and personality.

What do I notice in other people besides myself in terms of how they deal with conflicts and other stressors? First of all, because of that spaciousness, there is a lightness and luminosity that becomes apparent. Rarely do I see a conscious person taking themselves too seriously. They are marching to the beat of a different drummer. They are looking into the soul of another—observing the person instead of sizing them up to manipulate, enjoy, or defend against. This immediately lightens the load of a person who has been burdened with a certain egoic approach to relationships. The more conscious beings I am acquainted with are fascinated with the unfolding story of existence and are not trying to control it. This approach takes a huge amount of anxiety and negatively laden emotion off the table. It is an entirely new way of life.

A person making the journey to soul is not upset when things do not go a certain way. For example, when someone cuts them off in traffic, they slow down and acknowledge to themselves that a person doing such a thing has no understanding of the way the world really works. Those in soul understand that the other person's reckless behavior will eventually cause harm—whether to themselves or others. This approach, developed by our spiritual practice, and mapped out on the Enneagram's return to soul, evokes compassion for the "troublemaker." The conscious individual sees the unenviable and ultimately self-defeating consequences of the behavior. It is only then that we become aware that the ego's response of retaliation makes us part of the problem. The conscious response is compassion.

All people argue, even the conscious. However, the highly conscious ones are not invested in winning an argument. Their consideration is not for who wins but, rather, what issues are brought out and explained. For a conscious individual, the ultimate interest, even in an argument, is how well we love. I have witnessed many conscious people simply drop arguments that had turned ugly. I have found in my own life that if I truly believe my truth, and if the other person is adamant in theirs, we can prevent negative outcomes by simply agreeing to disagree.

Using the Enneagram to Bring Consciousness

As my own consciousness expanded and as I taught from that state, people began to be very interested in this model of teaching and learning about the Enneagram. Ministers, priests, and clergy from all religions wanted training in these principles and spiritual ideas. Regular businesswomen and men wanted to learn this, as did physicians, attorneys, and individual seekers who had no particular role in religion or mental health. These dear people wanted me to offer more than conferences and workshops: they desired training opportunities for their own personal spiritual growth. Some of the participants in one of my conferences wanted to go deeper and they asked for an extended period of study with me. One day, one of these students said to me, "You need to put all these handouts in a book. That way we could keep up with all the information that you are coming up with by referencing the book." When I asked this small group of students if they would like to assist Lark and me in conducting conferences on the Spirituality of the Enneagram and Consciousness Studies, they all said, "Yes, when do we start?" The many handouts formed the beginning of my first book on the Enneagram: *Becoming Conscious*.

Little did I know then, this very small group of students was to become the first faculty of a school, The Institute for Conscious Being. Since 2011, this school has educated scores of individuals of all walks of life using the principles of consciousness and spirituality of the Enneagram. The faculty, which now exceeds eighteen persons in total, handles all meetings in a conscious state, with meditation before each meeting. Over the years, we have dealt with all our differences among the faculty (and there have been some heavy issues) through the collective consciousness of our group, held in a container of love. For us, our soul types are just as useful to knowing and respecting one another as our ego types. The faculty provides teachings at each event, including conferences open to the public as well as intensives: the weekend trainings we offer. The faculty leads small groups in inquiry and personal growth as well as in more physical activities, such as bodywork, creativity workshops, dance, and theater.

Why do we do this and why has this work expanded so? People are crying out for something more. They are searching for a way to understand and transcend their personal pain. They are hungry for a supportive, like-minded community of others who are searching for inner peace but are unconvinced by society's more common answers or those offered by many types of organized religion. They realize that this thing called life is very complicated and individual and their needs must be addressed by teachings that speak deeply to each individual's unique circumstances.

They are hungry for new food for their spirits. They want an intellectually sound method of growth but do not want to sacrifice the element of mystery. They want to be respected for who they are in all their foibles and strengths and they seek to be part of something greater than themselves.

Those who best understand this work are acutely aware that only those of us who strive for higher consciousness can form answers to inner and outer chaos. They are also aware that the success of such an endeavor rests upon reaching a critical mass of conscious people, after which societies and cultures all over the world would become increasingly conscious. However, rising consciousness is a slow-moving phenomenon. History tells us that wars, famine, plagues, and oppression will either make a society re-examine its values or cause it to crumble. Slowly, most of the world has emerged from the dark ages. Slowly, codified laws have replaced chaos in many cultures.

However, even with the Herculean advancements of science and technology, we do not have a critical mass of conscious people on the planet to put these advancements to use. In fact, many turn a deaf ear to scientific findings and refuse to acknowledge that technology and collective action could save the planet from the worst of climate change. World powers remain in conflict and nuclear war is still a possibility. We have not discovered how to deal with tribalism or long-standing cultural and religious feuds. Deep-seated hatred between ethnicities plagues the world and hinders peace efforts; meanwhile, most of the planet operates based on who has the money: proof that the ego controls the world. This paradigm creates racism, misogyny, xenophobia, slavery, colonialism, and all sorts of oppression that set people against one another. All these factors block the possibility of a concerted rise in worldwide consciousness that would solve the problems that will eventually destroy us.

Our planet is slowly dying; we are watching our very air, water, and land drastically deteriorate, all because so many of us are disconnected from conscious reality. That same unconsciousness makes people lash out against taking a vaccine that has been proven to save lives. Many are so unconscious that they would spend their lives asleep to the happenings of the world. They are not aware of invasions of countries such as Ukraine and the murder of children and innocents. In unconsciousness, so many of us turn a deaf ear to racial hatred, White supremacy, and the oppression they engender. On top of these issues is the total unconsciousness of gun violence, the causes of which are completely ignored by many of those with the power to make desperately needed changes.

We say this is unconscionable, yet we live in a world where the unconscionable reigns. This is where the need for consciousness is imperative; it increases the respect, health, and safety of all. What is missing in the world is a new concept spoken in a new language: the language must transcend all cultural biases; the concept must be built on enduring truths that free us from our unhealthy egos—individually and collectively.

Outer Peace

Up until this chapter, I have focused on rediscovering and manifesting our individual souls by means of the spiritual map known as the Enneagram. But what if collectives such as families, organizations, or societies contained enough individuals who used this map? What if a critical mass of individuals were conscious enough to understand the rudimentary concept that, while the ego can be wonderful, it has a distorted sense of reality at times? Would that collective emanate more of its shared spiritual purpose (collective soul) than one dominated principally by an unchecked, unhealthy common ego? For example, some may assert that the US concept of Manifest Destiny was the product of a period when the country was dominated by an unchecked collective ego. On the flip side, some may say that when in the 1960s the US sent its state representatives to a Congress that then passed civil rights legislation, it was an expression of America's soul.

No soul lives in its own inner peace detached from others; we are all connected and therefore participate in each other's spiritual evolvement. Our individual essence proceeds from the greater essence, so like brothers and sisters who are connected by their common parents, all souls share a common divine source. By virtue of this invisible connection, we are constantly affecting one another on all levels of interaction. Researchers have determined that we can pick up on the invisible atmosphere in a room, whether it be negatively or positively charged. Clearly observable emotions, spoken language, body language, and chemosignals[4] transmit emotions and various mental states. Millions of ripple effects of these states spread from one individual to the next, throughout families, groups, regions, and nations. Collective mental and emotional states are transmitted across the planet, especially since the exponential growth of global technology. Our individual consciousness is greatly affected by the collective in which we are embedded and vice versa.

If this is true, might there be an emotional atmosphere or even a state of consciousness that is predominant within a family, an organization, or even a nation? If so, how does that collective send out its message—in actions, spoken attitudes, or unspoken attitudes? What is today's spoken or unspoken collective message of the United States, or any nation? What are the spoken or unspoken messages of the organizations to which we belong? of our family? What if the ripple effects of those collective messages came not from the collective's ego, but its soul? Would the world and our species stand a better chance of surviving, thriving, and evolving? If the answer is "Yes," how is this realistically achievable?

The most viable way that consciousness can be transmitted is by example to our neighbors and our young. Knowing the principles of

---

4. de Groot et al., "Chemosignals Communicate Human Emotions."

consciousness would put school-age children and all newcomers to this wisdom at an advantage. If they understand their ego, its necessity, and its propensity to block accurate perception, they can understand reality. Organizations such as the International Enneagram Association already teach and apply the principles and theory of consciousness throughout the world. Likewise, the Institute for Conscious Being teaches those principles and helps its students apply the truths to their situations and relationships. Yet the number of people touched by just a few conscious organizations is relatively small compared to those people who are never exposed to these principles. Worse, vast numbers of egocentric organizations across the globe promote the egoic way of experiencing the world.

When we review the increasing global tensions, conflicts, nuclear, and environmental threats, it seems that humankind is taking only baby steps toward consciousness and peace. I submit that teaching the principles of consciousness and the Enneagram to the young at home and in school would allow them to understand their ego, its strengths, and its distortions at an early age. Likewise, they would be familiar with the soul qualities that bring peace to the individual and the collective. They would not bypass ego development but would be aware of the ego as it develops. In awareness, they could understand the ego's potential to misrepresent the world. Children who are afforded the truths of the Enneagram would be able to put them into practice and ultimately spread them to future generations.

Because the Enneagram's truth is not tied to one religion, creed, culture, nation, or philosophy, it could be shared among groups and nations over the globe. In conflict-torn and high-tension areas, peace and reconciliation efforts would have a new language with which groups and nations could communicate and create solutions.

The Collective Soul

Every individual has a soul, which is their truest nature. When two souls come together to form a union, the couple forms a united soul, with its own spiritual purpose and intention; its qualities, core values, and spirit transcend those of the individuals that comprise it. When a family is formed, that soul enlarges to include others who are in the family, such as children, extended family, and even close friends. Neighborhoods have souls which encompass their common spiritual intentions and desires.

Regions have souls, as do countries. Souls are the truest spiritual nature and intention of any group. The collective souls of entire cultures and movements are composed of the souls of successively smaller collectives (e.g., families and individuals).

The key concept in describing any collective is the common denominator shared by the majority of its individuals (e.g., essential spirit, core values, etc.). The people of the country of Ukraine, for example, share a common *raison d'être*. Similarly, a baseball team's members' individual souls, when blended together as a group, form a common overall spirit and core meaning that is the combination of all the energies of each team member. That would be the team's collective soul.

Figure Twelve
The Soul Points of The Enneagram of Soul

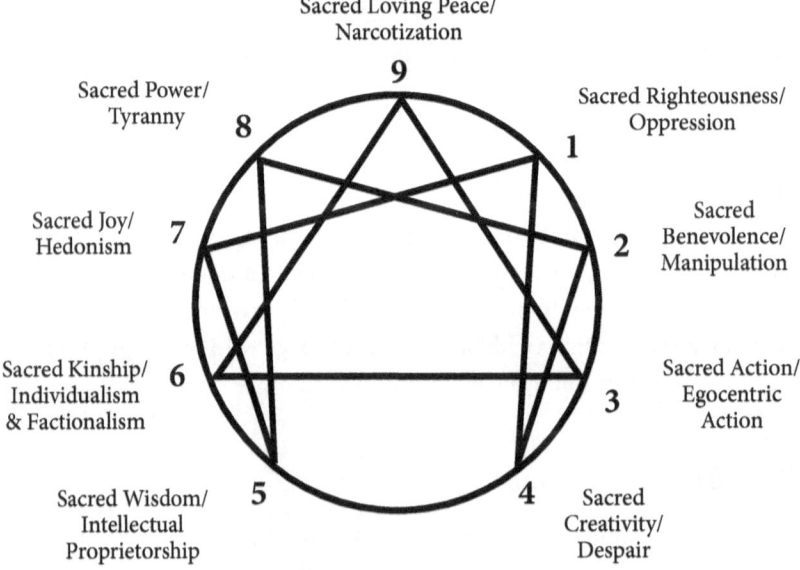

The Enneagram of Soul for Individuals and Collectives

Psychiatrist Carl Jung had a similar but non-spiritual concept about what groups share. He referred to "the collective unconscious":[5] that part of the mind common to humankind as a whole that contains memories and impulses of which the individuals are not aware.

Just as no one can fully know or understand my soul except me, the souls of collectives may only be known, understood, or accurately described by the individuals that make them up. A soul is not a material thing that can be broken down into absolute and scientifically measurable components. It is composed of invisible qualities that—like love itself—are beyond measurement.

The clearest way to define a collective's soul would be for all its individuals to describe it. Lacking that, we must rely on that group's customs and actions to represent its soul. I believe that the broadest characterization of any collective soul, as with any individual soul, is found at one of the nine points of the Enneagram of Soul. As the collective soul repeatedly journeys through all nine energies, it expresses its divine qualities to the outer world. If the collective does not manifest its soul qualities, this either means that it is in a holding pattern, ruled by inertia, or it is on a downward spiral of disintegration.

The Enneagram of Soul (Figure 12) illustrates the passageways to soul consciousness and soul regression in collectives.

Soul Growth and Regression in Collectives

Using the figure above, we can trace the growth or regression of any collective. You can see that the points are the same for individuals and collectives (see chapters 5 and 6). As a collective soul grows and evolves, it follows the Enneagram's inner flow, passing through each point on the Enneagram of Soul again and again, creating an upward spiral of growth. Just as souls have wings that are their alter-egos (see chapter 1), so do collectives. Therefore, collective soul types move with their wings through all the points, according to the arrows.

Similarly, collective soul types can regress, distorting the positive identity achieved on the upward spiral. When they regress, they switch back to the Enneagram of Collective Personality and continue in their downward spiral of disintegration.

---

5. Jung, "Psychological Types," 82–83.

Soul Progression of Collectives on the Inner Triangle

As an example of a collective's progress on the inner triangle, we will start randomly at point Six, where a critical amount of Sacred Kinship accumulates among the collective's members. This Sacred Kinship is formed by common higher beliefs and affinities that hold the collective together and move it forward in the world, promoting expanded kinship among its members and beyond to others outside of the collective.

After the group is solidified, it progresses against its arrow to Sacred Loving Peace at Point Nine. Sacred Loving Peace is not peace alone, but peace derived from affirmation between the members according to the Law of Love. This is a form of communal love that manifests from the collective's internal stability: the coherence between its stated beliefs and their application, its allocentric vs. egocentric methods of settling differences, and its attention to its members' welfare.

The collective then proceeds against its arrow to Sacred Action at Point Three. Here, the collective manifests and advances its beliefs. Sacred Action serves the common good by creating new systems and putting them into action. It improves methods, tools, and materials for the promotion of that collective's stated beliefs and the larger world.

We find an example of collective soul progression in the formation of the United States of America. Like all collectives, this country has progressed and regressed throughout its history. Its formative periods as a nation were largely ones of improvement regarding the collective consciousness. The new country would not have developed had it not shared Sacred Kinship among its founders (Point Six on the Enneagram of Soul.) Colonists had common interests apart from the English Crown, whom they considered abusive. Shared concerns about land, taxation, and autonomy took hold in the colonists' collective consciousness. As a result, they moved to Nine on the Enneagram of Soul, where they conceived of a land of peace, equality, freedom, and the pursuit of happiness. The idea of Sacred Loving Peace led to Sacred Action at Point Three. Though war is not associated with higher consciousness, at that time, war against England was the only action they knew of to gain independence from an oppressive and authoritarian power. In the collective of the early American colonists, Sacred Action included formulating a new government and a new democratic nation. This collective, however, does not include Native Americans; nor does its progression address the matter of slavery.

Collectives, like the people that comprise them, are complex, sometimes contradictory entities.

Soul Progression of Collectives on the Hexad

On the hexad, soul growth goes from any starting point to include all six points. Soul Point Two is Sacred Compassionate Benevolence: the altruism of a collective among its members. However, this compassionate benevolence extends outside the collective's borders/boundaries. Sacred Compassionate Benevolence proceeds from a collective heart of nurturing but does not foster unhealthy dependencies.

Next is Soul Point Four, where the collective is creative in problem-solving, governing, and bringing beauty to all things. This Sacred Creativity reflects the Divine, benefiting and inspiring all the members to their highest and best.

After this comes Soul Point One, which embodies Sacred Righteousness: the sense of discerning and applying the right principles and directions for all the members and therefore the collective.

At Point Seven is Sacred Joy. This is not synonymous with jubilation, although it may include that state at times. Sacred Joy is a state of being that is beyond mere emotions. This Joy is the spiritual well-being and contentment at the foundation of the collective. It is the deepest antidote for disheartenment. Sacred Joy is a fundamental state of being that is an inherent quality of the collective and its outreach.

After Sacred Joy is Sacred Wisdom, found at Soul Point Five, which manifests magnificent wisdom beyond mere knowledge. It is the inner knowing of a truth or set of truths that, when applied, ultimately brings higher consciousness and solutions to problems for all—problems that knowledge alone could not supply.

Finally, before completing the circuit, we progress to Sacred Power at Soul Point Eight. It represents the strength of the collective as it powerfully charts its course and handles the obstacles to progress. Sacred Power incorporates the powers of vulnerability and mercy found at its core.

The International Enneagram Association (IEA) serves as a great example of collective soul progression on the hexad. If we begin at Point Five on the Enneagram of Soul, we can understand Sacred Wisdom as the energy driving the organization's founders, who revered the Enneagram's teachings and imagined its potential.

From their shared Wisdom sprang Sacred Power at Point Eight. The Enneagram's Wisdom was inherently so powerful that the association's founders felt it necessary to organize its territory, proprietorship, and shared agreements to make it more accessible to the public. Opposition was dealt with by the joint strength of the small group.

From Power, Sacred Compassionate Benevolence manifested. The Enneagram now had a common forum where its teachings could be shared with all who were interested.

Next, Sacred Creativity enhanced the organization through the innovative development of programs and events that captured many people's imaginations worldwide.

After Sacred Creativity manifested fully, the leadership derived the best course for the future and the organization's best practices (Point One: Sacred Righteousness, the alignment with universal laws of truth).

Sacred Joy manifests at events and between members and visitors, and the deep joy is palpable.

We return to Sacred Wisdom at a higher level of consciousness, ready to begin the spiral of soul progression again.

Soul Regression of Collectives on the Inner Triangle

Sacred Kinship can devolve into Factionalism if fear predominates. Instead of the collective relying on the interdependent village within, it either degenerates into an "every person for themselves" mentality or dissolves into clusters of individuals with similar motives who cling to one another (Factionalism).

Likewise, if the collective soul of Sacred Loving Peace devolves, it indicates that a critical mass of its members has collectively gone to sleep on reality (Narcotization) and lost the integrative force that kept them together. A society that has gone to sleep eventually awakens when it is invaded. The result is pervasive anxiety. Now on the Enneagram of Collective Personality, it disintegrates into fear; the collective is distracted from attending to its own welfare and those of the groups with which it is interconnected.

Meanwhile, Sacred Action devolves into Egocentric Action: the collective loses its inner harmony, division occurs, and the collective is reduced to focusing its action on its own welfare and establishing its superiority over other collectives. As collective Sacred Action morphs into egocentricity, it reverts from the Enneagram of Collective Soul to the Enneagram of the Collective Personality. There, it loses all desire to move forward and—numb to its standards—follows the arrows of disintegration.

When thinking of collective soul regression on the triangle, we can use the example of a church whose members' Sacred Kinship devolved into Factionalism. There was a controversy about the historical church's cemetery: space was limited and one faction wanted to reserve the precious land that remained for senior members of the parish. Another faction wanted the remaining space to be made into a memorial garden; another wanted to leave it open as a burial space for whomever in the parish might need it. Yet another faction wanted to use the unused space for a columbarium.[6] The final faction wanted to enlarge the cemetery by buying an adjacent vacant lot. It was a highly fraught, emotionally charged issue for the collective. Divided, they devolved by falling back to the Enneagram of Collective Personality. At Point Three (Egocentric Action), each faction broke into its own "church," and members withdrew their pledges from the collective. Then, at Point Nine (Narcotization), people lost interest and went their separate ways, and the church as a whole finally dissolved.

Soul Regression of Collectives on the Hexad

Sacred Compassionate Benevolence is reduced to Manipulation when it no longer engenders empathy and support. The collective devolves into creating unhealthy dependencies within and without its ranks. If those who are dependent on the collective do not supply that which it demands, then the collective asserts control by withdrawing what it would otherwise supply, forcing compliance. Then, the collective re-enters the Enneagram of Collective Personality and continues the disintegration process (see above).

Sacred Power devolves into Tyranny. When this collective disconnects from its soul, it no longer uses its power for the well-being of its members or those outside. Power now builds a wall around the collective so that all the resources and people within are under the domination of the collective's power structure. This kind of power is ruthless in securing its dominance. Those who are disloyal to the power structure are

---

6. A building with niches to house funeral urns.

discarded. This collective soul further deteriorates on the Enneagram of Collective Personality.

Sacred Wisdom degenerates into Intellectual Ownership. Wisdom in the collective is no longer a freely shared quality. It is downgraded to knowledge, which is then compartmentalized and owned by certain members. This collapses the collective into a body of loosely associated proprietors who own separate bodies of knowledge. The collective has no core of communal wisdom.

Sacred Joy degenerates into Hedonism: the seeking after pleasure. True joy is replaced by the pleasure principle. Immediate gratification from all types of pleasure becomes the collective's core value. This is societal or group self-absorption in the sense that the overriding concern is gaining pleasure while denying reality. This collective drifts into a shared fantasy that pleasure and gratification will cancel out the ills of the collective.

Sacred Righteousness devolves into Oppression; the collective loses its connection to righteousness and justice. Righteousness is no longer based on the growth of its members but on a rigid code of "right" and "wrong" attitudes and behavior as agreed upon by the collective, unetethered to any external principles of conscience. Its members begin to be punished oppressively for breaking the code.

Sacred Creativity disintegrates into Despair. The collective loses its creative energy. Problem-solving is done by rote and becomes a cheerless responsibility. The energy to bring the beautiful into the collective and beyond is siphoned off by collective self-absorption. When no creative force motivates the collective, its members lose faith in its ability to generate the best solutions and sink into hopelessness and despair.

When any of the points on the Hexad of Collective Soul devolves, the collective immediately returns to the Enneagram of Collective Personality and continues its disintegration. An example is a college fraternity that started with a collective soul of harmony and joy. Founded on the Joy of brotherhood and all the benefits of shared ideals, the fraternity had a soul of Sacred Joy.

As the fraternity matured, it won many accolades for its spirit and accomplishments. However, its celebrations slowly turned into extravagant parties, which in turn, became lavish events at exotic destinations, and the group's soul shifted from Sacred Joy to Hedonism. The shift returned the fraternity to the Enneagram of Collective Personality, where its disintegration continued. The members denied their departure from their original standards. False righteousness at Point One replaced the fraternity's founding principles. Self-absorbed at Point Four (Despair), they disintegrated into Point Two's blinding pride and codependent relationships (Manipulation). When questioned by the university, the group was arrogant and domineering at Point Eight (Tyranny). From there, the fraternity withdrew into isolation at Point Five (Intellectual Ownership) and continued disintegrating at Point Seven, where it began.

Planet Earth's Collective Soul

If consciousness were to spring forth en masse, what would be the global effect? What number of conscious individuals would be needed to create the critical mass necessary to shift the planet's energy from adversarial to cooperative, and from egocentricity to soulcentricity? The collective soul of the planet determines its collective mind, its emotional tenor, and its collective body, but the collective ego can hijack that role and send the collective into egocentricity.

When I was a small child in the 1950s, there were many children's shows like *The Howdy Doody Show*,[7] but one of my favorite shows for adults was called *Life Is Worth Living*.[8] I did not understand what was being said, but I liked to listen to the man who was the show's host. He wore a cape, a wide metallic belt, and a small cap on his head. He had flashing eyes and a booming voice. More than this, however, I loved the song that ended the program. Its words were sung by the unseen voices of a choir while a picture of the globe filled the TV screen. The words were, "If everyone lit just one little candle, what a bright world this would be."

As an adult, I have learned that the show's stirring and captivating host was Archbishop Fulton Sheen. In the 1950s he spoke to a live studio audience about faith. In my recent review of some of his telecasts, I understood why my soul child was so drawn to this man's mere presence; when I watched his television program as an adult, I felt his magnetism, again. His messages were perfectly aligned with consciousness studies and the Enneagram.

On one of his telecasts I recently reviewed, he proposed that the soul of the Soviet Union was obscured when the individuals' rights and

---

7. *The Howdy Doody Show*. Aired 1947–60 on NBC.

8. *Life Is Worth Living*. Hosted by Bishop Fulton J. Sheen. Aired 1952–55 on DuMont and 1955–57 on ABC.

property were placed under state control. Bishop Sheen referenced the importance of the collective soul and how the individual soul and personality make up the healthy or unhealthy collective. His implication was that there were not enough individuals living in soul in that country to create a critical mass of those desiring freedom.

My "take away" as a child was the closing song of Bishop Sheen's show. Though I didn't understand his mature thoughts, the short song at the end touched my body, mind, and heart, and I have sung those lyrics under my breath ever since I was a soul child. "If everyone lit just one little candle, what a bright world this would be."[9] With a picture of the luminous globe on the TV screen, I imagined everyone in the world lighting a candle to create that glow. At ages four, five, and six, my soul child was learning by metaphor the power of the individual to affect the collective.

If the candle symbolizes the light of consciousness, how do we encourage our fellow humans to light theirs? This is not an easy feat but the answer lies in understanding our motivations. We are hugely motivated by enjoying pleasure and avoiding pain. So, we have to feel enough desire for the pleasure of consciousness or enough unconscious pain to seek healing for our suffering. But even if we seek these, if we have no resources, maps, or wisdom to consult—and most essentially, no living examples of that consciousness—then we are hopeless.

The Peace of Spiritual Consciousness

To seek the pleasure of spiritual consciousness, we must first have experienced spiritual unconsciousness. The depravity of being spiritually unaware drives us deeper and deeper into external gratifications, such as materialism, status, and power, sometimes to the point of addiction. But these are only facsimiles of the love we are searching for, and when they are exhausted, our lack of a sense of fulfillment is intensely painful.

There is an interrelationship between pleasure and pain. Our pain drives us to search for what will actually make us whole: the greatest pleasure of all. This is when we notice, possibly for the first time, someone with a lighted candle. They are conscious and they live in it. They are not angels, saints, or spiritual giants—they are imperfect humans striving for

---

9. "One Little Candle." Music by George Myself, with lyrics by Joseph Maloy Roach. © Music Sales Corporation, 1952.

consciousness whose light shines and illuminates their way. When we ask the person with the lighted candle, "How did you receive your light?" we are awed by their story. In this way, we too have begun the journey toward becoming conscious.

What these teachers tell us is not one word or phrase, not a credo or set of external laws; they tell us the story of their personal journey and their tools for continuing in consciousness. Theirs is the authority of the "living document," whose story, actions, and words we experience daily. Our spiritual teachers' lives are their testament.

The pleasure of spiritual consciousness is as sweet as honey, as light as the breeze, and as infinite as the stars. Many of my teachers have passed to another realm, yet I receive new ones all the time. Whatever deficit I have in my spiritual understanding and practice, an appropriate teacher seems to come my way. I first see their light and I covet it. I ask for their light and they invite me to hear their story. Their candlelight becomes mine as I am healed of my deficit and can enjoy the supreme pleasure of my lighted candle.

Pain as a Motivator for Spiritual Consciousness

Those of us in pain are most teachable because we want relief as soon as possible. However, there are some instances in which people thrive on pain. Called the pain-body, this phenomenon is the indwelling pain from previous generations that has come to feed on us.[10] It is so much a part of who we are that we have ego-identified with it as part of our identity and are unconscious of our attachment to it. Only those who truly want to be relieved of their pain-body can receive light for their candle.

For the most part, we experience our zenith of pain when we suffer a tremendous loss or when we disintegrate into more and more egocentricity, which brings on other great losses. This can be a loss of a dream, a person, a job, a home, our health, or any other thing that we have greatly relied on and are attached to. Power, status, and the like do not soothe or even address the pain of abject loss. This pain is the result of being driven to our very lowest and we see no way out. We experience no spaciousness, only abject emptiness and deficiency. Yet, this is the pivotal instance when we are most apt to see the reality that we have been blind to all our lives. This is the moment when we need hope. This is the moment when

---

10. Tolle, *New Earth*, 129–60.

we are searching for somebody with a candle: someone to teach us and to listen to our stories.

We need teachers who do more than sympathize. Real teachers at this point are ministers to us. We can follow their ministry because their lives are believable: they too have been healed from similar and sometimes even greater losses than our own, yet their candles are brightly lit. In the warmth of their glow, we listen to their story and witness them as a transformed individual.

We are all teachers with something to offer the world. The teachers of consciousness, however, have the calling and the empathy to be present for those in pain and to share healing presence with them at their time of deepest need—when they are most receptive to the light of our candle of the spirit.

Spreading the Light

The same thread of truth runs throughout all my teachers' wisdom: the light of the soul is our truest identity and the unchecked ego obscures this light. My teachers have shared with me that the greatest obstacle to our fulfillment is the unrealistic beliefs we hold of ourselves. When we become truly conscious, we know the real, luminous, and beautiful soul that we are. This is why the Enneagram is such an important map—it directs us to who we are as an unrealistic ego personality, as well as who we are in our truest nature, our soul. This is the spark of truth that, once realized, lights our candle.

The Enneagram, once it is known and applied, is a tool for consciousness that we can share with almost anyone, including children. When we know the spirituality of the Enneagram, we can offer it as a map out of darkness to anyone searching to fulfill their existence. We can familiarize people of all walks of life with its basic truths. The Enneagram pulls down the veils of lies we have between ourselves and our true being. It names exactly what blocks us, as an individual, from peace. Our unchecked ego spins its own idea of reality. The Enneagram reveals our narrative to be based on the false stories of how our egos want life to be. It brings into focus the all-pervading preoccupation we have with our ego: in our unceasing attempts to please it, we live according to its false story in the hope that story will bring the love we so desperately want. When the ego's suffering is too great, the Enneagram shows us how to escape by way of contact with our soul.

To understand and live out of the divine truth reflected by the Enneagram is to be able to give each searching soul we meet a light for their candle. Soul by soul, person by person, family by family, we can bring peace to this world. Yet this shall never happen until there are enough of us who embrace peace in ourselves and can be present for those searching for spiritual consciousness. The best way is to know our souls. If the collective soul of earth can be more conscious of its true nature, as Meister Eckhart says, we will have a new creation with compassion.[11]

For many, the Enneagram is just another personality quiz like the plethora of such typing instruments too numerous to count. However, those of us looking for something to transform us, reach for it instead as a system that meets those deeper needs. And, like a toothpick among thousands of lookalikes, the Enneagram, like no other spiritual tool, makes sense of our spiritual selves and provides a map to our soul. This map, if followed, helps to transform us and to heal the world.

---

11. Fox, *Meditations with Meister Eckhart*, in *Works of George Fox*.

Ego/Soul Traits

Ego Type One

Soul Point Seven: Sacred Joy

Holy Idea: Perfection

SP Native HI: Wisdom, Work, Plan

Point of Disintegration: Four: Despair

Soul's Essential Aspect: The Yellow/Joy

Idealized Aspect: Brilliancy

Ego Virtue activated at Soul Point: Serenity

Soul Virtue native to Soul Point: Sobriety

Avoidance: Anger/Being wrong

Passion: Anger

Fixation: Resentment

Trap: Perfection

Beatitude: reviled and persecuted

Ego Type Two

Soul Point Four: Sacred Creativity

Holy Idea: Will and Freedom

SP Native HI: Origin

Point of Disintegration: Eight: Tyranny

Soul's Essential Aspect: The Point/I am being

Idealized Aspect: Merging Gold

Ego Virtue activated at Soul Point: Humility

Soul Virtue native to Soul Point: Equanimity

Avoidance: Neediness

Passion: Pride

Fixation: Flattery

Trap: Freedom

Beatitude: meek

Ego Type Three

Soul Point Six: Sacred Kinship

Holy Idea: Harmony, Law, Hope

SP Native HI: Strength and Faith

Point of Disintegration: Nine: Narcotization

Soul's Essential Aspect: Will

Idealized Aspect: The Pearl

Ego Virtue activated at Soul Point: Veracity/Truthfulness

Soul Virtue native to Soul Point: Courage

Avoidance: Failure

Passion: Deceit

Fixation: Vanity

Trap: Efficiency

Beatitude: poor in spirit

Ego Type Four

Soul Point One: Sacred Righteousness

Holy Idea: Origin

SP Native HI: Perfection

Point of Disintegration: Two: Manipulation

Soul's Essential Aspect: Brilliancy

Idealized Aspect: The Point

Ego Virtue activated at Soul Point: Equanimity

Soul Virtue native to Soul Point: Serenity

Avoidance: Despair/Loss of true self

Passion: Envy

Fixation: Melancholy

Trap: Authenticity

Beatitude: persecuted for righteousness

Ego Type Five

Soul Point Eight: Sacred Power

Holy Idea: Transparency and Omniscience

SP Native HI: Truth

Point of Disintegration: Seven: Hedonism

Soul's Essential Aspect: The Red/Strength

Idealized Aspect: Diamond Guidance

Ego Virtue activated at Soul Point: Detachment

Soul Virtue native to Soul Point: Innocence/Simplicity

Avoidance: Emptiness

Passion: Stinginess

Fixation: Stinginess

Trap: Knowledge

Beatitude: hunger/thirst for righteousness

Ego Type Six

Soul Point Nine: Sacred Loving Peace

Holy Idea: Strength and Faith

SP Native HI: Love

Point of Disintegration: Three: Egocentric Action

Soul's Essential Aspect: Living Daylights

Idealized Aspect: Will

Ego Virtue activated at Soul Point: Courage

Soul Virtue native to Soul Point: Action/Diligence

Avoidance: Deviance

Passion: Fear

Fixation: Cowardice

Trap: Security

Beatitude: pure in heart

Ego Type Seven

Soul Point Five: Sacred Wisdom

Holy Idea: Wisdom, Work, and Plan

SP Native HI: Transparency and Omniscience

Point of Disintegration: One: Oppression

Soul's Essential Aspect: Diamond Guidance

Idealized Aspect: The Yellow

Ego Virtue activated at Soul Point: Sobriety

Soul Virtue native to Soul Point: Detachment

Avoidance: Pain

Passion: Overindulgence

Fixation: Planning

Trap: Idealism

Beatitude: those who mourn

Ego Type Eight

Soul Point Two: Sacred Benevolence

Holy Idea: Truth

SP Native HI: Will and Freedom

Point of Disintegration: Five: Intellectual Proprietorship

Soul's Essential Aspect: Merging Gold

Idealized Aspect: The Red

Ego Virtue activated at Soul Point: Innocence/Simplicity

Soul Virtue native to Soul Point: Humility

Avoidance: Weakness

Passion: Arrogance

Fixation: Vengeance

Trap: Justice

Beatitude: merciful

Ego Type Nine

Soul Point Three: Sacred Action

Holy Idea: Love

SP Native HI: Harmony, Law, Hope

Point of Disintegration: Six: Individualism/Tribalism

Soul's Essential Aspect: The Pearl

Idealized Aspect: Living Daylights

Ego Virtue activated at Soul Point: Action/Diligence

Soul Virtue native to Soul Point: Veracity/Truthfulness

Avoidance: Conflict

Passion: Arrogance

Fixation: Indolence

Trap: Seeker of others

Beatitude: peacemakers

Bibliography

Addison, Howard A. *The Enneagram and Kabbalah: Reading Your Soul*. 2nd ed. Woodstock, VT: Jewish Lights, 2006.
Almaas, A. H. *Essence: The Diamond Approach to Inner Realization*. New York Beach, ME: Weiser, 1986.
———. *Facets of Unity: The Enneagram of Holy Ideas*. Boston: Shambhala, 2012.
———. *Keys to the Enneagram: How to Unlock the Highest Potential of Every Personality Type*. Boulder, CO: Shambhala, 2021.
Appleton, George. "A Gathering Prayer." In *Jerusalem Prayers for the World Today*. 1974. Reprint, London: SPCK, 1986.
Beesing, Maria, et al. *The Enneagram: A Journey of Self Discovery*. Denville, NJ: Dimension, 1984.
Bennett, John. *Gurdjieff: Making a New World*. New York: Harper & Row, 1973.
Buber, Martin. *I and Thou*. New York: Scribner, 1958.
Casiday, Augustine M. *Evagrius Ponticus*. London: Routledge, 2006.
Dancy, Russell. *Plato's Introduction of Forms*. Cambridge: Cambridge University Press, 2004.
de Groot, Jasper, et al. "Chemosignals Communicate Human Emotions." *Psychological Science* 23.11 (Sept. 27, 2012).
de Salzmann, Jeanne. *The Reality of Being: The Fourth Way of Gurdjieff*. Boston: Shambhala, 2011.
Erikson, H. Erik. *Childhood and Society*. 1950. Reprint, New York: Norton, 1993.
Fox, George. *The Works of George Fox*. Philadelphia: Marcus T. C. Gould; New York: Isaac T. Hopper, 1831.
Gulpaygani, Ali. *Discursive Theology, Vol. 1*. New Charleston, SC: CreateSpace, 2015.
Gurdjieff, G. I. *Views from the Real World: Early Talks of Gurdjieff*. New York: Dutton, 1973.
Howell, Joseph B. *Becoming Conscious: The Enneagram's Forgotten Passageway*. Bloomington, IN: Balboa, 2012.
Ichazo, Oscar. "The Arica Psycho-Catalyzers/Holy Ideas/Mind Catalyzers." Handout with Holy Ideas definitions. Dobbs Ferry, NY: Arica Institute Press, 1972.
Interviews with Oscar Ichazo. New York: Arica Institute Press, 1982.

Jacobson, Edmund. *Progressive Relaxation: A Physiological and Clinical Investigation of Muscular States and Their Significance in Psychology and Medical Practice.* Chicago: University of Chicago Press, 1974.

James, William. *The Varieties of Religious Experience: A Study in Human Nature.* The Gifford Lectures. London: Longmans, Green, and Co., 1908.

John of the Cross. "The Dark Night of the Soul." https://www.poetryfoundation.org/poems/157984/the-dark-night-of-the-soul.

Johnson, Robert A. *Inner Work: Using Dreams and Active Imagination in Personal Growth.* New York: HarperOne, 2009.

Jung, Carl G. *Good and Evil in Analytical Psychology.* 1948. The Collected Works of C. G. Jung, Vol. 10. Revised by R. F. C. Hull and translated by H. G. Baynes. Princeton, NJ: Princeton University Press, 1992.

———. "Psychological Types." In The Collected Works of C. G. Jung, Vol. 6. Revised by R. F. C. Hull and translated by H. G. Baynes, 82–83. Princeton, NJ: Princeton University Press, 1974.

Kahn, Saad. "8 Gates of Jannah in Islam & Who Will Enter from Them." *IslamKaZikr.* https://islamkazikr.com/8-gates-of-jannah-in-islam/.

Katz, Brigit. "Scientists Grew Palm Trees from 2,000-Year-Old Seeds." *Smithsonian Magazine*, February 7, 2020, https://www.smithsonianmag.com/smart-news/scientists-grew-palm-trees-2000-year-old-seeds-180974164/.

Kazdin, Alan E., ed. *Encyclopedia of Psychology.* American Psychological Association. Oxford: Oxford University Press, 2000.

Kircher, Athanasius. *Arithmologia.* Rome: Varese, 1665.

Llull, Ramon. *Ars Brevis 1313.* Crerar Ms 245. Chicago: Hanna Holburn Gray Special Collections Research Center, University of Chicago Library.

Maitri, Sandra. *The Enneagram of Passions and Virtues: Finding the Way Home.* New York: Penguin, 2005.

———. *The Spiritual Dimension of the Enneagram: Nine Faces of the Soul.* New York: Putnam, 2000.

Moccia, L., et al. "The Experience of Pleasure: A Perspective between Neuroscience and Psychoanalysis." *Frontiers in Human Neuroscience* 12.359 (2018). doi:10.3389/fnhum.2018.00359.

Moody, Raymond. *Life After Life.* Covington, GA: Mockingbird, 1975.

Myss, Caroline. *Sacred Contracts: Awakening Your Divine Potential.* New York: Three Rivers, 2003.

Nouwen, Henri J. M. *Adam: God's Beloved.* Maryknoll, NY: Orbis, 1997.

Nouwen, Henri J. M., and M. Bodo. *The Inner Voice of Love: A Journey through Anguish to Freedom.* Cincinnati, OH: St. Anthony Messenger, 2001.

Ouspensky, Peter D. *In Search of the Miraculous.* 1949. Reprint, New York: Harcourt, Brace, & World, 2001.

Perls, Fritz. *The Gestalt Approach and Eye Witness to Therapy.* New York: Bantam, 1981.

Piaget, Jean. *The Origins of Intelligence in Children.* New York: International University Press, 1952.

Pine, Red. *The Platform Sutra: The Zen Teaching of Hui-neng.* Berkeley, CA: Counterpoint, 2008.

Plato. *Plato's Meno.* Translated by George Anastapio and Lawrence Berns. Newburyport, MA: Focus, 2004.

Porter, Frank C. "The Pre-Existence of the Soul in the Book of Wisdom and in the Rabbinical Writings." *Journal of Theology* 12.1 (1908) 53–115.
Riso, Don Richard, and Russ Hudson. *The Wisdom of the Enneagram*. New York: Bantam, 1999.
Rogers, Dale Evans. *Angel Unaware*. Westwood, NJ: Revel, 1953.
Singer, Jerome L. *Imagery and Daydream Methods in Psychotherapy and Behavior Modification*. London: Academic Press, 1974.
Tajadod, Nahal, and Robert Bononno. *Rumi: The Fire of Love*. London: Duckworth, 2011.
Tazewell, Charles. *The Littlest Angel*. Chicago: Children's Press, 1946.
Thich Nhat Hanh. *Being Peace*. Berkeley, CA: Parallax, 1996.
Tillich, Paul. *Systematic Theology, Vol. 1*. Chicago: University of Chicago Press, 2012.
Tolle, Eckhart. *A New Earth: Awakening to Your Life's Purpose*. New York: Dutton Penguin Group, 2005.
———. "Small Group Lectures." Live event at the Jewish Community Centre, Vancouver, BC, 2010.
Tournier, Paul. *The Meaning of Persons*. New York: Harper, 1957.
Tripolitis, Antonia. *The Doctrine of the Soul in the Thought of Plotinus and Origen*. New York: Libra, 1978.
Vernier, Nancy. *The Primal Wound*. Baltimore: Gateway, 1993.
Wagner, Jerome. *Nine Lenses on the World: The Enneagram Perspective*. Evanston, IL: NineLens, 2010.
Webb, James. *The Harmonious Circle: The Lives and Work of G. I. Gurdjieff, P. D. Ouspensky and Their Followers*. New York: Putnam's Sons, 1980.
The Wisdom of the Desert Fathers and Mothers. Translated by Henry L. Carrigan, Jr. Brewster, MA: Paraclete, 2010.
Yousafzai, Malala. "UN Speech on Youth Education." United Nations, New York City, New York, July 12, 2013.

Index

Note: n indicates footnotes, and italicized page numbers indicate illustrations.

Adam (Nouwen), 39
Addison, Rabbi Howard, 61
Almaas, A. H. (A. Hameed Ali), 7–8, 49, 82, 144
Angel Unaware (Evans), 38
Arica Institute, 6–7, 49
Arithmologia (Kircher), 32
Authenticated Idealized Aspects of the Ego
    amalgamation of the, 169–70, 178
    barriers to soul and components of the unobstructed soul, 123, 128, 130–31
    and ego virtues, 121
    reading the map of the Enneagram of Personality, 30
    and the soul child, 80, 91

beatitudes
    of the ego types, 147, 149, 152–53, 155, 158, 160–61, 163, 223–27
    Soul Points excluding, 128
    soulality in the, 58–61
Becoming Conscious: The Enneagram's Forgotten Passageway (Howell), 20, 79, 206
Beesing, Maria, 1, 7

Body Center of Intelligence
    dominant emotion of each type in the, 13–14
    Enneagram's passageways to inner and outer peace, 197
    history and development of the Enneagram, 4
    self-remembering, soulality, and the, 50–53, 56–57
    soul and its pain, 61–62
    soul child's qualities in the, 104
    types within the, 12–13, *12*
    wounding of the soul child, 88
Bon Vivant. *See* Seven, Ego Type
Brilliancy, 59, 82, 86, 121–22, 126, 130–31, 146–47, 223, 225

Carnegie, Dale, 138
Catholicism, 7
Centers of Intelligence
    dominant emotion of each type in the three, 13–14
    Enneagram's passageways to inner and outer peace, 197
    history and development of the Enneagram, 4
    self-remembering, soulality, and the, 50–57
    soul and its pain, 61–62

Centers of Intelligence (*cont.*)
   soul child's qualities in the, 100–104
   types within each of the three, 12–13, *12*
   wounding of the soul child, 88
Christianity, 7, 32, 43
Coexistence, 44
Commander. *See* Eight, Ego Type
Congress, U.S., 208
Courage, 28–29, 47, 126–27, 168–69, 189, 224, 226
Creator. *See* Four, Ego Type

Daniels, David, 8
"The Dark Night of the Soul" (St. John of the Cross), 141
Despair, 26, 122, 126, 216–17, 223, 225
Diamond Approach, 7–8, 82
Diamond Guidance, 83–84, 86, 125, 127, 131, 155, 225–26
Diamond Heart Retreat Group, Ridwhan School, 8
Divine Aspects of the Soul. *See* Essential Aspects of the Soul
Down Syndrome, 38

Eckhart, Meister, 221
ego, spiritual transformation and amalgamation of our, 164–81
ego, traits of the, 223–27
Ego Points, 82, 115–16, 130
Egocentric Action, 127, 214–15, 226
Egocentricity, 44
Egyptology, 32
Eight, Ego Type
   avoidances of, 26, 123, 227
   basic description of, 11
   beatitudes of, 149–50, 227
   blessings of, 60
   dominant emotion of, 13
   Ego Virtues of, 28–29, 47, 227
   Enneagram of Personality types, 3
   Essential Aspect of, 82, 86, 227
   Five as Stress Point for, 20, 136, 227
   fixations of, 27, 123, 227
   Holy Ideas of, 30, 49, 60, 77–78, 120, 148–49, 227
   Idealized Aspect of, 85–86, 227
   Kabbalah correlations with, 61
   as part of the Body Center of Intelligence, 13
   passions of, 26, 47, 123, 227
   qualities of, 60
   soul child of, 78
   and soul development levels, 20
   Soul Virtues of, 227
   summary of, 227
   traps of, 27–28, 123, 227
   Two as Soul Point for, 18, 30, 77–78, 120, 130, 137, 148–49, 227
Eight, Soul Point
   barriers to soul of Ego Type Five, 126
   components of the unobstructed, 127
   Ego Virtues of, 127
   Essential Aspect of, 84, 127, 161, 225
   Holy Ideas of, 120, 127, 161, 225
   Idealized Aspect of, 127, 225
   as one of the Hexad points, 25
   as part of the Body Center of Intelligence, 12–13
   portrait of, 160–62
   qualities of, 131
   as Soul Point for Five, 18, 74, 120, 131, 137, 160–62, 225
   soul progression on the hexad, 213–14
   soul regression on the hexad, 217
   Soul Virtues of, 127
   as Stress Point for Two, 19, 133, 224
Eight Gates of Jannah, 33
Emerging Souls, 182, 186–89
English Crown, 212
The Enneagram: A Journey of Self Discovery (Beesing et al.), 7
The Enneagram and Kabbalah: Reading Your Soul (Addison), 61
Enneagram Institute, 7
Enneagram of Business, 20, 22–23
Enneagram of Collective Personality, 211, 214–16
Enneagram of Collective Soul, 211–17
Enneagram of Holy Ideas, 47–50, 68
The Enneagram of Passions and Virtues (Maitri), 31, 46, 122

Index

Enneagram of Personality
  about the, 2–4
  amalgamation process on the, 175–76, 178
  categories of applications of the, 20, 22–23
  comparison to the Enneagram of Soul, 116, 137
  diagram, 3
  discovering our type on the, 8
  history and development of the, 6–7
  Holy Ideas of the, 49, 68, 117
  integration and higher consciousness on the, 113–15
  knowing in order to get to the Enneagram of Soul, 31, 33
  major ego structures on the, 166
  numbers as limiting on the, 93
  reading the map of the, 24
  soul development levels on the, 186
  Soul Points on the, 128
  Stress Points on the, 132, 132
  virtues on the, 121
Enneagram of Soul
  about the, 109–36
  amalgamation process on the, 165, 168–70, 175–76, 178
  categories of applications of the Enneagram of Personality, 20
  comparison to the Enneagram of Personality, 116–17, 137
  knowing the Enneagram of Personality in order to get to the, 31, 33
  major soul structures on the, 166
  passageways to inner and outer peace on the, 210, 211–13
  and the soul child, 91
  soul development levels on the, 186, 188
  Soul Points on the, 81, 128
  soul types of the, 137–63
  Stress Points on the, 132
  virtues on the, 121
Enneagram of Transformation, 20, 23–24
Erickson, Erik, 65
Esalen Institute, 7
Essence/Soul Child, 44

Essence/Transformed Soul, 44
Essential Aspects of the Soul
  and amalgamation of our ego and soul, 169–70, 176, 178–80
  and ego/soul traits, 223–27
  and our virtues, 121
  reading the map of the Enneagram of Personality, 29–30
  and the soul child, 66, 79–88, 85, 91–92, 105, 122–27
  and soul development levels, 189–90
  in Soul Points, 128, 146, 149–51, 153, 155, 157, 159, 161, 163
  in a state of soulality, 141
Evagrius of Ponticus, 32
Evans (Rogers), Dale, 38–39

Facets of Unity (Almaas), 8
Factionalism, 124, 214–15
Five, Ego Type
  avoidances of, 26, 126, 225
  basic description of, 10
  beatitudes of, 161, 225
  blessings of, 60
  dominant emotion of, 14
  Ego Virtues of, 28–29, 47, 225
  Eight as Soul Point for, 18, 74, 120, 131, 137, 160–62, 225
  Enneagram of Personality types, 3
  Essential Aspect of, 84, 86, 225
  fixations of, 27, 126, 225
  Holy Ideas of, 30, 49, 60, 74–75, 120, 161, 225
  Idealized Aspect of, 84, 86, 225
  Kabbalah correlations with, 61
  as part of the Head Center of Intelligence, 13
  passions of, 26, 47, 126, 225
  qualities of, 60
  Seven as Stress Point for, 19, 134–35, 225
  soul child of, 74–75
  Soul Virtues of, 225
  summary of, 225
  traps of, 27–28, 126, 225
  using and misusing personality typing, 21

Five, Soul Point
  barriers to soul of Ego Type Seven, 125
  components of the unobstructed, 125
  Ego Virtues of, 125
  Essential Aspect of, 83, 125, 155, 226
  Holy Ideas of, 120, 125, 154–55, 226
  Idealized Aspect of, 125, 226
  as one of the Hexad points, 25
  as part of the Head Center of Intelligence, 13
  portrait of, 154–56
  qualities of, 130–31
  as Soul Point for Seven, 18, 76–77, 120, 131, 137, 154–55, 182, 226
  soul progression on the hexad, 213
  soul regression on the hexad, 217
  Soul Virtues of, 125
  as Stress Point for Eight, 20, 136, 227
Four, Ego Type
  avoidances of, 26, 122, 225
  basic description of, 10
  beatitudes of, 147, 225
  blessings of, 59
  dominant emotion of, 14
  Ego Virtues of, 28–29, 47, 175, 225
  Enneagram of Personality types, 3
  Essential Aspect of, 82, 86, 225
  example of amalgamation, 173–77
  fixations of, 27, 122, 225
  Holy Ideas of, 30, 49, 59, 73–74, 120, 147, 225
  Idealized Aspect of, 83, 86, 225
  Kabbalah correlations with, 61
  One as Soul Point for, 18, 73, 120, 130, 137, 146–47, 174, 225
  as part of the Heart Center of Intelligence, 13
  passions of, 26, 47, 122, 225
  qualities of, 60
  soul child of, 73–74
  Soul Virtues of, 225
  summary of, 225
  traps of, 27, 122, 225
  Two as Stress Point for, 19, 134, 225
Four, Soul Point
  barriers to soul of Ego Type Two, 124
  components of the unobstructed, 124
  Ego Virtues of, 124
  Essential Aspect of, 83, 124, 153, 224
  Holy Ideas of, 120, 124, 152–53, 224
  Idealized Aspect of, 124, 224
  as one of the Hexad points, 25
  as part of the Heart Center of Intelligence, 12–13
  portrait of, 152–54
  qualities of, 130
  as Soul Point for Two, 18, 71, 120, 130, 137, 152–54, 224
  soul progression on the hexad, 213
  soul regression on the hexad, 217
  Soul Virtues of, 124
  and the Spiral of Consciousness, 115
  as Stress Point for One, 19, 133, 223
The Fourth Way (Gurdjieff), 4
Fox, George, 40

Gestalt therapy, 7
God
  and amalgamation of our ego and soul, 181
  asking your soul child about, 100
  creation as cosmic purpose of, 78
  Enneagram's passageways to inner and outer peace, 195–96
  expressing aspects of as Holy Ideas, 68, 157
  love as connection to, 163
  soul as part of, 37, 40, 44
  soul child's expression of, 80, 154, 161
  soul created around time of conception by, 43
  and soul development levels, 192
  Soul Point Three as embodiment of, 59, 152
  three aspects of, 69
  unity with through personal hardship, 141
Goodall, Jane, 203
Gregory, Pope, 32
Gurdjieff, George Ivanovich, 4–6, 31, 47

Harmonizer. *See* Nine, Ego Type

Index

Head Center of Intelligence
    dominant emotion of each type in the, 14
    Enneagram's passageways to inner and outer peace, 197
    history and development of the Enneagram, 4
    self-remembering, soulality, and the, 50, 55–57
    soul and its pain, 62
    soul child's qualities in the, 102–3
    types within the, *12*, 13
Heart Center of Intelligence
    dominant emotion of each type in the, 14
    Enneagram's passageways to inner and outer peace, 197
    history and development of the Enneagram, 4
    self-remembering, soulality, and the, 50, 53–57
    soul and its pain, 62
    soul child's qualities in the, 101–2
    types within the, 12–13, *12*
Heart Points. *See* Soul Points
Hedonism, 216, 225
Hexad points, 24–25, *24*, 113, 115, 120, 198, 213–17
Holy Faith
    activated, 120, 130–31
    and amalgamation of our ego and soul, 167–68, 179
    and the beatitudes, 60
    expressed, 131
    Holy Ideas by ego type, 30, 49–50, 226
    Holy Ideas by soul type, 125, 127, 157, 162–63, 224
    and the soul child, 67, 75
    and soul development levels, 189
Holy Freedom
    activated, 120, 130
    and the beatitudes, 59
    expressed, 130
    Holy Ideas by ego type, 30, 49, 224
    Holy Ideas by soul type, 123, 149, 152–53, 227
    and the soul child, 71–72
    and the Spiral of Consciousness, 115
Holy Harmony
    activated, 119–20
    and the beatitudes, 59
    expressed, 131
    Holy Ideas by ego type, 30, 49, 224
    Holy Ideas by soul type, 124–25, 150–51, 157, 227
    and the soul child, 72–73, 92
Holy Hope
    activated, 119–20
    and the beatitudes, 59
    expressed, 131
    Holy Ideas by ego type, 30, 49, 224
    Holy Ideas by soul type, 124–25, 150–51, 157, 227
    and the soul child, 72–73, 92
Holy Ideas
    activated, 118–21, 130–31
    and amalgamation of our ego and soul, 167–69, 174–75, 178–80
    by ego type, 29–30, 70–78, 223–27
    Essential Aspects as, 82
    as foundations of our soul, 66–69
    history and development of the Enneagram, 6
    of our Soul Points, 119–21, 127–28
    and our virtues, 121
    personality and soulality, 141
    reading the map of the Enneagram of Soul, 117–19, *118*
    self-remembering, soulality, and, 47–50
    and the soul child, 48, 69–79, 87–89, 91–93, 105, 118–19, 128–31
    and soul development levels, 189–90
    by soul type, 122–27, 145–55, 157, 159, 161–63, 223–27
    and soulality in the beatitudes, 58–61
    and the Spiral of Consciousness, 115
Holy Law
    activated, 119–20
    and the beatitudes, 59
    expressed, 131
    Holy Ideas by ego type, 30, 49, 224
    Holy Ideas by soul type, 124–25, 150–51, 157, 227
    and the soul child, 72–73, 92

Holy Love
  activated, 118–20, 131
  and amalgamation of our ego and
    soul, 168–69
  and the beatitudes, 61
  expressed, 130
  Holy Ideas by ego type, 30, 49, 227
  Holy Ideas by soul type, 124, 127,
    150–51, 163, 226
  and the soul child, 67, 78, 93
Holy Omniscience
  activated, 120, 131
  and the beatitudes, 60
  expressed, 131
  Holy Ideas by ego type, 30, 49, 225
  Holy Ideas by soul type, 125, 127,
    155, 161, 226
  and the soul child, 74
Holy Origin
  activated, 120, 130
  and amalgamation of our ego and
    soul, 174–75
  and the beatitudes, 59
  expressed, 130
  Holy Ideas by ego type, 30, 49, 225
  Holy Ideas by soul type, 122, 124,
    146–47, 152, 224
  and the soul child, 73
Holy Perfection
  activated, 120–21, 130
  and amalgamation of our ego and
    soul, 174–75
  and the beatitudes, 59
  expressed, 131
  Holy Ideas by ego type, 30, 49, 223
  Holy Ideas by soul type, 122, 126,
    147, 158, 225
  and the soul child, 70
Holy Plan
  activated, 120, 131
  and the beatitudes, 60
  expressed, 131
  Holy Ideas by ego type, 30, 49, 226
  Holy Ideas by soul type, 125–26,
    154–55, 158, 223
  and the soul child, 76–77
Holy Strength
  activated, 120, 130–31

  and amalgamation of our ego and
    soul, 167–68, 179
  and the beatitudes, 60
  expressed, 131
  Holy Ideas by ego type, 30, 49–50,
    226
  Holy Ideas by soul type, 125, 127,
    157, 162–63, 224
  and the soul child, 67, 75
  and soul development levels, 189
Holy Transparency
  activated, 120, 131
  and the beatitudes, 60
  expressed, 131
  Holy Ideas by ego type, 30, 49, 225
  Holy Ideas by soul type, 125, 127,
    155, 161, 226
  and the soul child, 74
Holy Trust, 120
Holy Truth
  activated, 120, 131
  and the beatitudes, 60
  expressed, 130
  Holy Ideas by ego type, 30, 49, 227
  Holy Ideas by soul type, 123, 127,
    148–49, 161, 225
  and the soul child, 77
Holy Will
  activated, 120, 130
  and the beatitudes, 59
  expressed, 130
  Holy Ideas by ego type, 30, 49, 224
  Holy Ideas by soul type, 123, 149,
    152–53, 227
  and the soul child, 71–72, 81
  and the Spiral of Consciousness, 115
Holy Wisdom
  activated, 120, 131
  and the beatitudes, 60
  expressed, 131
  Holy Ideas by ego type, 30, 49, 226
  Holy Ideas by soul type, 125–26,
    154–55, 158, 223
  and the soul child, 76
Holy Work
  activated, 120, 131
  and the beatitudes, 60
  expressed, 131

Index

Holy Ideas by ego type, 30, 49, 226
Holy Ideas by soul type, 125–26,
    154–55, 158, 223
and the soul child, 76
How to Win Friends and Influence People
    (Carnegie), 138
The Howdy Doody Show [TV show], 217
Howell, Ben, 41, 112–13, 116–17, 143,
    167–72, 179, 188, 195–97
Howell, Lark, 9, 40–41, 65, 112, 143,
    188, 191–92, 195–97, 200, 205
Howell, Lauren, 9, 41, 112, 196
Howell, Trevor, 38
Hudson, Russ, 7, 144

Ichazo, Oscar, 6–7, 23, 49, 67–69, 82, 144
Idealized Aspects of the Ego
    amalgamation of the, 92, 169–70, 178
    barriers to soul and components of
        the unobstructed soul, 128
    defining the, 80–86
    diagram, 85
    and ego virtues, 121
    reading the map of the Enneagram
        of Personality, 30
    and the soul child, 66, 88, 91
IEA (International Enneagram
    Association), 7–8, 209, 213
The Iliad (Homer), 93
In Search of the Miraculous
    (Ouspensky), 6
Inner (Primary) Triangle, 24, 25, 113,
    115, 120, 199, 212, 214–15
Institute for Conscious Being, 202, 206,
    209
Intellectual Ownership, 136, 216–17
International Enneagram Association
    (IEA), 7–8, 209, 213
Islam, 33, 43

Jacobsonian relaxation, 200
James, William, 57
Jannah, 33
Jesuit Retreat House (Center), 1, 7
Jesuits. *See* Society of Jesus
Jesus Christ, 32, 38, 43, 59
Johnson, Robert, 98
Jones, Anna, 38

Joy (Yellow), 84, 86, 125–26, 131, 159,
    185, 223, 226
Judaism, 43
Jung, Carl, 46, 211
Jungian philosophy, 98

Kabbalah, 32, 61
Kircher, Athanasius, 32

Law of Love, 212
Law of One, 4
Law of Seven, 4, 6
Law of Three, 4
Life After Life (Moody), 40
Life Is Worth Living [TV show], 217
Lincoln, Abraham, 203
Linthicum, Deborah, 109
Linthicum, Patsy, 109
The Littlest Angel [story], 38
Living Daylight, 79–81, 86–87, 124, 127,
    131, 163, 169, 179, 189, 226–27
Llull, Ramon, 32

Maitri, Sandra, 8, 25, 31, 46, 82, 117,
    122, 144
Mandela, Nelson, 190
Manifest Destiny, 208
Manipulation, 215, 217, 225
Matthew, Gospel of, 32
Merging Gold, 82–83, 86, 123–24, 130,
    149–50, 224, 227
Mind Center of Intelligence. *See* Head
    Center of Intelligence
Missildine, Hugh, 201
Mixture, 186
Moody, Raymond, 40
Mother Teresa, 190
Mullis, Buddy, 195–96
Mullis, Charlotte, 195–96
Muslims. *See* Islam
Myss, Caroline, 48

Naranjo, Claudio, 7–8, 144
Narcotization, 214–15, 224
Native Americans, 180, 212
near-death experiences (NDEs), 40
Neo-Freudianism, 201

Nine, Ego Type
  avoidances of, 26, 123, 227
  basic description of, 11
  beatitudes of, 152, 227
  blessings of, 61
  dominant emotion of, 13–14
  Ego Virtues of, 28–29, 47, 227
  Enneagram of Personality types, 3
  Essential Aspect of, 83, 86, 227
  fixations of, 27, 123, 227
  Holy Ideas of, 30, 49, 61, 78–79, 118–19, 120, 150–51, 227
  Idealized Aspect of, 86, 227
  Kabbalah correlations with, 61
  as part of the Body Center of Intelligence, 13
  passions of, 26, 47, 123, 227
  qualities of, 61
  Six as Stress Point for, 20, 136, 227
  soul child of, 79
  Soul Virtues of, 227
  summary of, 227
  Three as Soul Point for, 18, 78–79, 119–20, 130, 137, 150–52, 227
  traps of, 27–28, 123, 227
Nine, Soul Point
  barriers to soul of Ego Type Six, 127
  components of the unobstructed, 127
  Ego Virtues of, 127
  Essential Aspect of, 86–87, 127, 163, 226
  example of Enneagram's passageways to inner and outer peace, 212
  Holy Ideas of, 120, 127, 162–63, 226
  Idealized Aspect of, 127, 226
  as one of the Primary Triangle points, 25
  as part of the Body Center of Intelligence, 12–13
  portrait of, 162–63
  qualities of, 131
  as Soul Point for Six, 15, 18, 75, 80, 93, 116, 120, 131, 137, 143, 162–63, 168–69, 197, 226
  soul regression of collectives on the inner triangle, 215
  Soul Virtues of, 127

  as Stress Point for Three, 19, 133–34, 224
Nine Lenses on the World: The Enneagram Perspective (Wagner), 8
Nobel Peace Prize, 175
Nogosek, Robert, 1, 7
Nouwen, Henri, 39, 147
Nurturer. *See* Two, Ego Type

Obscured Souls, 182–86
Ochs, Father Robert "Bob," 7
The Odyssey (Homer), 93
O'Leary, Patrick, 1–2, 7, 144
One, Ego Type
  avoidances of, 26, 126, 223
  basic description of, 10
  beatitudes of, 160, 223
  blessings of, 59
  dominant emotion of, 13
  Ego Virtues of, 28, 47, 121, 223
  Enneagram of Personality types, 3
  Essential Aspect of, 84, 86, 223
  fixations of, 27, 126, 135, 223
  Four as Stress Point for, 19, 133, 223
  Holy Ideas of, 30, 49, 59, 70–71, 120, 159, 223
  Idealized Aspect of, 82, 86, 223
  Kabbalah correlations with, 61
  as part of the Body Center of Intelligence, 13
  passions of, 26, 47, 126, 223
  qualities of, 59
  Seven as Soul Point for, 18, 70–71, 120, 131, 137, 159–60, 192, 223
  soul child of, 70–71
  and soul development levels, 185, 192
  Soul Virtues of, 223
  summary of, 223
  traps of, 27, 126, 223
  as wing of Ego Type Two, 115
One, Soul Point
  Authenticated Idealized Aspects of, 123
  barriers to soul of Ego Type Four, 122

Index

components of the unobstructed, 122–23
Ego Virtues of, 123, 146
Essential Aspect of, 82, 122, 146, 225
Holy Ideas of, 120, 122, 147, 225
Idealized Aspect of, 225
as one of the Hexad points, 25
as part of the Body Center of Intelligence, 12–13
portrait of, 146–48
qualities of, 130
as Soul Point for Four, 18, 73, 120, 130, 137, 146–47, 174, 225
soul progression on the hexad, 213–14
soul regression on the hexad, 217
Soul Virtues of, 123, 146, 175
as Stress Point for Seven, 20, 135, 226
Oppression, 216, 226
Origen, 43
Ouspensky, Peter, 6

Palmer, Helen, 8
Palpable Souls, 183, 189–94
Pearl, 83, 86, 124–25, 130–31, 151–52, 224, 227
Piaget, Jean, 55
Plato and Platonism, 2, 37, 43, 68, 144
Point, 83, 86, 123–24, 130, 153, 224–25
Points of Disintegration. *See* Stress Points
Points of Integration. *See* Soul Points
Post-Traumatic Stress Disorder, 52
Primary Triangle. *See* Inner (Primary) Triangle
Pythagoreanism, 2

Quakerism (Society of Friends), 40

Red (Strength), 84–86, 123, 127, 130–31, 161–62, 225, 227
Ridhwan School, 7–8
Riso, Don, 7, 144
Rogers, Dale Evans, 38–39
Rogers, Robin, 38–39
Roman Empire, 32

Sacred Action, 130, 150–52, 212, 214, 227
Sacred Benevolence, 130, 148–50, 213–15, 227
Sacred Compassion, 130, 213–15
Sacred Contracts (Myss), 48
Sacred Creativity, 130, 152–54, 213–14, 216, 224
Sacred Diligence, 130
Sacred Joy, 131, 159–60, 213–14, 216, 223
Sacred Kinship, 131, 156–58, 212, 214–15, 224
Sacred Loving Peace, 131, 162–63, 212, 214, 226
Sacred Power, 131, 160–62, 213–14, 225
Sacred Righteousness, 60, 71, 130, 146–48, 213–14, 216, 225
Sacred Wisdom, 130–31, 154–56, 213–14, 216, 226
Salzmann, Jeanne de, 4
Sarmoung Brotherhood, 4
Scholar. *See* Five, Ego Type
Seekers After Truth (SAT), 7
Sephirot, 33
Sermon on the Mount, 59
Seven, Ego Type
avoidances of, 26, 125, 226
basic description of, 11
beatitudes of, 155–56, 226
blessings of, 60
dominant emotion of, 14
Ego Virtues of, 28–29, 47, 226
Enneagram of Personality types, 3
Essential Aspect of, 83, 86, 226
Five as Soul Point for, 18, 76–77, 120, 131, 137, 154–55, 182, 226
fixations of, 27, 76, 125, 226
Holy Ideas of, 30, 49, 60, 76–77, 120, 154–55, 226
Idealized Aspect of, 84, 86, 226
Kabbalah correlations with, 61
One as Stress Point for, 20, 135, 226
as part of the Head Center of Intelligence, 13
passions of, 26, 47, 125, 226
qualities of, 60
soul child of, 77

Seven, Ego Type (*cont.*)
   Soul Virtues of, 226
   summary of, 226
   traps of, 27–28, 125, 226
   using and misusing personality typing, 21

Seven, Soul Point
   barriers to soul of Ego Type One, 126
   components of the unobstructed, 126
   Ego Virtues of, 126
   Essential Aspect of, 84, 126, 159, 223
   Holy Ideas of, 120, 126, 159, 223
   Idealized Aspect of, 126, 223
   as one of the Hexad points, 25
   as part of the Head Center of Intelligence, 13
   portrait of, 159–60
   qualities of, 131
   as Soul Point for One, 18, 70–71, 120, 131, 137, 159–60, 192, 223
   soul progression on the hexad, 213
   soul regression on the hexad, 217
   Soul Virtues of, 126
   as Stress Point for Five, 19, 134–35, 225

Sheen, Archbishop Fulton, 217–18
Singer, Jerome, 200

Six, Ego Type
   Authenticated Idealized Aspect of, 169–70
   as author's personal type, 8–9, 138, 143, 167–69, 179, 189, 197
   avoidances of, 26, 127, 167–68, 226
   basic description of, 10–11
   beatitudes of, 163, 226
   blessings of, 60
   dominant emotion of, 14
   Ego Virtues of, 28–29, 47, 168, 189, 226
   Enneagram of Personality types, 3
   Essential Aspect of, 86–87, 169–70, 179, 189, 226
   fixations of, 27, 127, 169, 226
   Holy Ideas of, 30, 49, 60, 75–76, 120, 162–63, 226
   Idealized Aspect of, 84, 86, 169–70, 226
   Kabbalah correlations with, 61
   Nine as Soul Point for, 15, 18, 75, 80, 93, 116, 120, 131, 137, 143, 162–63, 168–69, 197, 226
   as part of the Head Center of Intelligence, 13
   passions of, 26, 47, 127, 168–69, 226
   qualities of, 60
   soul child of, 75–76, 81
   and soul development levels, 189
   Soul Virtues of, 168–69, 226
   summary of, 226
   Three as Stress Point for, 19–20, 116, 135, 226
   traps of, 27–28, 127, 171, 226

Six, Soul Point
   barriers to soul of Ego Type Three, 125
   components of the unobstructed, 125–26
   Ego Virtues of, 126
   Essential Aspect of, 84, 92–93, 125, 157, 224
   example of Enneagram's passageways to inner and outer peace, 212
   Holy Ideas of, 120, 125, 157, 224
   Idealized Aspect of, 125, 224
   as one of the Primary Triangle points, 25
   as part of the Head Center of Intelligence, 13
   portrait of, 156–58
   qualities of, 131
   Six returning to, 143, 163, 170
   as Soul Point for Three, 18, 72–73, 119–20, 131, 137, 156–58, 224
   Soul Virtues of, 126
   as Stress Point for Nine, 20, 136, 227
   using and misusing personality typing, 21

Smith, Eric Parkman, 191–94
Society of Friends (Quakerism), 40
Society of Jesus, 7, 32
Socrates, 37

soul child
   barriers to and components of the unobstructed, 122–36
   defining the, 63–94

development of the, 182, 189
emerging profile of your, 105
Enneagram's passageways to inner and outer peace, 198, 200–204, 217–18
and Essential Aspects of the Soul, 79–86
finding through our soul type, 137, 143, 148, 150, 152, 154–55, 157, 159, 161–62
and Holy Ideas, 29, 48, 66–79, 81, 87–89, 92–93, 118–19, 128–31
and Idealized Aspects of the Ego, 30, 80–86
identifying your, 79–80, 95–105
integration into our consciousness, 93–94
journey of the, 90–92
knowing your, 110
listing qualities of your, 101–4
meeting your, 98–101
mischief and naughtiness in the, 86–88
and Soul Points, 25, 128–31
and the Spiral Continuum of Being, 44
and Stress Points, 134, 136
transformation and amalgamation of our ego and soul, 164, 166, 171–72, 174–75, 178, 180
and virtues, 121
wounding of the, 88–90
Soul Level One, 20, 182–86
Soul Level Three, 20, 183, 187–94
Soul Level Two, 20, 182, 186–89
Soul Points
and amalgamation of our ego and soul, 167–70, 174–75
as antidote to distortions and suffering, 15
contents of the, 129, 130–31
Enneagram's passageways to inner and outer peace, 197–99, 202, 210, 213
Essential Aspects of our, 80–84, 86
Holy Ideas of our, 30, 70–78, 117, 119–21, 127–28
identifying personality types in order to find, 4, 33, 223–27

and levels of soul development, 182, 192
reading the map of the Enneagram of Personality, 24–25, 137
reading the map of the Enneagram of Soul, 116
soul children as, 79, 87, 92
and soul types, 150–51, 154, 158–59, 163
using arrows to follow ego type to, 16–18, *16*, *17*, 113
virtues of our, 121–27, 223–27
soulality
in the beatitudes, 58–61
defining as qualities of our unique soul, 37–62
discovering the soul child, 63–94
discovering your soul child, 95–105, 110
Enneagram's passageways to inner and outer peace, 198–99, 202, 204
personality and, 139–43
self-remembering, the Centers of Intelligence, and, 51–58
self-remembering, the Enneagram of Holy Ideas, and, 47–50
self-remembering, the shadow, and, 46–47
soul and its pain, 62
and soul development levels, 186, 189–90, 192
and soul types, 145
and the transformation and amalgamation process, 176
Soulcentricity/Soulality, 44
Spiral Continuum of Being, 44–45, *45*, 158, 182, 186
Spiral of Consciousness
amalgamation process on the, 165, 177
diagram, *114*
inner flow of the enneagram, 93, 199, 202
integration and growth on the, 113
progression of your soul, 112
soul levels on the, 186
The Spiritual Dimension of the Enneagram (Maitri), 8, 25

Spirituality of the Enneagram and Consciousness Studies, 205
St. Francis of Assisi, 190, 192
St. John of the Cross, 141
Standard Bearer. *See* One, Ego Type
Strength (Red), 84–86, 123, 127, 130–31, 161–62, 225, 227
Stress Points, 17–20, *17*, 25–26, 116, 131–36
Sufism, 4

Taliban, 175
Team Player. *See* Six, Ego Type
Third Order of Francis, 32
Three, Ego Type
    avoidances of, 26, 125, 224
    basic description of, 10
    beatitudes of, 158, 224
    blessings of, 59
    dominant emotion of, 14
    Ego Virtues of, 28–29, 47, 224
    Enneagram of Personality types, 3
    Essential Aspect of, 84, 86, 92–93, 176, 224
    example of amalgamation, 176
    fixations of, 27, 125, 135, 158, 224
    Holy Ideas of, 30, 49, 59, 72–73, 120, 157, 224
    Idealized Aspect of, 83, 86, 224
    Kabbalah correlations with, 61
    Nine as Stress Point for, 19, 133–34, 224
    as part of the Heart Center of Intelligence, 13
    passions of, 26, 47, 125, 224
    qualities of, 59
    Six as Soul Point for, 18, 72–73, 119–20, 131, 137, 156–58, 224
    soul child of, 73
    Soul Virtues of, 224
    summary of, 224
    traps of, 27, 125, 224
    using and misusing personality typing, 21
    as wing of Ego Type Two, 115
Three, Soul Point
    barriers to soul of Ego Type Nine, 123
    components of the unobstructed, 124
    Ego Virtues of, 124, 151
    Essential Aspect of, 83, 124, 151, 227
    example of Enneagram's passageways to inner and outer peace, 212
    Holy Ideas of, 120, 124, 150–51, 227
    Idealized Aspect of, 124, 227
    as one of the Primary Triangle points, 25
    as part of the Heart Center of Intelligence, 12–13
    portrait of, 150–52
    qualities of, 130
    as Soul Point for Nine, 18, 78–79, 119–20, 130, 137, 150–52, 227
    soul regression of collectives on the inner triangle, 215
    Soul Virtues of, 124, 151
    as Stress Point for Six, 19–20, 116, 135, 226
    Three returning to, 93
Tolle, Eckhart, 22, 61, 145
The Trip to Bountiful [movie], 93
True Being, 169, 174
Two, Ego Type
    avoidances of, 26, 124, 224
    basic description of, 10
    beatitudes of, 153, 224
    blessings of, 59
    dominant emotion of, 14
    Ego Virtues of, 28, 47, 224
    Eight as Stress Point for, 19, 133, 224
    Enneagram of Personality types, 3
    Essential Aspect of, 83, 86, 224
    fixations of, 27, 124, 224
    Four as Soul Point for, 18, 71, 120, 130, 137, 152–54, 224
    Holy Ideas of, 30, 49, 59, 71–72, 120, 152–53, 224
    Idealized Aspect of, 83, 86, 224
    Kabbalah correlations with, 61
    as part of the Heart Center of Intelligence, 13
    passions of, 26, 47, 124, 224
    qualities of, 59
    soul child of, 71–72
    Soul Virtues of, 224

and the Spiral of Consciousness, 115
summary of, 224
traps of, 27, 124, 224
Two, Soul Point
 barriers to soul of Ego Type Eight, 123
 components of the unobstructed, 123
 Ego Virtues of, 123, 149
 Essential Aspect of, 82, 123, 149–50, 227
 Holy Ideas of, 120, 123, 148–49, 227
 Idealized Aspect of, 123, 227
 as one of the Hexad points, 25
 as part of the Heart Center of Intelligence, 12–13
 portrait of, 148–50
 qualities of, 130
 as Soul Point for Eight, 18, 30, 77–78, 120, 130, 137, 148–49, 227
 soul progression on the hexad, 213
 soul regression on the hexad, 217
 Soul Virtues of, 123, 149
 as Stress Point for Four, 19, 134, 225
Tyranny, 215, 217, 224

United Nations, 176

University of Virginia, 40

The Varieties of Religious Experience (James), 57
Vietnam War, 67, 138

Wagner, Jerry, 8
Wagner Enneagram Personality Style Scales (WEPSS), 8
Will, 81, 84, 86, 125, 127, 131, 157, 169, 176, 224, 226
Winner. *See* Three, Ego Type
The Wisdom of the Enneagram (Hudson and Riso), 7
World War II, 67, 109

Yale Divinity School, 39–40, 200
Yellow (Joy), 84, 86, 125–26, 131, 159, 185, 223, 226
Your Inner Child of the Past (Missildine), 201
Yousafzai, Malala, 175–77

Zen, 94
Zoroastrianism, 4

Please use the QR code to visit the Institute for Conscious Being's information page.

Dr. Joseph Howell and Mrs. Lark Howell founded the Institute for Conscious Being in 2014. Our mission is to promote living in spiritual consciousness. We teach this through The Spiritual Approach to Enneagram and Consciousness Studies.

The school accepts those of all spiritual paths and grants certifications at different levels of study. Dr. Howell, and the faculty of the Institute for Conscious Being conduct in-person as well as on-line events.

You may also want to visit ICB's official website at www.theicb.org to learn more about our school. On line Applications are provided at this site.

To engage Dr. Howell for speaking events, workshops and retreats, address emails to: drjoehowell@theicb.org

www.ingramcontent.com/pod-product-compliance
Lightning Source LLC
Chambersburg PA
CBHW031804220426
43662CB00007B/525